METHODOLOGY

WHO NEEDS IT?

SAGE has been part of the global academic community since 1965, supporting high quality research and learning that transforms society and our understanding of individuals, groups, and cultures. SAGE is the independent, innovative, natural home for authors, editors and societies who share our commitment and passion for the social sciences.

Find out more at: **www.sagepublications.com**

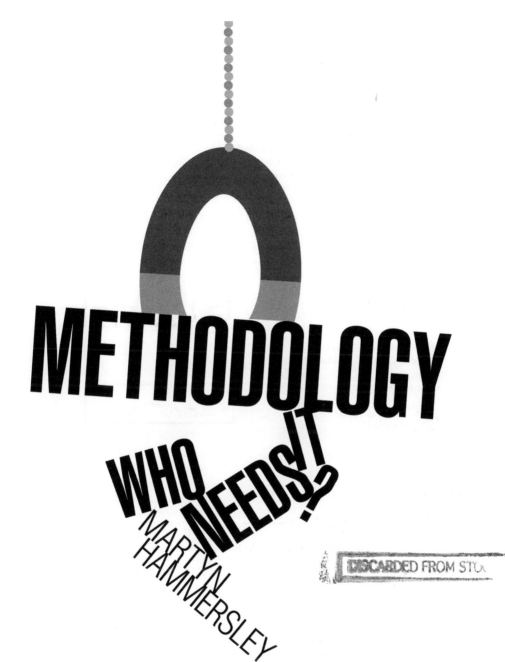

METHODOLOGY

WHO NEEDS IT?

MARTYN HAMMERSLEY

SAGE

Los Angeles | London | New Delhi
Singapore | Washington DC

SAGE Publications Ltd
1 Oliver's Yard
55 City Road
London EC1Y 1SP

SAGE Publications Inc.
2455 Teller Road
Thousand Oaks, California 91320

SAGE Publications India Pvt Ltd
B 1/I 1 Mohan Cooperative Industrial Area
Mathura Road
New Delhi 110 044

SAGE Publications Asia-Pacific Pte Ltd
33 Pekin Street #02-01
Far East Square
Singapore 048763

Library of Congress Control Number: 2010925800

British Library Cataloguing in Publication data

A catalogue record for this book is available from the British Library

ISBN 978-1-84920-204-6
ISBN 978-1-84920-205-3 (pbk)

Typeset by C&M Digitals (P) Ltd, Chennai, India
Printed in India at Replika Press Pvt Ltd
Printed on paper from sustainable resources

05513146

For all 'no-nonsense academics'

CONTENTS

Acknowledgements   ix

Introduction   1

Part 1: The role of the researcher: limits, obligations and virtues   15

1   Methodology, who needs it?   17

2   On the social scientist as intellectual   43

3   Should social science be critical?   75

4   Objectivity as an intellectual virtue   89

5   Too good to be false? The ethics of belief   105

Part 2: The dialectic of knowledge production   121

6   Models of research: discovery, construction, and understanding   123

7   Merely academic? A dialectic for research communities   138

8   Academic licence and its limits: the case of Holocaust denial   159

Epilogue   185

References   188

Name Index   209

Subject Index   212

ACKNOWLEDGEMENTS

My thanks to Richard Palmer for providing me with an unpublished paper on Gadamer, and especially to Susan Haack for keeping me well supplied with her publications, and thereby helping to preserve my sanity.

An earlier version of Chapter 3 appeared in *Philosophy of the Social Sciences*, 35, 2, pp. 175–95, 2005. Chapter 4 was published in *The Sage Handbook of Methodological Innovation*, London, Sage, 2010.

I have been working on many of these chapters for a long time. Earlier versions have been given as papers:

Chapter 1: To a British Society for Research into Learning Mathematics meeting at the Open University in 1992, to the Sociology Society, University of Warwick, in 1993, and later at seminars at the Universities of Stirling and Keele.

Chapter 3: At the British Educational Research Association Annual Conference in 2000 and also at the University of Sussex that year, and later at Cardiff University, Nottingham Trent University and the Institute of Education.

Chapter 5: To a seminar at the School of Education, University of Durham, April 2005.

Chapter 6: At Oxford Brookes University in 2002 and at University College, Worcester in 2003.

I am grateful to all those who commented on my ideas at these events.

INTRODUCTION

Only if [one] experiences how easy it is to err, and how hard to make even a
small advance in the field of knowledge, only then can he [or she] obtain a
feeling for the standards of intellectual honesty, a respect for truth, and a disregard
of authority and bumptiousness. But nothing is more necessary today than the
spread of these modest intellectual virtues. (Popper 1945: 283–4)

In the twentieth century, academic social science flourished in universities. Today it
is under increasing threat. It faces unprecedented challenges, in both intellectual and
material terms: its institutional and attitudinal preconditions are being eroded.
Indeed, key elements of the rationale that underpinned it have come to be abandoned by many social scientists, and are explicitly championed by very few. The
essays in this book seek to clarify, develop and defend this kind of work. This is not
done in the belief that its declining fortunes can be easily reversed, or that the
alternatives to it are worthless. However, I believe that, at the very least, we need
to know what we are losing: in the modern world, much is lost through forgetfulness
(Todorov 2001: 11–12).

Of course, the nature of academic social science is not, and was never, beyond
dispute. But generally recognised features include that it is relatively autonomous
from practical and political goals, being aimed at generating factual – not evaluative
– knowledge that is of universal or at least very general value, rather than serving
immediate practical needs or demands for evidence. As with natural science, the key
claim, implicit or explicit, is to produce findings whose likely validity is significantly
greater than information from other sources. And it is assumed that, for this to be
possible, what is to be investigated, and how it is to be investigated, must be determined by academic researchers exercising independence within an intellectual community that is largely self-governing.[1]

---

[1] I recognize that there are other sorts of social science, and the value of these, see Hammersley
(2002a: ch. 6). For influential accounts of the academic model in the context of natural
science, see Polanyi (1962), Merton (1973b) and Ziman (2000). For a discussion of 'the
academic ethic' in general terms, and of the threats to it in the United States and elsewhere,
see Shils (1972).

Current challenges to this academic ideal in social science include the following:

1   Demands from external 'stakeholders' that research findings be directed towards immediate practical or political benefit, such as improving national economic performance and 'quality of life', shaping or challenging policies, solving social problems, etc.
2   Commitment on the part of many social scientists to the idea that their main task is critically to evaluate policies, practices, or social arrangements, this sometimes being formulated as an insistence that the researcher take on the role of public intellectual.
3   Challenges to the assumption that sound knowledge of the kind pursued by academic enquiry is best produced in detachment from practical or political concerns, or indeed denials that inquiry *can* be detached from practical value commitments – it being argued instead that research must be engaged directly with 'action'.
4   Scepticism about whether social science can produce knowledge that is in any way superior to that which is available by other means, along with political and/or moral objections to the idea that it should propose to do this. From this point of view, subverting the claims to expertise made by social science, and amplifying other voices, becomes an important task.

In one form or another, challenges to the possibility and value of academic social science have always been present. In the past, these tended to focus on whether social scientists study the world in ways analogous to those employed by natural scientists, and whether this is possible or desirable. However, then, these challenges were largely kept at bay, whereas today they are much more powerful, and operate *within* as well as outside research communities and universities. Here I can do no more than sketch how this situation has come about.

CHANGES IN INSTITUTIONAL ENVIRONMENT

There have been long-term changes within universities and in their relations with outside agencies, especially governments, that have brought about the present situation. One is the increasing role of governmental and commercial research contracts in relation to natural science and technology; another is the growing prominence of professional schools within universities, in the United States especially but also elsewhere (see Nisbet 1971). However, more recently there have been other rapid changes that have exacerbated the situation. In particular, it is now commonly demanded by governments, as funders of universities, that academic research be judged by the value of its products to external 'users'. In the past, in some countries, the public funding of research was guided by what we might call a state patronage system. Here, the knowledge produced by research was treated as of value in itself, or assumed to be of likely practical value (in necessarily unspecifiable ways) in the future, rather than required to be of immediate, demonstrable value. Moreover, researchers were assumed to know best how to pursue such knowledge. Today, by contrast, an investment model is increasingly being adopted. Here, funding is directed to those forms of research, or specific projects, that successfully claim to offer a substantial and specified return, as regards economic and social benefit. Thus, governments that fund research now often demand that it be geared more directly to meet their requirements for information and/or be designed to generate 'knowledge transfer' with commercial organisations, in order to boost economic competitiveness in the 'knowledge economy'.[2]

This has sometimes been described as a redrafting of the 'contract' between researchers and the state or the national society (Stokes 1997 and 2009; Demeritt 2000). In part, this can be understood as reflecting the rise of the 'new public management', so that what is happening to research is simply a reflection of wider changes in governance of the public sector (Pollitt 1990; Ferlie et al. 1996; Clarke and Newman 1997; Power 1997). Central here is the rhetoric of the market: the assumption that production must be demand-led in order to maximise benefit. Where market forces are not directly involved, it is believed that regulation and accountability are required: of kinds that set up incentives and disincentives mimicking those of the market. Here, investment is tied to past 'outcomes' in relation to targets, and may be accompanied by the imposition of modes of good practice through inspection regimes. An equally important component of the 'new public management', especially relevant as regards research, is a strand of populist or anti-elitist political rhetoric which demands that the expenditure of public funds must result in direct and clear benefit to the wider public, often accompanied by the accusation that, previously, funding has served only to satisfy the interests, or finance the leisure, of an intellectual elite.[3]

A slightly different interpretation of this changing institutional environment views it as part of an evolutionary shift to postmodernity, or at least as reflecting a major change in the nature of modern societies, whereby the crucial productive factors are no longer material resources, such as coal and electricity, but knowledge or information.[4] It has been argued that this shift demands a transformation of scientific enquiry, away from that characteristic of universities in the past ('Mode 1') to a 'transdisciplinary' form that is more distributed and is directly linked with business and commerce ('Mode 2') (Gibbons et al. 1994; Gibbons 2000; Nowotny et al. 2001).

---

[2]Of course, even in patronage systems there is a tendency for patrons to interfere, and indeed to place specific demands upon the producer, but this takes place within a framework where recognising the expertise of the latter is the default position. Patronage systems can of course take different forms, see Turner (1990). The investment model reallocates the necessary expertise to outsiders, for example to some sort of accountant or auditor. Russell (1993) documents a key point in the shift to this model in the UK, in the late 1980s. See his discussion of the distinction between universities being accountable to the state as to whether funds have been spent on activities for which they were allocated, and their being accountable in the sense of demonstrating to the satisfaction of outsiders that teaching and research were carried out in the best way, and in an efficient manner (pp. 48–51).

[3]Ignatieff (1997: 399) refers to a 'sullen populism'. See also Furedi (2006).

[4]See Stehr (1994), Webster (1995) and Rule and Besen (2008). An early, and locally very influential, argument about how universities would need to change, given the shift to the information society, was presented by Douglas Hague (1991), speechwriter for and adviser to Margaret Thatcher as UK Prime Minister and later Chairman of the Economic and Social Research Council.

In part, this reflects changes in the character of much natural science, what Ziman (2000) has referred to as the shift from academic to post-academic science, along with the fact that in the increasingly interventionist modes of 'research governance' that are now operating this has been taken as the template for all forms of academic enquiry. So, in natural science there has been an increasing shift away from the academic model towards one in which the identification of problems to be solved, the allocation of resources, the organisation of research teams, etc., have increasingly been conducted in ways that are modelled on practices in applied science and technological development (see Ravetz 1971; Cozzens et al. 1990; Ziman 1994; 2000). This has been a product of a variety of factors. One is increasing cost of the equipment needed to carry out research in many fields, and the requirements placed upon the allocation of funds by funding bodies, governments and universities. Another, also associated with increased dependence on complex equipment, is the development of elaborate technical divisions of labour, resulting in large, often transdisciplinary, teams of researchers collaborating on the same project. Increased pressure on time available for research arising from higher teaching and administrative workloads within universities may also have been a factor in this.

Nowotny et al. (2003) identify three elements of the environment in which scientific research now operates and regard these as key signs of a fundamental shift. First, there are greater attempts by governmental agencies, at national and international level, to 'steer' research priorities in such a way as to meet what are identified as pressing social and economic needs. Secondly, there is the 'commercialisation of research', an increasing turn to private sources of funding, and a preoccupation on the part of universities with gaining control of the 'intellectual property' generated by their research. Thirdly, there is the application of accountability regimes to scientific research that purport 'transparently' to assess its effectiveness and quality, regimes that have been increasingly internalised within universities in the form of strategic management systems of various kinds. Nowotny et al. report that: 'as a result of these and other trends, the research that is variously described as "pure", "blue-skies", fundamental, or disinterested, is now a minority preoccupation – even in universities' (2003: 184).

A variety of attitudes can be adopted towards these developments, including: wholehearted endorsement of what is believed to be an overdue transformation of 'the research industries' to make them more effective and efficient; a pragmatic resistance which insists that all that one can hope to do is nudge inevitable changes in better rather than worse directions; Marxist and post-Marxist analyses of the significance of these changes as reflecting the nature of late capitalism or postmodernity, which may or may not allow for the possibility of successful resistance; and conservative despair at a world that has gone off the rails. There is something to be said for all of these stances, but I have least sympathy for the first.

CHANGES IN ATTITUDE AMONG ACADEMICS

In addition to institutional changes, there have also been significant shifts in the attitudes and behaviour of social scientists themselves. In the UK, by around the middle of the twentieth century, social science had been largely assimilated into the academic ethos, despite its origins in reform movements and other practical ventures (Abrams 1972; Kent 1981; Bulmer 1984). However, academics recruited from the 1960s' generation of university students, among whom social scientists were a much increased proportion, probably had rather different attitudes towards the functions of research and of universities from previous generations, both because they came from a wider range of social backgrounds and as a result of the significant changes in socio-political climate that took place in that decade in some Western societies.[5] Moreover, later generations of academics have probably inherited an even more diluted version of the academic ethos, and have been more subject to the changes in institutional conditions mentioned in the previous section, and the ideas associated with these.

The result is that many academic social scientists now reject central elements of the academic ethos, though usually without abandoning it completely, in practice at least. One aspect of this has been loss of belief in the idea that the sole immediate task of academic research is to pursue knowledge, and that such knowledge is of value in its own right. In place of this there has been an emphasis on the pragmatic goals that knowledge can serve, and often a conviction that research can bring about significant change in society; indeed that it cannot be justified if it does not have practical effect or political value. This has been reflected, for example, in the growth of 'critical' forms of enquiry – including those motivated by feminism, anti-racism and disability activism – and of 'action research' of various kinds. Of course, what resulted by no means always took an explicitly oppositional form – the weakening of the academic ethos was also associated with the growth of university research aimed at serving governments, commercial organisations, or occupational practitioners of particular kinds.

As this makes clear, one of the components of the academic ethos that was rejected was the idea that research should be 'detached', in the sense of the researcher either foregoing any impulse to evaluate what was being investigated or being disengaged from practical or political action. Such detachment came to be widely regarded as condemning social research to irrelevance and triviality or, even worse from some points of view, allowing it inadvertently to support the status quo. For it to be of value, the argument went, it had to be directly engaged with some desirable practical goal or with 'progressive' politics.[6]

The theoretical resources that were drawn on by social scientists from the 1970s onwards carried another consequence for commitment to the academic ideal. An influential strand in many quarters consisted of various kinds of epistemological radicalism. The starting point for these, often, was the idea, drawn from Marxism and critical theory, that forms of 'knowledge' presenting themselves as objective and neutral are in fact social products that serve to promote particular interests and/or to preserve the existing social order. From this, there was a rapid move by many to the idea that *all* knowledge is a social product, with the false implication drawn that we are all necessarily engaged in constructing different 'knowledges', some becoming much more powerful than others, none of which can claim epistemic priority, in

---

[5] On socio-cultural changes in the UK, see Martin (1981) and DeGroot (2008).

[6] For critical assessments of this argument, see Hammersley (1995; 2000a).

terms of truly representing reality. The conclusion derived from this, often, was that knowledge claims must be assessed in non-epistemic terms: political, ethical or even aesthetic (Smith 2004; Denzin and Lincoln 2005; Hammersley 2008a; Eaglestone 2004: 169). One effect of this was to stimulate the production of fiction, poems, autobiographical accounts, plays and other arts-based forms by some qualitative researchers.[7]

In the second half of the twentieth century, this shift towards epistemological radicalism was greatly aided by the huge influence, within social science, of Thomas Kuhn's (1970) *The Structure of Scientific Revolutions*. This was frequently interpreted (wrongly) as demonstrating that even natural science simply involves the construction of competing interpretations of the physical world, none of which can claim epistemic superiority over the others. Kuhn was treated as arguing that a particular paradigm comes to be dominant through the exercise of persuasion and power, only to be toppled later by another paradigm through exactly the same social processes.[8] Of course, Kuhn's work was not the only stimulus to epistemological radicalism: the influence of relativistic readings of phenomenology and structuralism, philosophical hermeneutics, and various strands of 'postmodernism', were also important, especially in later years.

Under the influence of these kinds of epistemological radicalism, there have been recurrent paradigm wars (Gage 1989) within social science, so that academic discussion has increasingly come to be understood as a form of battle.[9] The battles have been interspersed with periods of détente, characterised by a distinctive attitude of toleration according to which radically different approaches are to be allowed so long as they are themselves tolerant towards their competitors. However, this kind of toleration does not encourage productive debate about the issues that divide the various approaches. Indeed, the epistemological radicalism on which it is based actually denies that any such engagement is possible, because different approaches are 'incommensurable': they do not share sufficient in common for discussion even to get off the ground. Instead, it is insisted, we must simply adopt one or another approach, and respect the different decisions other people have made.

Increasingly, then, social scientists dismiss key elements of the academic ethos, appealing to alternative rationales that propose quite different forms of research. For example, it has become standard to ridicule the idea of pursuing knowledge for its own sake, and the requirement that researchers should attempt to be value neutral or objective. Similarly, in many quarters, the words 'truth', 'reality' and 'knowledge' are placed in scare quotes, when they are used at all, to deny that (perish the thought!) the author is committed to their having genuine meaning. Instead, it is widely accepted that academic research must be directed towards bringing about practical

---

[7]See, for example, many articles in *Qualitative Inquiry* and in *International Journal of Qualitative Studies in Education*. In a prescient article, Lovejoy (1917) contrasted the goal of objective knowledge with that of edification, a contrast whose evaluative slant Rorty (1982: 169–79) later reversed. Lovejoy commented that, if edification is the goal, 'poetry is surely a happier medium' (p. 131).

[8]For excellent accounts of Kuhn's work, see Hoyningen-Huene (1993), Bird (2000), Sharrock and Read (2002). See also Kuhn (2000).

[9]This continues today, a recently published book on qualitative research by Denzin (2010) has the subtitle 'a call to arms'.

outcomes of one sort or another; or that it should be designed to exemplify some practical value, for example social justice; or that its function is to challenge dominant ideas, and/or to subvert the socio-political status quo.

Even among those who pursue academic research, rather than explicitly adopting one of these other orientations, there is extreme reticence about defending it in its own terms. This reflects the fact that its rationale is at odds with powerful themes within the contemporary political cultures of the West. For researchers to claim to produce superior knowledge is likely to be interpreted as implying that lay people are ignorant, and that society should be governed by experts; in other words, it will be dismissed as undemocratic. Similarly, the notion that it is possible and desirable to try to be objective, and any claim that objectivity has been approximated, is down-played for fear that it will be rejected as self-interested rhetoric, as all claims to have acted in line with moral principles now tend to be. That academic research should pursue knowledge for its own sake is also rarely defended because it is likely to be interpreted as implying that such research is worthless. Indeed, in gaining the resources to carry out social scientific work in the UK today, from external agencies and within universities themselves, it is now required to specify what sort of practical 'impact' it is likely to have.

These cultural themes reflect broader institutional changes. One is the growth in technological research funded by companies in a range of fields – notably pharmaceuticals, computing and telecommunications – and the ways in which this model has shaped ideas about research. Other relevant changes are those that have taken place in the orientation of the mass media, and especially the growth of lob-bying, public relations agencies, and think tanks of various kinds, many of these claiming the title to research. To a large extent what we have now in many Western societies is a political culture characterised by 'spin', in which the production and presentation of information and misinformation is governed by commercial or political interests of various kinds, sometimes overt but often covert. In such a culture, distrust is endemic, and this is increasingly extended to academic research.

The changes in institutional and attitudinal conditions I have discussed are major threats to academic social science.[10] My aim in this book is to clarify and develop an account of its character and requirements, and the rationale underpinning it. In the next section, I will provide a slightly more detailed overview of what it involves, before outlining the contents of subsequent chapters.

THE ACADEMIC MODEL

A first point to make is that academic research implies the exercise of some licence, often labelled 'academic freedom' (Pincoffs 1975; Russell 1993; Menand 1998). This involves recognition that producing academic knowledge may involve exploring topics, questioning assumptions, and producing findings in ways that lay people may regard

---

[10]There are many who would deny this. For a recent argument to the effect that academic science has long been shaped by non-epistemic values and that this is no threat to objectivity, see Douglas (2009). For an assessment, see Hammersley (2010b).

as unintelligible, pointless, trivial, shocking, immoral, or even dangerous. It can entail asking about or observing things which are judged to be indecent; drawing on sources that are viewed as disreputable; taking seriously lines of argument that are regarded as unacceptable in ethical or moral terms; or publishing findings that could have bad consequences, for example by being used in ways that many (including researchers themselves) find highly objectionable. At the very least, and more usually, it involves expending a great deal of time and effort investigating small matters whose significance can only be understood in the context of a particular discipline, and from a relatively long time-perspective.

In my view, preserving this sort of licence is essential if the academic model of knowledge production is to flourish, or even to survive. However, this model also imposes some significant obligations on researchers. Indeed, in some ways these are simply the obverse of the licence outlined above. The relationship between the freedom and the responsibilities of social scientists was central to Max Weber's defence of academic freedom in the face of state encroachment on it in Germany in the early 1900s (Weber 1974). He recognised that academic freedom would be allowed by a state only in exchange for academics focusing on the tasks that are distinctive to them: producing knowledge and inducting students into this knowledge. Moreover, he did not see this 'contract' as a matter of sheer expediency, he regarded it as essential not just to the effective pursuit of academic knowledge but also to the existence of a liberal society.[11]

Against this background, I want to try to identify some of the virtues that are required of academic researchers. A first one is *dedication* to the task of producing knowledge. While this requirement may seem obvious, it is not just a matter of high-level commitment to academic work, it also implies that the pursuit of knowledge should not be subordinated to, or indeed combined with, other goals. This runs against influential demands, mentioned earlier, that social scientists go beyond the production of knowledge, for example that they should serve as 'organic' or 'public' intellectuals, that they ought to work to maximise the practical or political 'impact' of their work, and so on. Combining knowledge production with other goals requires compromises that cannot avoid obstructing the most effective means of pursuing enquiry (Hammersley 2008b).

It is important to note that achieving knowledge which reaches the threshold of likely validity required by academic work is extremely demanding. It entails what might be called slow thinking (Pels 2003; see also Law 2004: 10). Very often, the task will have to be broken down into sub-tasks whose value would not be recognised by lay audiences. Furthermore, researchers must be prepared to recognise that at any particular point in time there may not be sufficient compelling evidence to come to a sound conclusion about a particular issue, and they will often need to acknowledge that much further research is required before this can be achieved. Difficult judgements are involved, and these must be protected from practical and political pressures to resolve the issue within a specified time.

---

[11]Bruun (1972) emphasises that Weber saw value-freedom/value-neutrality as a defence against scientism. On Weber, see also Ciaffa (1998). On the issue of neutrality more generally, see Simon (1994).

What are involved here are very different imperatives from those that govern most other social roles, including those that researchers take on in other areas of their lives. These requirements are also widely ridiculed – with academic knowledge being dismissed as irrelevant or trivial, as outdated by the time it appears, as subject to excessive qualification, as never conclusive, and so on. Many social scientists feel such criticism acutely, accommodate to it, or even agree with it. This has been true for some time – here is an example from 1975:

> A common conclusion of studies in the social sciences is for the author to write that 'more research is needed'. But that kind of conclusion has become something of a bad joke and it is not my conclusion. That kind of conclusion should be recognised for what it is: a way of dodging the problem of arriving at a conclusion, burying one's head in the uncertainty which only scholars understand. (Pearson 1975: x)

What I have referred to as dedication involves an obligation to defend the value of academic research in the face of such criticism and to respect the nature of its distinctive task. There is a duty to uphold the importance of this kind of research, not acquiesce in downgrading or dismissing its value. To flout these obligations amounts to a betrayal of the ideals to which any academic researcher ought to be committed.

A second important requirement, alongside dedication, is that, in doing their work, researchers should have a heightened sense of methodological awareness, as regards potential threats to validity and how to deal with them. The need for this is obvious given the demanding nature of the kind of knowledge that is to be produced. This means that the field of methodology should be central to research: it should not be viewed as of relevance only to students and novices, or as getting in the way of 'the real business'. Even in everyday life, we are all usually aware of at least some ways in which our beliefs could be undercut by error; and, on those occasions where major costs are involved, we will often check these out very carefully. However, the responsibility of the social scientist, indeed of any academic researcher, is much greater: he or she must engage in sufficient checking of potential sources of error to ensure that all conclusions reach a high threshold of likely validity.

Of course, the implication is not that the researcher must eliminate, or fully check, *all* potential sources of error. This could never be achieved, and the attempt to do so would result in no social scientific knowledge being produced at all. Moreover, the fact that what is required here is a matter of degree clearly allows for considerable variation in judgement about what findings are and are not sufficiently well-established to be treated as sound knowledge. And this leeway is potentially subject to the influence of various sorts of interest and bias, so that the task of remaining objective is by no means straightforward. Nevertheless, objectivity, in the sense of seeking to minimise the danger of systematic bias arising from background commitments and assumptions, is another essential virtue for the researcher. The fact that some researchers today seem to deny both the possibility and the value of objectivity is itself a threat to the survival of academic social science.

My account up to now might be taken to imply that what is required of academics is that they possess individual virtues, in forms that are distinctive to their particular occupation. This is certainly true, but it is essential to recognise that the process of producing academic knowledge is a collective one. I argue in this book that such knowledge is not discovered or constructed by individual researchers, each working on her or his own, but rather is generated through dialectical processes within research communities: through discussion, both oral and written, that is designed to come to conclusions about what is true, what is false and what is currently uncertain. The work of any individual researcher takes place against this background, and necessarily engages with it.

This collective character of enquiry places additional obligations on researchers, as regards how they present their work, how they respond to criticism and how they treat the work of colleagues. In large part, what is required here is that academic research takes place within an enclave that is protected from the practical considerations that are paramount elsewhere: those considerations must be suspended, and so too (generally speaking) must be any considerations deriving from the other identities of those acting as researchers. In particular, the political, ethical and practical implications or consequences that might be associated with any line of argument or research conclusion must be held in abeyance in order to focus entirely on its likely truth. Also suspended must be any characterisations that might conventionally be made of someone who puts forward this line of argument, entertains its possible validity, or opposes it. In other words, academic discussion must be protected from political and practical demands, so that the consequentiality of proposing, challenging, or even just examining particular ideas or lines of investigation is minimised.

It is worth noting that the model of academic enquiry I am putting forward is at odds with currently influential views about the *dissemination* of research findings. Today, it is often demanded, for example by funders and university managements, that researchers make the knowledge claims they generate widely available, or even that the 'impact' of these be maximised. In a similar way, many academic social researchers see their work as directly contributing to a process of discursive democracy, and this too demands that findings be widely publicised. However, according to the model I am presenting here, while the 'findings' of particular studies should be made public within research communities, they should not be disseminated to lay audiences. What *should* be communicated to those audiences, via literature reviews and textbook accounts, is the knowledge that has come to be more or less generally agreed to be sound within the relevant research community, through assessment of multiple studies.

This restriction on what is disseminated, and when, is essential if a context is to be preserved within academic communities in which research conclusions can be assessed solely for their likely validity. If findings are to be publicised immediately then researchers can hardly avoid considering the likely political or practical implications that will be attached to their work, or its possible consequences. Equally important, restricting the publicity given to initial research findings is also necessary if the public sphere is to be protected from findings being presented as if they had been validated by the research community when they have not. Lay people who are interested in using research findings often complain that these are contradictory. This problem arises, in part, because of the misguided imperative that is now placed upon researchers to disseminate the findings of each study, along with journalists' reporting of what they take to be newsworthy findings from particular studies.[12]

OUTLINE OF THE CHAPTERS

Earlier, I argued that methodological awareness and reflection are central to academic social science. In large part, this is what offers the prospect of producing findings whose likely validity is greater than that of information from other sources, which is the distinctive value of academic knowledge. In Chapter 1, I examine the field of social scientific methodology, noting that it is now very large and very diverse in character, and that there is considerable ambivalence among social scientists about its value. For many, methodology is only relevant to novices, while some regard it as a distraction from, or even a fetter on, the substantive business of actually doing research. Moreover, the situation is greatly complicated by the fact that the boundaries around what is included in the field of methodology have been widened dramatically over the past few decades, notably through the rise of what I refer to as methodology-as-philosophy and methodology-as-autobiography, alongside the previously dominant form of methodology-as-technique. This change reflects the influence of deepening divisions among social scientists, whereby methodological debates are now not just about how social research can best be carried out, but also about whether producing knowledge is a sufficient goal, and about the very possibility and desirability of this product.

My aim in this first chapter is to clarify the forms that methodological reflection currently takes, and to consider what its proper function ought to be. The main conclusion is that methodology, in the sense of continual reflexive awareness of potential threats to validity, must play a central role in every piece of social research. However, methodology should extend beyond reflection about particular studies to address more general issues; and this necessarily requires specialisation on the part of some social scientists. I also suggest that, while methodology must document how research is actually done and be realistic about what is possible, it is necessarily normative in character. Finally, there is the question of whether there can be too much attention given to methodology, as well as too little. I examine each of the three genres, considering the contribution they make, and the respects in which they may have become overdeveloped.

In the second chapter, the focus is on the influential idea that researchers should be intellectuals, rather than being 'mere technicians' or professionals. I examine different interpretations of the concept of the intellectual, ranging from the minimal sense of pursuing an 'intellectual' occupation, through being a witness to universal values in the public realm, to various sorts of 'engagement' with practical activities and political causes. As illustration, I use examples from France during the twentieth century, since these carry important, and often forgotten, lessons. I argue that, first

[12]This is a particularly serious problem in the field of health, but it occurs more widely.

and foremost, social researchers must be devoted to the intellectual character of their work, and I spell out what this means by drawing parallels with the concept of professionalism. While there is no reason why those who are pursuing social research should not also serve some other practical or public role, it is important to recognise that doing this is a separate task, not an intrinsic part of the research process; that researchers are not uniquely qualified to be public intellectuals; and that taking on this additional role reduces the time and other resources available for research, and may generate tensions that can damage its quality.

The next chapter develops this argument by focusing on the role of criticism in academic research, and the insistence by many social scientists that their work should have a 'critical' function, in the sense of challenging dominant ideas or institutional forms. Indeed, the charge that colleagues' work is 'uncritical' has become a common one, reflecting the fact that being critical is frequently taken to be an unalloyed virtue. However, there are important questions about what the term 'critical' means, about what we should be critical of, and about the form that criticism ought to take. My argument here is that criticism plays a crucial role in academic work, but that it must operate within specific parameters. I compare the proper role of criticism in academic communities with its role in public discussions of social problems and policy proposals. I argue that the kinds of criticism required in these two contexts are very different. Indeed, there are ways in which the dispositions that social scientists acquire, or should acquire, through their work may actually make them less effective as participants in the public sphere. In each context, there are proper limits to criticism; albeit different ones. Like anything else, criticism is not always a good thing.

What I am moving towards here is an account of the obligations and virtues that are imperative for academic social scientists. In Chapter 4, I address a key virtue that has come to be the subject of considerable debate: objectivity. A first task is to clarify the different meanings this word can have, and how these have changed over time. I then explore the implications of a commitment to objectivity within the context of academic research, drawing on the literature dealing with virtue ethics, and interpreting it as an obligation to minimise bias. Along the way, I challenge various attempts to deny the importance of objectivity in this sense, or to transform it into something else. Objectivity is closely related to what I referred to earlier as dedication. It assumes that pursuit of the occupational task, the production of academic knowledge, is the only immediate goal, and it involves seeking to ensure that commitment to other goals and values (as a person or citizen, for example) does not lead to false conclusions.

Chapter 5 starts from an observation that social scientists sometimes continue to treat research findings as true even when these have been shown to be false, or at least to be of uncertain validity; in other words, they are regarded as 'too good to be false'. At face value, this is clearly a vice, but it raises some important issues about the threshold of likely validity that a knowledge claim must reach if it is to be treated as true in the context of academic enquiry. Drawing on the arguments deployed in the dispute over 'the ethics of belief' in the late nineteenth and early twentieth centuries, I examine the differences between how we evaluate knowledge claims in the context of academic research and how we do this in most other activities. Central here are two sorts of epistemic risk: treating findings as true when they are false (false positives), and treating them as false when they are true (false negatives). I argue that in everyday life we respond variably to these types of error, according to their relative importance in the particular context. By contrast, there should be a standard, and asymmetrical, approach to these two types of error in academic research: we should err on the side of false negatives rather than false positives.

The second half of this book addresses the nature of academic knowledge production more directly. Chapter 6 compares three models of the research process. Two of these are widely employed, both explicitly and implicitly. Indeed, the first, the discovery model, was at one time, and remains among lay audiences, the standard view of scientific enquiry. The second, the construction model, has arisen partly as a reaction against the first, but also through the influence of various philosophical ideas, from Kant onwards, which raise questions about the idea that knowledge can correspond to the character of independent, real objects. However, this second model is also subject to serious criticisms. Both models omit or misrepresent important aspects of the enquiry process, and fit some kinds of enquiry better than others. I argue that they therefore need to be complemented with what I refer to as the hermeneutic or understanding model. This treats knowledge production as necessarily dependent upon the background assumptions and situation of the researcher, but at the same time as directed towards discovering features of the phenomena investigated whose existence does not depend upon the enquiry process. It is stressed that what is produced is not a 'picture' of some set of phenomena, even less an exhaustive representation of them, but rather answers to particular questions about them.

In Chapter 7, this model of academic knowledge production is developed further by examining the dialectical processes through which knowledge claims are assessed within academic communities. The aim here is to identify the norms that ought to govern researchers' engagement with one another's work. I begin by drawing on the ideas of three very different philosophers – Popper, Habermas, and Gadamer – to spell out the basic commitments that should underpin academic discussion, whether in oral or written form. I then provide a more systematic and detailed account of these, drawing on the maxims that Paul Grice identified as regulating conversation. What results from this is a list of dispositions that relate to all stages of the communication process. These concern the following: when findings should be published and to what audience, what level of confidence in their validity should be expressed, what information and evidence need to be provided in support of them, what the response should be to criticism, and so on. What is outlined here is a powerful social mechanism that maximises the chances of discovering the truth – though, of course, it can never guarantee this outcome. In effect, what is involved is the setting up of a distinctive discursive environment in which the likely truth of knowledge claims can be assessed effectively; and in which the danger is minimised of this being distorted by concern with the value implications of those claims, or the perceived political or practical consequences – personal or social – of putting them forward as true or of rejecting them.

Returning to a theme mentioned earlier, the exercise of academic licence or freedom is central to the operation of academic communities. In the final chapter I examine what the limits to this licence should be and how they ought to be determined.

I do this by investigating the extreme case of Holocaust denial, which most people would treat as beyond the pale. I examine the extensive arguments that have surrounded this issue, and the different attitudes adopted towards it. I try to show that the only appropriate grounds for ruling out particular claims from consideration within academic communities are that they challenge or contradict what is already well-established knowledge without sufficient warrant, or that the manner in which they are presented breaches the constitutive rules of academic discussion. Some of the arguments about Holocaust denial accuse it of normalising what was a uniquely evil event. But this amounts to rejecting the idea that it can be studied via the kind of academic enquiry I have defended in this book. I argue that claims that the Holocaust must be treated as inexplicable or absolutely unique should be rejected. At the same time, I emphasise that academic research cannot provide us, on its own, with an appropriate response to the Holocaust, or to any other event; or offer practical advice for avoiding its repetition. This extreme case also brings out a more fundamental point: that, while academic enquiry aims at neutrality in relation to practical values, it is not compatible with all religious, ethical, or political perspectives. There is a direct parallel here with liberal forms of government, which also presuppose some substantive values, however 'thin' by comparison with governments that are dedicated to the promotion of particular conceptions of the good life. Neutrality is always relative to some range of alternatives; it cannot be defined in an absolute way.[13]

In the chapters that follow, then, I examine various methodological aspects of academic social science and of the rationale for it. I hope that this enterprise, as outlined here, can be saved from what many claim is, or should be, its demise. But I am not optimistic.

---

[13]The term 'value-neutrality' or 'value-freedom' is a very problematic one. When introduced, by Max Weber, it meant impartiality on the part of scientists in relation to practical (that is, non-epistemic) values in the assessment of knowledge claims; and, more broadly, an exclusive immediate commitment to the pursuit of knowledge. This seems to me to be central to the academic ideal, but so too is what Lacey (1999) refers to as autonomy: while, in social science at least, research questions must be selected partly in relation to some value-relevance framework, they should be set by academic researchers themselves, not by funders, sponsors, university managers, or governments.

PART 1

THE ROLE OF THE RESEARCHER: LIMITS, OBLIGATIONS AND VIRTUES

1

METHODOLOGY, WHO NEEDS IT?[1]

[…] sociology is the science with the greatest number of methods and the least results. (Poincaré 1908: 19–20)

Methodologists remind me of people who clean their glasses so thoroughly that they never have time to look through them. (Freud, cited in Sterba 1982: 120)

Methodology is too important to be left to the methodologists. (Becker 1970: 3)

The literature on social research methodology is now very large. Indeed, it may still be increasing at an increasing rate. It is so substantial that it is unlikely anyone could read all of it; or perhaps even keep up with the latest publications. In part, this growth in the literature results from the fact that, in the UK and elsewhere, substantial 'training' in methodology has become institutionalised in many postgraduate programmes, notably as a result of requirements laid down by research funding bodies. There has also been increased emphasis on 'research capacity building', aimed at improving the methodological knowledge and skills of practising researchers, and this has included the promotion and dissemination of 'methodological innovation' (see Travers 2009).

The sheer scale and growth of the methodological literature might be taken as a sign that social science is in robust health. But it is also possible to draw a very different conclusion: that there is an excessive preoccupation with methodology on the part of social scientists, perhaps amounting to a cancer on the face of research. Approximations to both these views can be found, suggesting that there is some ambivalence towards methodology among social scientists at the collective, and perhaps even at the individual, level. Attitudes no doubt vary according to researchers' degree of involvement in this type of work, from those

---

[1]My title echoes Howard Schwartz's (2003) 'Data: who needs it?', though my concerns and arguments are different from his.

who call themselves methodologists and/or contribute substantially to the literature, through to those who do not write about it, believe that it is only of relevance to novice researchers, or perhaps even regard it as a major distraction or obstruction.

Ambivalence towards methodology has been evident for a long time. In the first decade of the twentieth century, Max Weber complained about a 'methodological pestilence' in German social science (quoted in Oakes 1975: 13), with researchers becoming preoccupied with epistemological issues; yet, at the same time, he himself produced a batch of highly influential methodological writings (Weber 1949; 1975; 1977). Around the middle of the twentieth century, when the importance of meth-odological training was beginning to be emphasised in US sociology, C. Wright Mills wrote a paper entitled 'On intellectual craftsmanship' that was later developed into an appendix to his book *The Sociological Imagination*, and was reprinted in various forms in other places. It became a classic methodological text for sociologists. Yet, in this text, Mills declares that much methodological discussion simply 'disturb[s] people who are at work', as well as leading to 'methodological inhibition' (Mills 1959a: 27). So, here we have a methodological text which warns of the dangers of methodology. Mills also complains about 'the fetishism of method and technique' (Mills 1959b: 224), and others have echoed this, referring to 'methodological narcissism' (Nisbet 1963: 148), the 'myth of methodology' (Kaplan 1964: 24) and 'methodolatry' (Gouldner 1965; Janesick 1994: 215).

In this chapter, I will begin with a very brief sketch of the methodological ideas that have shaped social science in the past 50 years, and then examine three genres to be found in the methodological literature today and the ambivalence towards methodology to which they have given rise. Towards the end of the chapter, I will consider the role that methodology *ought to* play in social research, reflecting on the value of each of the genres but also on how they can lead us astray.

A BRIEF HISTORY

There has not just been an increase in the amount of methodological literature over the past few decades, its content has also changed considerably; this varying, of course, according to disciplinary area as well as across national contexts and language com-munities. Around the middle of the twentieth century, methodological texts gener-ally treated natural science as the model to be followed, with *method* being seen as the driving force behind science.[2] It was widely believed that the development of experimental method in the sixteenth and seventeenth centuries had been crucial to the remarkable success of the natural sciences, enabling them subsequently to make startling discoveries about the nature of the Universe, the constituents of matter, and the character and development of living organisms. Not surprisingly, much effort was soon made to apply 'scientific method' to the task of understanding the social world. Furthermore, it was widely assumed that this could lead to progress in overcoming

---

[2]This idea can be traced back at least to the writings of Francis Bacon. For a sophisticated account of Bacon's views in their historical context, see Gaukroger (2001).

the increasingly serious problems faced by large, complex industrial societies. The expectation was that social science could deliver parallel benefits to those which science-based technology had brought to many material aspects of human life.

Despite widespread adoption of natural science as a model, from the beginning there were important differences in views among social scientists about the nature of scientific method; as well as conflicting ideas about whether social science is distinctive in its goal or in the nature of the phenomena with which it deals; and, if so, about whether and how scientific method should be adapted to take account of this. Debates about these matters go back to the nineteenth and early twentieth centuries, when there were philosophical conflicts between inductive and hypothetico-deductive views of science, and also between those who took physics – rather than, for example, biology – as their model. In addition, there were arguments about the necessary methodological distinctiveness of the historical and social sciences (see Hammersley 1989: ch. 1). Moreover, by the middle of the twentieth century, there was an awareness on the part of many social scientists that their disciplines had not achieved the demonstrable progress characteristic of natural science in the nineteenth century, nor the same practical payoff. One response was to insist on the continuing immaturity of, and difficulties faced by, the social sciences. At the same time, this sense of failure undoubtedly stimulated the promotion of approaches that rejected the natural science model, and in some cases the very idea of *science* itself (Bateson 1984: ix; Smith 1989; Harding 1991; Denzin and Lincoln 2005; Hutchinson et al. 2008; Peim 2009).

In the second half of the twentieth century, there were also significant changes in attitude towards natural science in the wider society. Its beneficent image began to be tarnished by public recognition of its negative side: of the uses to which its methods and products had been put, for example in warfare and in the Holocaust; of the environmental consequences of the new industries it stimulated; of the disturbing possibilities it opened up in biogenetics; and even of the means it employed, such as animal experimentation. As a result, there was a shift in view about the nature and value of scientific knowledge. As long ago as 1972, the philosopher of science Mary Hesse noted the consequences:

> Various intellectual and moral tendencies are currently combining to dethrone natural science from the sovereignty of reason, knowledge, and truth which it has enjoyed since the seventeenth century. Far from being the paradigm of objective truth and control which will make us free of all natural ills and constraints, science is increasingly accused of being a one-sided development of reason, yielding not truth but a succession of mutually incommensurable and historically relative paradigms, and not freedom, but enslavement to its own technology and the consequent modes of social organisation generated by technology. (1972: 275)

These wider challenges to natural science tended further to undermine its role as a theoretical or methodological model for many social scientists. One consequence of this, in the second half of the twentieth century, was the emergence of a fundamental division between quantitative and qualitative approaches within many fields of social science. Views of method as requiring quantitative measurement and the control of variables that were dominant in many areas began to be abandoned by a growing number of social scientists, on the grounds that these were based upon a false, positivist philosophy. Furthermore, qualitative researchers started to draw on very different ideas about the proper nature of social enquiry: from nineteenth-century philosophies like hermeneutics or pragmatism to influential strands in twentieth-century continental philosophy, such as critical theory and post-structuralism. Over time, qualitative research increasingly fragmented into competing approaches that marked themselves off from one another in the name of conflicting philosophical and political commitments: interpretive, 'critical', feminist, constructionist, postmodernist, etc. And these developments led to a considerable diversification of the methodological literature.

THREE GENRES

We can identify at least three broad genres within the literature on social research methodology today:

1   Methodology-as-technique
2   Methodology-as-philosophy
3   Methodology-as-autobiography

In each case, a particular kind of methodological writing is treated as central, on the basis of various assumptions about the nature of social enquiry, what it can produce, and the conditions for doing it well.[3]

METHODOLOGY-AS-TECHNIQUE

In the 1950s and 1960s, methodological writing tended to focus on research designs concerned with hypothesis testing, the details of experimental and survey method, measurement strategies, and techniques of statistical analysis.[4] What was involved here was a particular conception of social scientific research, whereby the questions to be addressed needed to be identified and made explicit at the outset, and quantitative methods were generally assumed to be required for a scientific approach; though non-quantitative methods were sometimes included as supplements. Furthermore, it was assumed that research method could be quite closely specified in terms of rules to be followed.

---

[3]These three genres are, of course, ideal types. Particular examples of methodological writing only approximate to them. Nevertheless, the typology provides a crude map of the field that may be of some use.

[4]For early examples of texts within the methodology-as-technique tradition, see Goode and Hatt (1952), Festinger and Katz (1953) and Galtung (1967).

Here, methodology was treated as providing the knowledge and skills that are essential for effective social science practice. This involved spelling out the nature of scientific method and its implications for doing social research, along with the provision of advice about how to approach the various decisions involved. There was also great emphasis on the need for social researchers to be *trained* in methodological procedures, especially in statistical techniques, so as to be able to carry out scientific work well.

Later in the twentieth century, methodological texts became broader in their coverage, generally giving more attention to qualitative methods, though they often preserved the emphasis on technique. This emphasis was even true of many early books that were specifically devoted to qualitative method, in the sense that they were primarily concerned with offering practical guidance.[5]

At its simplest, methodology-as-technique is an attempt to codify the methods social scientists use, specifying their character and proper application in relation to the different research tasks, indicating the grounds on which choices among methods should be made, and so on. And the primary audience here is often students and other novices who need to learn how to do research. The aim is to make method explicit and thereby to provide a basis for learning and improving it. Generally speaking, in this genre of writing, an apparently consensual image of how to pursue research is presented. Even where different methodological philosophies are recognised, these tend to be reduced to a relatively small number of clearly defined options that are to be chosen either according to fitness for purpose or as a matter of taste.

At its most extreme, what is involved here is what might be referred to as proceduralism: the idea that good practice amounts to following a set of rules that can be made explicit as a set of prescriptive dos and don'ts, or even in the form of recipes. Quantitative research is often believed to be codifiable in this way; but there is a temptation to try to proceduralise qualitative research as well, on the grounds that this must be done if it is to be scientific, and/or if newcomers are to be taught how to do it. However, the literature within this genre varies considerably in how closely it approximates to the procedural model.

The early methodology-as-technique texts came to be criticised because of the way they privileged quantitative work, for their 'positivist' philosophical orientation, and/or for their encouragement of recipe following. They increasingly came to be seen as at odds with the spirit of qualitative enquiry, not least because of the latter's emphasis on the importance of creativity in research, and on the role of personal, social and cultural factors in shaping it. Proceduralism, in particular, was rejected for being ideological: that it systematically obscures the fact that research is done by people with distinctive characteristics in particular socio-historical locations, and that it is based on philosophical assumptions.

---

[5]Examples include Junker (1960), Glaser and Strauss (1967), Denzin (1970), Lofland (1971) and Schatzman and Strauss (1973). More recently, a form of literature has emerged covering both quantitative and qualitative methods that is very practice-focused and instrumental in character. See, for instance, Bell (2005), Phillips and Pugh (2005), Denscombe (2007; 2009) and O'Leary (2009). Such books would also come under the category of methodology-as-technique.

METHODOLOGY-AS-PHILOSOPHY

One of the effects of the rise of qualitative approaches and associated criticism of quantitative method, and of subsequent disputes amongst proponents of competing qualitative paradigms, was the flourishing of a new genre, what I will call methodology-as-philosophy. Early textbooks, and other publications, in the methodology-as-technique genre had often included some coverage of philosophical ideas about the nature of science, but this was usually restricted to brief preliminaries. Moreover, philosophical debates were generally presented as either already largely resolved or as of minimal practical significance for how research ought to be done. There was rarely much indication that there were sharply conflicting views among philosophers of science or that there are unresolved philosophical problems surrounding social science; despite the fact that, by the end of the 1950s, the philosophy of science was in turmoil, older positivist ideas having collapsed largely as a result of internal criticism (Suppe 1974).

As already noted, many of the early introductions to qualitative method adopted a primarily practical focus, and they too generally gave relatively little space to philosophical issues – by comparison with many later treatments. However, there were already signs of the emergence of a different emphasis. In their influential book *The Discovery of Grounded Theory*, Glaser and Strauss (1967) argued for a distinctive methodological approach, against the preoccupation with testing hypotheses that dominated quantitative research, and also against the tendency towards a descriptive orientation in much qualitative work. While they make little appeal to the philosophical literature, what they address here are nevertheless philosophical issues: as I noted earlier, there had been a long-running philosophical debate about inductive versus hypothetico-deductive interpretations of scientific method (see Gillies 1993). The year before Glaser and Strauss's book, Bruyn's *The Human Perspective in Sociology* (1966) appeared, and this was largely concerned with outlining the competing epistemological and ontological principles he identified as underpinning qualitative, as against quantitative, enquiry.

Subsequently, the amount of philosophical discussion in the methodological literature increased considerably, as 'new' qualitative paradigms sought to distinguish themselves from earlier ones. Furthermore, the character of the philosophical ideas that were appealed to by qualitative researchers changed over time: the influence of nineteenth-century hermeneutics, pragmatism, Marxism and critical theory was later accompanied or displaced by appeals to structuralism, philosophical hermeneutics, deconstruction and other forms of post-structuralism and 'postmodernism'. In the course of the battles that took place, older philosophical rationales tended to be rejected under the catch-all term 'positivist', this becoming an example of what Passmore calls a 'dismissal-phrase' (Passmore 1961: 2).[6]

---

[6]For an account of positivism and an argument that what this term refers to still has value, see Hammersley (1995: ch. 1). Ringer (1969: 298–301) notes a similar tendency to brand all that is anathema with the label 'positivist', this time among German academics at the beginning of the twentieth century. He highlights the context-dependent and variable meaning that the term had acquired even then.

Many of these developments raised fundamental issues. For example, within Marxism the question arose: in what sense can there be scientific study of the social world that escapes ideology, and what requirements must be met to achieve this? Pragmatism raised the question, among others, of in what sense human behaviour can be segmented into units among which determinate causal relations operate, and therefore in what sense such behaviour is amenable to scientific investigation. For hermeneutics, the issue was whether and how we can understand other cultures; and, later, what the implications are of the fact that all understanding is a product of socio-historical location. Ethnomethodology generated questions about what would be required for a fully scientific approach to the study of the social world, in the sense of one that does not trade on commonsense knowledge, and about whether social phenomena have the determinate character that is required for scientific investigation. From post-structuralism, there was the issue of whether discourse, perhaps of any kind, can escape being a reification of the world, an imposition on it and an expression of power.

Central to this new literature, often, has been a very different view about the relationship between research and philosophy from that which had informed the earlier concern with methodology-as-technique. The latter treated philosophy as providing a specification of what a scientific approach required, thereby paving the way for a technical approach to research that left philosophy itself behind, relying instead, for example, on statistical theory. In fact, the sort of positivism that underpinned this early literature often assumed that philosophy itself could and should become scientific, with logic as its core (see Friedman 2001: ch. 1). By contrast, many of the philosophical sources on which qualitative researchers drew did not treat science as distinct from philosophy, and certainly not as superior to it or as uniquely exemplifying rationality – unless rationality was itself being dismissed. Some viewed science as a mode of rational thought that was broadly philosophical in character. Others challenged science of the kind that had become prevalent as based on a false philosophy, and therefore as representing a form of intellectual and political oppression.[7]

In addition, a change took place in ideas about the history of natural science over the course of the twentieth century, with the emphasis shifting away from the role of experimental method towards a stress on how philosophical ideas had shaped scientific development (see Burtt 1924; Koyré 1957). The implications of this, and of increasing criticism of positivist philosophy of science, were embodied in Thomas Kuhn's (1970) enormously influential *The Structure of Scientific Revolutions*. The impact of this book was much greater in the social than the natural sciences, despite the fact that Kuhn specifically sidelined these as 'pre-paradigmatic' and therefore as pre-scientific. For Kuhn, a mature science generally operates within a largely taken-for-granted framework or paradigm of theoretical and methodological ideas, embodied in major discoveries that are treated as exemplars of scientific work in the field concerned. However, when some of the problems that scientists are working on within a paradigm come to be recognised as recalcitrant, and when an alternative framework is available, fundamental change can occur. In such a 'scientific revolution',

---

[7]Influential sources for these various views are Habermas (1968), Gadamer (1975), and Lyotard (1993).

philosophical debates emerge about the phenomena being studied, how they should be conceptualised, and what constitutes evidence about them. As a result of this, eventually, the paradigm that had previously been taken for granted may be replaced by another. This sets up a new range of 'puzzles' that scientists in the field tackle, and in doing this they treat the new framework of paradigmatic assumptions as given, so that once again science becomes a largely technical activity.[8]

A key feature of Kuhn's account here is his argument that different paradigms are incommensurable: there is neither an overarching framework that can provide a means of assessing them nor an independent body of data that can adjudicate among their conflicting theoretical and methodological assumptions. This notion of incommensurability undermined the previously influential conception of science as accumulating knowledge over time through the application of a distinctive method. As a result, it became very common for social scientists to see the different approaches in their field as competing, incommensurable paradigms. Furthermore, whereas the natural science paradigms that Kuhn identified differed solely in their assumptions about the nature of the phenomena being studied and how these could best be investigated, social scientific paradigms came to differ also in ideas about what the purpose of research is, as well as about its relationship to politics and various forms of organisational and occupational practice. Indeed, as noted earlier, the model of science itself came to be abandoned by some, in favour of alternatives that included political commentary, autobiography, imaginative literature and art. From these perspectives, the main declared goal of social research sometimes became political change, personal or professional development, the realisation of ethical ideals, and/or aesthetic impact.

As should be clear, methodology-as-philosophy took discussion in methods texts into some of the most contentious areas of philosophical enquiry, including the following:

1   Whether research can identify causal processes operating in the social world, or whether what it documents are social constructions that people produce through their interpretations of and interactions with one another.

2   Whether enquiry is a process of discovery, in which extant features of the social world are documented, or whether research itself necessarily *constructs* the phenomena that it claims to document.

3   Whether any account of the world necessarily reflects the social and personal characteristics of the person(s) who produced it, in a way that undercuts claims to representational accuracy.

4   The differences, if any, between social scientific research reports and fictional writing, such as novels.

5   The political and ethical responsibilities that researchers have in 'representing' the people they study, one issue here being: how can these people and their lives be portrayed 'authentically'?

6   Whether objectivity is possible or desirable; and, in fact, what the term means. There is a host of sub-questions here: Is it possible to represent 'objects' in the world as they are in their own terms? Should people be viewed as objects? Is

---

[8]For a post-Kuhnian elaboration of the role of philosophy in the development of natural science, see Friedman (2001: 20–4).

it possible to produce accounts of social phenomena that are unbiased; and, if it is not, what are the implications of this for the (at least implicit) claim of social science to produce knowledge that is valid or true?

7   Whether enquiry can and should adopt an orientation that is detached from social or political practice. In particular, there is the question: should it be directed towards bringing about some kind of social change, serving the interests of a particular group or category of people, improving some practice, etc.?

8   Whether social research should be pursued as a distinct enterprise in its own right or should take the form of 'action research'. And, within this context, there is the issue of whether equity requires that the relationship between researchers and those they are 'researching' be one of partnership, or even involve the researcher adopting a subordinate role.

Needless to say, these are challenging questions, and a wide variety of stances towards them can now be found in the methodological literature, often amounting to what Smith (2004: 51) has referred to as 'deep heterogeneity'.

So, in place of the earlier focus on scientific method, on rules and procedures, there came to be an emphasis in much methodological writing on the philosophical assumptions underpinning various forms of research practice; on the creativity of research, with convergences to imaginative literature and art; on the centrality of ethics and politics; and on the need to be reflexive, continually questioning one's philosophical and political assumptions. This last notion, the commitment to reflexivity, was also central to the third main genre of methodological writing, which also arose largely as a result of the growing popularity of qualitative work.

METHODOLOGY-AS-AUTOBIOGRAPHY

In 1955 William Foote Whyte published a 'methodological appendix' to his classic qualitative study *Streetcorner Society*.[9] In this, he offered an autobiographical account, or 'natural history', in which he told the story of how he came to do the research on which his book was based: how he had gained access to the Italian community that he was studying in Boston, how his relations developed with informants, the problems that he faced and how he sought to resolve them, and so on. His account became very influential and there was an explosion of such accounts of particular studies in the late 1960s, 1970s and 1980s.[10] This 'methodology-as-autobiography' literature often took the form of chapters or appendices in books or theses, but there were also journal articles and a considerable number of *collections* of research biographies appeared. There were even some whole books devoted to explicating the research process involved in particular studies (see, for example, Rabinow 1977; Cesara 1982).

---

[9]Whyte's appendix was reprinted and extended in later editions, see Whyte (1993). This was not the first example of methodology-as-autobiography, for example Laura Bohannon had already published a pseudonymous fictional account of her anthropological fieldwork in Africa (Bowen 1954).

[10]For a listing of many of these, see Hammersley (2003a).

These 'reflexive accounts' grew to form a very large corpus; and, in addition, there was increased use of autobiographical material, and of other people's accounts of their research, as a source of illustration in qualitative methods texts (see, for example, Johnson 1975; Hammersley and Atkinson 1983).

From early on, some information about the design, data collection and analysis procedures employed in studies had, of course, been included in research reports. But the content, amount, and tone of later more autobiographical accounts were different. Where previously most of the information had been basic methodological facts about how the research had been carried out, perhaps with some technical problems mentioned, the new natural histories often *emphasised* the problems faced, especially those concerning relations with people in the field, how these were dealt with, the researcher's own personal responses to the research process, and so on. Furthermore, what was stressed, often, was how, in practice, research deviated from textbook accounts; natural histories sometimes thereby opened researchers up to methodological and moral criticism.[11]

The rationales provided for this third genre varied considerably. One involved criticism of the role of standard methodological texts in preparing newcomers to do research. It was argued that they did not cover all relevant aspects of the research process, especially as regards qualitative work. In particular, textbook accounts tended to say little in detail about social relations in the field and the problems that could arise in this area, yet these could be major obstacles. Closely related was an argument to the effect that much of the existing literature was relatively abstract, giving only *general* guidance. It was pointed out that concrete examples could be more illuminating for those learning how to do research. There was also concern about the picture of research presented in methodological textbooks: that it was, to a large extent, a rational reconstruction of the research process, portraying how it *ought to be*, rather than how it *actually is*. The suggestion was that beginning researchers often experienced a huge gap between how methodology texts told them research should be done and their own experience of it, leading to a sense of incompetence and failure, when in fact what they had experienced was normal. So, part of the rationale for methodology-as-autobiography was to provide a more realistic account of the research process for students.

Closely associated with all this was the idea that research is a craft, with the implication that how to do it cannot be learned as an abstractly formulated set of rules or techniques, or derived from some idealised model, but rather only through first-hand experience, and/or through accounts of actual studies produced by other researchers, these providing a basis for vicarious learning.[12] The argument here was that

---

[11]Bell and Newby report that they invited the contributors to the volume they were editing to 'own up' (1977: 11). Also influential was the publication in 1967 of the diaries that Bronislaw Malinowski had written while carrying out his early fieldwork. These provoked consternation at the disparaging remarks he made about the people he was studying (see Wax 1971).

[12]Around the same time as the growth of published natural histories, there was an increasing tendency to introduce project components into research methods courses, so as to give students direct experience of actually *doing* research. Note, though, that this had long been central to the education of neophyte sociologists at the University of Chicago, where case study work had been pioneered; see Bulmer 1984.

research is a practical rather than a technical activity: it necessarily involves making judgements, often on the basis of uncertain and inadequate evidence. This stems, in part, from the fact that it is subject to all manner of contingencies to which the researcher must respond. These contingencies are especially severe in the case of qualitative research. For instance, Everett Hughes argued that 'the situations and circumstances in which field observation of human behavior is done are so various that no manual of detailed rules would serve'; though he insisted that the basic problems faced by all field researchers are more or less the same (Hughes 1960: x). In other words, doing research in 'natural' settings – that is, under conditions that are not specifically designed for carrying out research – and often over relatively long periods of time, mean that it is essential to adapt the research process to the situation and to any significant changes in it. This may be necessary even just to 'survive' in the field so as to continue the research. However, there are also specifically methodological reasons why qualitative research cannot usually be a matter of following some prespecified plan. For one thing, failure to adapt to the situation being studied is likely to maximise reactivity and thereby to threaten the validity of the findings. Furthermore, the open-ended approach to data analysis which is characteristic of qualitative work means that ideas about what data are required will change over time; the requirements cannot be identified completely at the beginning.

Thus, it was argued that social research involves improvisation on the basis of past experience, plus situated judgements about what is and is not possible and desirable in particular circumstances. And the conclusion drawn from this by many qualitative researchers was that while methodology can supply heuristics, such as 'tricks of the trade' (Becker 1998), it cannot provide recipes for doing research or even specific guidelines. Moreover, these heuristics are best conveyed by concrete examples derived from actual research experience.

We can find many of these arguments in the introduction to one of the earliest and most influential collections of natural histories, that of Bell and Newby (1977). But these authors add another point as well. Besides complaining that textbooks do not represent the research process accurately, they also reject what they describe as their 'normative' character (p. 10). It is the emphasis on 'what ought to be done', they suggest, that leads to textbooks presenting a misleadingly 'context-free' account of research. In particular, what are neglected are the political aspects of research: 'everything from the micropolitics of interpersonal relationships, through the politics of research units, institutions and universities, to those of government departments and finally to the state'; and they argue that 'all these contexts *vitally* determine the design, implementation and outcome of sociological research' (p. 10). What is required, from this point of view, is a descriptive rather than a normative approach to methodology.[13]

Another argument underpinning methodology-as-autobiography was that textbook accounts present a false image of the researcher. For example, Whyte complained that these accounts place the discussion 'entirely on a logical–intellectual basis':

---

[13]This blends with ideas about the sociology of sociology that were influential at the time, see Friedrichs (1970) and Gouldner (1970).

they fail to note that the researcher, like his informants, is a social animal. He has a role to play, and he has his own personality needs that must be met in some degree if he is to function successfully. Where the researcher operates out of a university, just going into the field for a few hours at a time, he can keep his personal social life separate from field activity. His problem of role is not quite so complicated. If, on the other hand, the researcher is living for an extended period in the community he is studying, his personal life is inextricably mixed with his research. A real explanation, then, of how the research was done necessarily involves a rather personal account of how the researcher lived during the period of study. (1955: 279)

In fact, Whyte's argument here subsequently came to be applied even to those only 'going into the field for just a few hours at a time'. It was emphasised that in all research the decisions made in the field will necessarily reflect the social identity, personality, and feelings of the researcher – including her or his reactions to the events and people being studied.

As this indicates, a crucial issue is the effect of doing research on the researcher. Bell and Newby, for example, note that in the course of their own work 'we became different people' (1977: 16). They, and other commentators, emphasised that research can be a stressful process, and that how the work is done will inevitably be shaped by how researchers feel about the people they are studying, their fears about what might happen, etc. So one of the major themes in the methodology-as-autobiography literature came to be the emotional dimension of research (Henry and Saberwal 1969; Carter and Delamont 1996).

Whereas in methodology-as-technique the image is of the researcher as a rational actor deploying technical skills to resolve standard problems, and remaining much the same throughout the process, in methodology-as-autobiography the researcher is very often portrayed as at the mercy of events; as coping or failing to cope with contingencies; as winning through by luck as much as by expertise; and as changing in attitude and feeling over time. It came to be argued that reflexive accounts should reveal 'at least some of the human costs, passions, mistakes, frailties, and even gaieties which lie behind the erstwhile antiseptic reports of most social scientists' (Bell and Newby 1977: 14).

An important aspect of this argument, emphasised by some commentators, was that most textbook accounts of social research tended to portray it as a smooth, cooperative process. What came to be highlighted instead, often, were the conflicts that researchers often found themselves involved in with some of the people they were studying, especially those in powerful positions. And this was sometimes taken to signal that researchers might need to adopt a strategic, even a Machiavellian, approach in order to get the data required, on the model of investigative journalism (see, for example, Douglas 1976).

Another strand of argument promoting methodology-as-autobiography was concerned with what readers need to be provided with if they are to be able to assess the findings of a study. As noted earlier, prior to the emergence of this genre, studies had offered some information about how the research had been done, but this was quite limited in character. Since research was assumed to involve following particular methods, or applying specific techniques, minimal information about the researcher was thought to be necessary. However, once it was recognised that qualitative research cannot take a pre-designed and standardised form, it followed that a much fuller account was required of the research and of the researcher, if readers were to be in a position to assess or even interpret the work.

One version of this argument was that researchers should provide an 'audit trail', so that how they came to the conclusions they reached is made available to readers for checking (Lincoln and Guba 1985; Schwandt and Halpern 1988; Erlandson et al. 1993). This was seen as constituting an alternative form of rigour to that character-istic of quantitative research. In place of the argument that rigour involves following rules, thereby allowing replication as a test for the reliability and validity of the find-ings, it was suggested that the demand for rigour could be met by continual and careful reflection on the research process by the researcher, in terms of possible sources of error, plus documentation of this reflexive monitoring for readers, so that the latter could make their own assessments of likely validity.

Other writers took this notion of reflexivity in a different, more radical epistemo-logical direction.[14] Here it was argued that any research is necessarily infused by a distinctive personal perspective. As a result, notions of bias and error are eclipsed: research reports are not to be evaluated in terms of impersonal criteria, but should rather be judged in relation to the person and process that generated them. This involves a move away from the idea that research findings can accurately reflect the nature of the phenomena studied, in favour of a more constructivist point of view. On this basis, it often came to be argued that any account is necessarily partial and subjective, and as such should be assessed in ethical or aesthetic, rather than epistemic, terms.[15]

Also relevant here are ethical views which see reflexivity in terms of fairness: that if a researcher is asking people to expose themselves by providing information about their lives, then the researcher's own character and life ought to be included within the focus of the research. Not to do this, it was sometimes argued, is to imply the superiority of the researcher, to suggest that he or she is or could be a god looking down on the world, offering 'a view from nowhere'.[16] This led to the argument that natural histories of research should not be separated off from the main body of the research report but incorporated into it, so that the whole report should have a self-reflexive character (see Stanley and Wise 1983; 2002).

These radical versions of reflexivity arose from increasing emphasis on the creative character of research, the insistence that 'the personal is political', and the growing use of literature and art as models, in place of natural science. One formulation, that of Denzin and Lincoln, portrays the researcher as a bricoleur, who draws on a variety of resources to produce images or impressions of the world, in ways that are analogous

---

[14]'Reflexivity' is a term that is used in a variety of ways. For an outline of these, as part of a critique of the sense of the term I am discussing here, see Lynch (2000). See also Hammersley (2004c).

[15]See, for example, Mauthner et al. (2002), Denzin and Lincoln (2005).

[16]This widely used phrase seems to derive from Nagel (1989).

to collage or jazz as art forms (Denzin and Lincoln 2005). An alternative would be the idea that the path which any research project follows is necessarily both contingent and constitutive; that it is under the control of nothing and no-one, and *represents* nothing and no-one – certainly not reality or rationality. In other words, it must be seen as a matter of necessarily arbitrary 'decisions' among incommensurable possibilities. Either way, we are as far as we could be from the idea that research involves following the procedures of scientific method. From this radically reflexive point of view, methodology – in the sense of a concern with specifying techniques and methods, how they should be used, what would count as valid measurement, etc. – is simply a distortion of the research process; one created through the ideological imposition of a natural scientific or technical model, under the influence of a false positivist philosophy.

THE RISE OF ANTI-METHODOLOGICAL RHETORIC

Earlier, I argued that there is considerable ambivalence about methodology among researchers. In part, this amounts to a reaction against methodology-as-technique; for example by those who insist that social scientists must not neglect philosophical or political issues (see Chamberlain 1999). What is being rejected here is not methodology per se, but a particular version of it; one that prescribes rules to be followed that constitute 'a system for offering more or less bankable guarantees' (Law 2004: 9).

However, there are more fundamental sorts of anti-methodological argument to be found in the methodological literature. One of these has its roots in the craft model of research associated with some versions of methodology-as-autobiography.[17] As we saw, this model generates scepticism about the value of abstract discussions of methods and of the rationales for them, whether these take a technical or philosophical form. Instead, it is argued that research problems can only be dealt with in concrete terms, in particular contexts. Thus, in his influential discussion of 'intellectual craftsmanship', C. Wright Mills comments that 'serious attention should be paid to general discussions of methodology only when they are in [...] reference to actual work', and he adds that if all social scientists followed this 'obvious and straightforward' practice, 'at least all of us would then be at work on the problems of [social science]' (1959a: 27).

This craft position does not amount to a total rejection of methodological writing. Rather, the latter is seen as playing a narrowly defined role, one that is very much subordinate to the actual practice of research. Thus, Clive Seale argues that 'intense methodological awareness, if engaged in too seriously, can create anxieties that hinder practice', but he recognises that 'if taken in small doses (methodology) can help to guard against more obvious errors' (1999: 475). Within the craft tradition, then, there is often an insistence on the limited and subordinate function of methodology in relation to the practice of enquiry. At most, the methodologist's role is that of an

---

[17]On the craft model, see Hammersley (2004b: 550–2).

under-labourer, clearing the ground for research, and offering guidance about dangers. If methodology is given too much weight, so the argument goes, it becomes a diversion from the real work of enquiry, and perhaps even a positive hindrance.

A rather different version of anti-methodological rhetoric emphasises the need for researchers to have the freedom to engage creatively with their data in finding answers to research questions, with methodology (at least of a certain kind) being seen as amounting to an unwarranted form of constraint. For example, in his critique of methodolatry, Chamberlain argues that:

> developing a good interpretation requires thought and creativity, and its out-comes should be provocative and insightful. Codified approaches to method and analysis have a particular problem in capturing and presenting this. (1999: 290)

Here, an objection to 'inflexible and inappropriate guidelines' can merge into a general opposition to codification on the grounds that this obstructs good-quality research, this requiring the exercise of free theoretical interpretation directed not towards the discovery of facts about the world but rather to the construction of perspectives that can shape practice in ways that bring about social change (see also Law 2004). We should perhaps note, though, that, from the point of view of the craft tradition, the solution to the problem of methodolatry Chamberlain proposes – that we start from epistemology, then move to the issue of theory, finally ending up with method (p. 294) – might be seen as a symptom of the illness rather than a cure, on the grounds that it involves an (over)emphasis on methodology-as-philosophy.[18]

Interestingly, these kinds of anti-methodological argument do not occur only among social scientists. They have been directed more widely against attempts to specify the nature of scientific method in the philosophy of science. For example, echoing Bridgman's (1955: 535) definition of science as 'nothing more than doing one's damndest with one's mind, no holds barred', but developing the point in a rather different direction, Feyerabend argued, in *Against Method* (1975), that methodological prescriptions not only do not accurately capture how successful natural scientists do their work but actually obstruct the process of scientific investigation. A slightly different version of this argument, developed in the humanities and relating to methodology-as-philosophy not just to methodology-as-technique, is the position of Fish. He writes:

> Historians do not gain credibility (or anything else) by becoming meta-historians, that is by giving big answers to large questions like, What is the nature of fact?, How does one determine what counts as evidence?, Can the past be reconstructed?, Can the distinction between the past and the present be maintained? Whatever answers you give to such questions will be entirely unhelpful and beside the point when you return from their airy heights to the questions historians appropriately ask. (Fish 2001a: 510; see also Fish 2001b)

---

[18]For this kind of judgement about much methodological writing, see Mann (1981).

These anti-methodological arguments fitted the spirit of some of the qualitative approaches that gained ground in social research in the second half of the twentieth century in many fields. And, ironically, this anti-methodological spirit has itself added to the methodological literature. For example, Phillips reports that his book *Abandoning Method* was written to justify a course in methodology (1973: xi). Much more recently, Law (2004) has suggested that we must move beyond 'method', recognising that the 'realities' that social science deals with are often 'messy' rather than well-defined, and therefore cannot be captured by rule-based procedures and theories, so that in an important sense social science 'makes' the phenomena it purports to describe and explain. On its back cover, his book is described as being 'essential reading for students, postgraduates and researchers with an interest in methodology'. We might interpret all this as suggesting that social scientists' ambivalence about methodology amounts to a futile revolt against the inevitable need both to try to spell out the methods they use and to engage in methodological and philosophical reflection. However, it also shows an awareness of the limitations and dangers involved in this.

Against the background of the diverse character of the methodological literature today, and ambivalence towards and within it, in the next section I want to try to determine its proper nature and role. I will look again at the three genres I have identified, emphasising both what they can contribute and the limits to their value.

THE FUNCTION OF METHODOLOGY: EVALUATING THE THREE GENRES

We need to begin by looking at the meaning of the word 'methodology', as currently used. In its core sense, this refers to a discipline concerned with studying the methods employed in carrying out some form of enquiry. However, its meaning also extends to include the body of knowledge built up through this methodological work. And, in the context of the diverse orientations within social research outlined above, it is a short step to the use of 'methodologies' to refer to distinct approaches to studying the social world that involve conflicting ideas not just about methods but also about the intended goal and products of research, the ontological and epistemological assumptions involved, how the role of research is defined in relation to other activities, and so on. As a result, 'methodology', when used to refer to an area of study, has now come to include not just discussion of methods but also discussion of the philosophical and political issues that differentiate the many approaches to social research that now exist.

In this section I will argue that there is a place for all three of the genres of methodological work that have been identified: they all serve important functions. However, at the same time, each is in danger of, and has been subject to, 'overdevelopment'.

Methodology-as-technique. It should be clear that some knowledge of the various methods available is essential for social researchers. Newcomers must learn what these are, how they differ from one another, what is involved in their use and the problems that may be faced. Also, more experienced researchers will often have to improve or revise their knowledge of methods when embarking on new projects, since few if any of them will have a comprehensive, in-depth knowledge of all the techniques and strategies available in their field. Moreover, new methods sometimes emerge, or new applications of old ones; and, sometimes, new problems can arise in the use of existing methods as a result of changing circumstances. For these reasons, methodology-as-technique will be relevant to experienced researchers as well as to new entrants.

In these terms, we could ask whether the methodological knowledge that most researchers have today is adequate. There are those who believe it is not. A currently influential charge is that many social scientists have a sound knowledge of qualitative method but lack the necessary grasp of quantitative techniques. There may well be some truth in this, but there are also those who would insist that there is a widespread lack of adequate knowledge about qualitative method too. Furthermore, a broader critique could be mounted, relating to both sides of the qualitative–quantitative divide. It might be suggested, for example, that many social scientists are not aware of the full range of data collection and analysis strategies that would be relevant to the projects in which they are engaged; that they tend immediately to adopt standard methods and standard forms of these. If any of these charges is sound, it would require that methodology-as-technique should be given even more emphasis than it currently is; though there will be disagreement about what form this ought to take, and about the methods that should be emphasised.

Of course, methodology-as-technique also carries dangers. The most important, already noted, is proceduralism: a belief that rules can be laid out for applying particular methods, for example on analogy with specification of the steps that must be followed in using software to carry out statistical tests, or in doing the calculations oneself. In fact, very little of the research process can be reduced to rule following of this kind: it is too uncertain and complex a business, so that a significant level of judgement is always required. Given this, attempts to specify rules will have negative consequences. One example of proceduralism – to be found in many general, introductory methods texts – is the reduction of research design to a fixed and standard sequence of steps. This requires the researcher to: turn research questions into specific hypotheses; operationalise the variables making up those hypotheses; establish procedures for the control of both the hypothetical cause and confounding variables; and identify the statistical techniques that will allow the resulting data to test the hypotheses and reach conclusions about their likely validity. While, in one form or another, these various activities constitute essential aspects of any piece of social research, it is a mistake both to assume that all research must start with hypotheses and be directed towards testing them, and to insist that these various activities must, can, or should be carried out in this fixed sequence and form, each being completed before the next is begun. Instead, research design should be seen as an iterative process in which judgements must be made about what it is best to do in relation to all these issues, given the purpose of the research and present circumstances, throughout the course of enquiry. Furthermore, this may even involve changes in research focus and in the kind of knowledge aimed at, and therefore in the ways in which the various tasks making up research design are approached (see Maxwell 2004).

Also involved in proceduralism is the idea that the research process can and should be made 'transparent', in other words that it can be fully specified, thereby allowing for replication by other researchers. It is certainly true that readers of research reports need to have information about how the work was carried out, and that in some cases replication can be a useful means of checking the results. However, just as doing research cannot be reduced to following procedures, so too it is not possible to give a complete account of how any piece of research was actually carried out; nor would it be productive to attempt this. Rather, a reader only needs *sufficient* information to be able to make an assessment of the likely validity of the findings. For the purpose of replication, the information required may be greater, but it is still selective. Moreover, the aim of replication is not simply to copy what was originally done, but to find out whether it is possible to produce the claimed results, and this may involve strategic variation in the methods used.

Given this, the fear that methodology-as-technique can put blinkers on the researcher, restricting creativity and innovation, is a genuine one. At the same time, creativity cannot operate in a vacuum. There is always a need for knowledge about existing methods and methodological ideas. While proceduralism is a danger, so too is ignorance.

Methodology-as-philosophy. Doing research always involves relying upon philosophical assumptions, and there will be times when these need to be reassessed. This can arise in a variety of ways. It may be that practical difficulties emerge in the course of an investigation, which then lead to doubts about what was previously taken for granted. Equally, though, doubts may be generated by external influences. As noted earlier, over the years social science has been shaped by ideas from a variety of philosophical traditions, and these have sometimes stimulated re-evaluations of the assumptions on which past work had relied. The belief that research can be an entirely technical or practical matter – philosophy-free, as it were – is an illusion; there must always be some reflection on what is being done and why, and sometimes this will involve issues that have preoccupied philosophers. Much can be gained from drawing on their work. Moreover, in a context where there are multiple conflicting external influences, and where there are often several competing approaches within any research field, attention to philosophical issues will normally be required in order to decide on and to justify the approach being adopted in any particular study.

However, there are also some dangers with methodology-as-philosophy. One is that philosophy will be plundered and misinterpreted in ways that are not helpful for the pursuit of social enquiry (see Hammersley 2006a). Many years ago, Tudor noted how sociologists have used philosophy 'much as the military might use a guided missile':

> Recognising the incipient power of labels borrowed from philosophy, sociologists have strewn them about with little regard to their detailed significance. Indeed, if armies were so irresponsible (and they may yet be) I should not be writing, nor you reading, this essay. We would have since vanished in clouds of nuclear fallout. (1982: 1–2)

Another problem is that attention may be given to philosophical issues that do not have major implications for actually going about social research. For example, while there are undoubtedly important differences between positivist and realist accounts of science (see Keat and Urry 1975), in my view it is doubtful whether these, in themselves, carry much import for social scientific work. There are two reasons for this. First, there is a great deal of variation within each of these philosophical approaches, so that what they can be taken to recommend overlaps substantially. It is only if we take extreme versions of both that clear water appears. Secondly, drawing inferences from each of them about how social research should be carried out is necessarily a process of interpretation, in which other assumptions are relied upon, for example about what is possible in a particular area of enquiry. So, for example, not all of those who have been influenced by positivism have given primary emphasis to quantification and measurement; and some of those doing quantitative work appeal to realism rather than to positivism.[19]

A third point is that there are some philosophical assumptions on which social scientists rely whose validity there is no point in their questioning *in the course of planning and carrying out their work*. This is because the assumptions concerned cannot be avoided if social research is the task. In *On Certainty*, Wittgenstein refers to these as 'hinge' assumptions. He provides an example: if we were to start doubting whether the past extended beyond living memory, suspecting that what we take to be signs of the more remote past are simply artefacts constructed so as to make us believe in its existence, the very possibility of most historical work would be undercut (Wittgenstein 1969: paras 206, 234, 311).[20] Similarly, to dismiss sequential time as 'a recent and highly artificial invention of Western civilisation' (Ankersmit 1994: 33), which privileges Western over non-Western ways of viewing the world, and which therefore should be abandoned, is not to 're-think' history (Jenkins 2003) but rather to abandon it (see Evans 1997: 141). More generally, to raise doubts about the very possibility or desirability of knowledge, in the sense of accounts that represent facts about the social world, removes the point of academic social science. We cannot do this kind of work if these assumptions are genuinely doubted. What results from abandoning them is not some new form of social scientific enquiry but rather turning it into something else: a form of philosophy, imaginative literature or political commentary; or into the blend of these that is characteristic of the diverse body of French writing that has come to be labelled postmodernist.

Questions about whether knowledge of the kind pursued by social science is possible and desirable can be usefully subjected to philosophical and other kinds of investigation, but these are not issues that there is any point in social scientists considering as part of their methodological deliberations. In doing social research we *must* believe that there are facts about the phenomena we are investigating that can be discovered, and that this knowledge is worthwhile. If we do not, then there is no point in pursuing the activity. Of course, outsiders – scholars in other disciplines and members of funding bodies or of the general public – may take a different view about these matters; and in response to this social scientists will have to address these

---

[19]For a different view about this issue, see Halfpenny (1982; 1997).

[20]There are some differences in the interpretation of Wittgenstein's argument here, see Kober (1996), Moyal-Sharrock and Brenner (2007).

questions in order to defend social science and sustain its funding. Similarly, individual social scientists may experience a crisis of faith about these matters. However, arguments about them cannot be part of methodology, they are not relevant to how researchers can best do their work. Despite this, there is currently much discussion of these matters in the methodological literature; along with arguments premised on the assumption that knowledge, in the ordinary sense of that word, is impossible or undesirable (see, for example, Denzin and Lincoln 2005; Peim 2009).

It should be added that *any* activity involves presuppositions on which it necessarily relies – without which it could not be pursued. These can always be questioned from the point of view of epistemological scepticism, as well as from other perspectives. Furthermore, there is no reason to suppose that the assumptions underpinning various kinds of empirical academic enquiry, including the social sciences, are any more open to reasonable doubt than those which structure other human activities, including those to which some qualitative researchers seem to want to turn: such as politics, ethics, literature, or art. Finally, in the most general terms, it makes no sense to doubt the possibility or value of knowledge, since in one form or another enquiry is integral to all human activity; nor does redefining 'knowledge' as belief or personal expression provide a satisfactory alternative.

So, there is a considerable amount of discussion today within the genre of methodology-as-philosophy that, in my view, is irrelevant or obstructive to the practice of social enquiry. Philosophical issues are frequently discussed in a manner that does not take proper account of the arguments developed to deal with them by philosophers. And they are sometimes treated as if they had direct and determinate implications for practice when they do not. Even more obvious is the way in which sceptical arguments about truth and value are deployed in much methodological discussion, in ways that flout the hinge assumptions of social enquiry. Inevitably, these arguments are used selectively – to criticise other positions – while their global implications are quietly forgotten when it comes to the critic's own position and form of work.

Methodology-as-philosophy is essential, then, since we cannot avoid relying upon philosophical assumptions, and these can be problematic. However, a considerable amount of methodology-as-philosophy is excessive.[21]

Methodology-as-autobiography. Above, it was argued that much writing under this heading was stimulated by what I referred to as the craft tradition. The fundamental idea here is that research is a practical activity: it is directed towards particular products, and depends upon judgements and learning in specific circumstances about how best to produce these. This is clearly at odds with any idea that research is a matter of following rules or procedures, but it also denies that the problems it faces can be resolved primarily by philosophical means. It places great emphasis on situated decision-making, and the wisdom that can arise from experience in doing research and reflecting upon it. To a large extent it is a matter of trying out various strategies in the context of particular projects, and the circumstances in which these are being pursued, and then reflecting upon what has happened and been produced, with a

---

[21]In some quarters excess is valued, notably under the direct or indirect influence of Bataille (1991). By contrast, my model here is Aristotle's notion of the mean; see Gottlieb (2009).

view to further practical decisions.[22] So we must see methodological reflection as a recurrent activity that is closely tied to the process of learning involved in doing research. Indeed, reflection in, and on, the research process is the core of methodology. The methodological literature is *secondary*: it comes out of the ordinary methodological thinking involved in carrying out research, even though it also feeds back into it.

There is a tendency for some commentators within the craft tradition to deny the value of more abstract forms of methodological thought and the literature this produces. Here, again, is Mills:

> As one begins his studies of some problem, he naturally turns first to studies that have already been done, and as he examines them, he certainly notices the methods their authors have used. He would be a fool if he did not do so. But once he goes beyond such an examination of the methods used in one area or another, and once he tries to transform methods into 'methodology', he often becomes quite abstracted. He loses firm connection with the kinds of problems for which given methods have been devised, and, in the end, makes quite formal, and often even useless, his examination of methods. Although not necessarily the case, this is surely a very real danger. (1959a: 26)

Clearly there is a genuine danger here, but any blanket rejection of more abstract methodological work can also be counterproductive. It is important not to see methodology as solely an individual, even less an idiosyncratic, pursuit.[23] The methodological thinking of the individual researcher or research team must be informed by collective discussion of methodological matters, and in such a way that progress can be made at least in understanding, if not in resolving, the problems that are faced by those working in the relevant area. Moreover, necessarily, this collective discussion will address more general questions than those which are specific to any particular project, and even to any single field.

So, one problem with methodology-as-autobiography is that its proponents often underestimate the value of methodological literature that goes beyond autobiographical accounts by individual researchers of particular projects. Sometimes what is in operation here is the idea that doing research is a matter of common sense, of ordinary knowledge and skills, and that the methodological literature renders it overly complicated and therefore opaque. Yet there *are* difficult problems, and there is much to be gained from noting differences between various kinds of work, following out the implications of particular lines of argument in fields that are different from those in which they were developed, addressing problems that face a wide range of kinds of work, and so on. The interaction between the specifics of what is involved in any particular project and more general reflection needs to be preserved. Without

---

[22]Here, I am blurring the ancient Greek distinction between *poiesis*, the making of things, including art works, and *praxis*, the kind of decision-making characteristic of life more generally and of politics in particular. This blurring is also a feature of much argument about the nature of professions, especially where a contrast is drawn with the work of technicians.

[23]It is striking in this context that Bell and Newby preface their introduction with the following quotation: 'idiosyncrasies of person and circumstance are at the heart not the periphery of the scientific enterprise' (Johnson 1975: 2; quoted in Bell and Newby 1977: 9).

this, every researcher is on her or his own, starting from scratch, and the result will be little methodological progress overall.

I have accepted that the core meaning of 'methodology' is the corpus of practical thinking and theory generated in actually doing research; so that in this sense *writing* about method is secondary. However, methodological writing is not simply the *inscription* of such thinking, it almost always involves its further development. It is an activity, or set of activities, that has a somewhat different, although no doubt overlapping, range of purposes even from oral discussion of methodology (and especially from the sort of internal dialogues in which researchers and research teams engage). Furthermore, writing about methodology can itself take a variety of forms, some closer to what is involved in oral methodological discussion, others further away. For example, blogging about method will be very different in character from writing a journal article or an introductory text. However, the value of more abstract kinds of methodological writing, for example drawing on specialised bodies of knowledge such as philosophy, mathematics, or literary theory, should not be dismissed.

There is also a problem with the concept of reflexivity, as this is sometimes interpreted within the methodology-as-autobiography genre. On some interpretations, it is taken to imply that researchers must somehow make their work fully transparent, explicating all that has gone into it, in terms of their own personal biography and philosophical-cum-political assumptions. Yet, not only is such self-explication impossible to achieve, since the process is never-ending, but the attempt to achieve it is likely to have very undesirable consequences for the pursuit of research. Taken to its logical conclusion, either no research will be done or the research that *is* done will not tell us much about what goes on in the world, but rather will be almost entirely preoccupied with explicating the 'subject positions' of the researcher. This is especially likely where 'reflexivity' is taken to signal that what is produced by research can be no more than a personal perspective on the part of the researcher, or a contingent co-construction with the people studied.

Another problem with methodology-as-autobiography is its insistence that methodology should be descriptive, not normative. Realistic reports of how particular studies were carried out are of great value, but they do not exhaust what is required. The fact that methodology is essentially normative follows directly from the practical character of research, which is central to the idea that it is a craft. The thinking that researchers engage in during the course of their work is about what they *ought to do*: whether what they have done was sensible, what they need to do now, what will have to be done later; and it will also extend to thoughts about the strengths and weaknesses of alternative strategies. Given that the function of methodological writing is to aid the practice of research, it must be normative. Even accounts of how researchers actually carried out particular pieces of work must be framed in ways that are relevant to practical concerns. In other words, they must be designed to lead into assessments of the advantages and disadvantages of different methods, the threats to validity associated with them, and so on. And they must be complemented by other kinds of writing that are more overtly normative in character. Of course, these must not be overly prescriptive – they must take account of inevitable variation in research goals and in the practical circumstances that researchers face. In other words, the methodological literature can only offer general, not specific, guidance. But offering guidance is its task; it is not equivalent to either the sociology or the philosophy of social science.

Indeed, there is a danger that realistic reports of how actual studies were carried out, taken alone, will legitimate adaptations to circumstances that amount to bad practice; in the sense of strategies that are not effective means of pursuing the goals of the research. What is expedient in a particular study is not necessarily sufficient to produce conclusions that are more likely to be true than information from other sources; yet this is what is required for academic enquiry to be worthwhile. So, the kind of 'realism' that is at the heart of methodology-as-autobiography must not be taken to entail that whatever it is possible to do in particular circumstances must be treated as sufficient to warrant drawing the conclusions reached. Instead, we will have to recognise, for instance, that some research questions are simply not answerable given the constraints under which we are operating, and that attempts to answer them are misguided. In short, the fact that research methodology must be realistic does not mean that whatever was, or can be, done should be treated as adequate. Normative assessment is essential.

A further danger associated with methodology-as-autobiography stems from the idea that every researcher must be her or his own methodologist (Mills 1959b: 224). In an important sense, this is correct. But it can lead to the false conclusion that there is no need for some social scientists to specialise in methodology, or indeed that such specialisation is undesirable. A rankling objection to specialist methodologists is evident in Mills' writing on method:

> I feel the need to say that I should much rather have one account by a working student of how he is going about his work than a dozen 'codifications of procedure' by specialists who as often as not have never done much work of consequence. (1959a: 28)

It is certainly true that there are dangers with specialisation, especially when this results in a cadre of methodologists who have little or no recent experience of actually carrying out social research, or where methodology becomes an enterprise with its own agenda that is not directed towards practical assistance and improvement of social research. But there are several reasons why a division of labour is desirable.

One is that researchers who have experience of a range of projects, perhaps of quite diverse kinds, or who have a talent for reflecting on methodological issues, can be an important source of insight and advice. A second point is that if methodological work is to be sound, and of value, then those doing it need to be familiar with the existing methodological literature. Contributions in this field, as in others, must take account of what has already been done and what is already known – if the same ground is not to be covered over and over again. Yet most practising social scientists do not have the time or resources to gain a reasonably comprehensive and deep understanding of what is now a very large literature. For any researcher, time taken reading the methodological literature is time not doing research. Given this, for most experienced researchers, most of the time, reading the methodological literature should be limited to searching for material relevant to specific, pressing problems. But, at the same time, there can be gains from some people specialising in methodology.

Of course, not all kinds of contribution to the methodological literature make great demands upon the writer in terms of familiarity with the methodological literature. We can identify a continuum in this respect, running from publications chronicling particular research experiences, through accounts that formulate those experiences in terms of particular sorts of methodological 'issue' or 'lesson', to sustained arguments about proper and improper use of particular research methods or strategies, their advantages and disadvantages, as well as more abstract discussions of fundamental methodological or philosophical issues. The first two types of contribution are important and do not demand much in the way of knowledge of the extant methodological literature. There is no need to become a specialist methodologist to produce them. By contrast, the last two sorts of contribution make much larger demands on methodological expertise if they are to be done properly. They may require the author to draw not just on the existing methodological literature but also on philosophy, social theory, psychology, literary criticism, statistical and mathematical theory, natural science, and so on. Indeed, some contributions to methodology may take the form of presentations of ideas from these fields that are relevant to the pursuit of social enquiry, outlining what their implications might be. And it is important that such contributions are based on a sound understanding of the material being used.[24]

I am arguing, then, that while methodological reflection is an essential element in the practice of research, and thus a necessary and proper activity for *all* researchers, a division of labour is required both in reading the methodological literature and even more so in making contributions to it, especially those of a more abstract and general kind. Furthermore, while methodological reflection is important for all researchers, generally speaking it must be limited for most of them to what is necessary for doing particular pieces of research, and to contributions that do not make great demands in terms of knowledge of the existing literature.

Specialist methodologists are under an obligation to disseminate the results of their work, whether through producing textbooks, reviews of portions of the literature, guides to ideas on particular methodological topics, or whatever. In other words, to provide resources that researchers can use in thinking about and tackling the problems they face. However, this activity, and the fact that it is essentially normative, raises the question of the extent and sort of authority that they can and should seek to exercise. Any division of labour involves an unequal distribution of authority, but this authority is always fallible and limited to particular issues. Needless to say, the response of individual researchers to recommendations and cautions in the methodological literature must be reflective, rather than a matter of automatic acceptance. Even if these recommendations and cautions are sound in general terms, they will

---

[24]It is equally important that they draw on good knowledge of the relevant methodological literature, rather than it being considered, as a starting assumption that the new perspective renders this obsolete. Law's (2004) application of ideas from 'the discipline of science, technology and society' (p. 8) to the field of methodology is open to this charge. The claim that 'the proof of new ways of thinking about method […] lies in their results and their outcomes, rather than in their antecedents' may be true, but the idea that this can be judged without learning from past methodological and philosophical discussions is a modernist illusion.

not usually apply straightforwardly to particular studies. At the same time, blanket scepticism about the value of the methodological literature is not wise; it will hamper or prevent improvements in social research.

There are many researchers who specialise in methodology today, not least as a result of the demands of postgraduate training programmes. Whether this division of labour works well is debatable. Those who write introductions to research methods, and make other general contributions to the methodological literature, do not always display knowledge of the most relevant previous discussions in that literature, or a sound understanding of the more specialist fields on which they draw. Indeed, it sometimes seems to be assumed that anyone who has done some research has what is needed to write sensibly about methodology. As a result, many contributions repeat what has already been covered, in apparent ignorance of what can be learned from the existing literature, and in the process they often perpetuate confusions that had previously been cleared up. Some also misrepresent and misuse previously well-understood ideas. Moreover, many stock assumptions that need to be questioned prevail in contributions to the methodological literature, about both quantitative and qualitative method. For example: that research is always necessarily political; that any enquiry must begin by specifying the methodological framework adopted and must stay within its limits; that the central assumption of positivism is that there is a real world, independent of our experience; that the findings of quantitative research are generalisable while those of qualitative work are not; that the sort of correlational analysis used by most quantitative research involves the effective control of confounding variables; that discourse analysis, in its usual forms, can avoid reliance upon a correspondence theory of truth; and so on.[25]

CONCLUSION

In this chapter I began with a brief history of social research methodology and outlined the diverse forms it takes today, distinguishing between methodology-as-technique, methodology-as-philosophy, and methodology-as-autobiography. I showed how the emergence of the last two genres stemmed from the rise of qualitative work, and how this had been associated with ambivalence towards methodology, resulting in influential anti-methodological strands within the methodological literature.

In the face of understandable scepticism about the value of methodology, in the second half of the chapter I outlined my own views about its nature and function. I argued that its core must be the sort of awareness of, and reflection about, methods in which researchers should normally engage during the course of enquiry, but that there is also a need for specialist methodologists (who must themselves also be engaged in research or be close to it). I insisted on the value of all three genres, but also outlined some boundaries that ought to be placed around methodology. In the course of this I highlighted ways in which it had come to be overdeveloped: the tendency for methodology-as-technique to encourage proceduralism; the irrelevance and destructive character of some methodology-as-philosophy; and the

---

[25]For discussion of these various issues, see Hammersley (1992a; 1995; 2009b).

tendency for advocates of methodology-as-autobiography to downplay the role of general discussion of methodological issues and methods, and to forget the necessarily normative character of the task.

The answer to the question in my title is that we all need methodology: it is an essential component of social scientific research, both at the practical level and in more specialised terms. However, the methodological literature today suffers from serious distortions in relation to all three of the genres I discussed, and from a failure to learn from its past, leading to both repetition and a lack of coordination (Hammersley 2004d). This is unfortunate given that social science of most kinds has, in my view, been a good deal less successful than is frequently claimed by many social scientists; and that it faces fundamental methodological problems that require a great deal more attention, and more thoughtful investigation, than is usually recognised.

2

ON THE SOCIAL SCIENTIST AS INTELLECTUAL

All men are intellectuals [...]; but not all men have in society the function of intellectuals. (Gramsci 1971: 9)

The intellectual is constantly betrayed by his vanity. God-like, he blandly assumes that he can express everything in words, whereas the things one loves, lives, and dies for are not, in the last analysis, completely expressible in words. (Lindbergh 1940: 6)

It is often argued today that social scientists should be public intellectuals: that an important part of their role is to participate in public discussions about social problems, political issues, or particular policies, and to engage directly with policy makers, political activists, campaigning organisations, and/or occupational practitioners of various kinds, in order to promote social change of one sort or another. In recent times, this has sometimes been portrayed as a matter of disseminating, and maximising the 'impact' of, their research findings; but it usually extends beyond this to include engaging in social and political commentary, championing neglected causes, and challenging dominant ideas and powerful interests.[1]

In the course of such arguments about the public role of social science, a contrast has often been drawn between 'the intellectual', on the one side, and the 'scientist',

---

[1] Burawoy's (2005) presidential address to the American Sociological Association in 2004, advocating 'public sociology', while recognising other kinds of work, exemplifies this commitment. This address generated considerable controversy; see for example www.savesociology.org/ and http://burawoy.berkeley.edu/PS.Webpage/ps.papers.htm. See also the argument and references in Holmwood (2007). Also relevant here is advocacy of action research, participatory enquiry, design experiments, interactive social science, or the co-production of knowledge, all of which propose some kind of integration between research and other activity. I have discussed these elsewhere, see Hammersley (2003a; 2004a).

the 'technician' or the 'professional', on the other.[2] This opposition goes back well into the twentieth century. Thus, C. Wright Mills picks up one aspect of it in his advocacy of 'the sociological imagination'. He bemoans a trend in which 'the idea of a university as a circle of professorial peers, each with apprentices and each practicing a craft, tends to be replaced by the idea of a university as a set of research bureaucracies, each containing an elaborate division of labor, and hence of intellectual technicians' (Mills 1959b: 103). What he is attacking in this passage is deviation from the scholarly ideal that I outlined in the Introduction of this book. However, in practice, Mills' conception of the role of the social scientist went well beyond this ideal, and in my view undermined it, extending to encompass forthright contributions to political debate on a range of issues, these being treated as a central part of his scholarly work (see Mills 1963; Horowitz 1983; Gillam 1977/8; Hammersley 2000a: ch. 2; Summers 2008). Indeed, Mills insisted that intellectuals should 'not split their work from their lives' (Mills 1959b: 195).

A little later, Gouldner's critique of the idea of value freedom within sociology involved a similar vision of academic communities whose work is necessarily linked to a radical political agenda (Gouldner 1970). Writing in the 1960s, he argued that there were still some sociologists who took on the role of the intellectual, but he lamented that the dominant drift of American sociology was towards seeing itself as a 'value-free profession' (Gouldner 1973: 16). He warned that 'if we today concern ourselves exclusively with the technical proficiency of our students and reject all responsibility for their moral sense, or lack of it, then we may some day be compelled to accept responsibility for having trained a generation willing to serve in another Auschwitz' (Gouldner 1973: 25). Against this technical, professional model, he argued that the sociologist should be a partisan, albeit in an objective manner (see Hammersley 2000a: ch. 4).

A couple of decades later, a similar contrast was drawn by Edward Said in his influential Reith Lectures, devoted to *Representations of the Intellectual*. He identified the true intellectual as an amateur, by contrast with professionals who are concerned solely with making a living, with avoiding 'rocking the boat', and with 'not straying outside the accepted paradigms or limits'; in short, with being 'uncontroversial and unpolitical, and "objective"' (Said 1994: 55). Interestingly, the terms of his discussion here are close to those in which the ideal of professionalism was being publicly challenged around the same time, from both Left and Right: for instance, professionals were attacked as claiming to be disinterested when their actions were actually self-serving (Hammersley 2009a).

More recent advocacy of the social scientist as intellectual has been in much the same spirit as that of Mills, Gouldner and Said, emphasising an obligation to champion progressive social change, to support marginalised and oppressed groups, to amplify subordinated forms of knowledge, and to challenge dominant ideas that support the political status quo, however defined (Robbins 1993; Fuller 1999; 2005; Goodson 1999; Michael 2000; Furedi 2006; Hollands and Stanley 2009). Similarly,

---

[2]See, for example, Coser (1965: viii–ix). Other, related, contrasts are drawn, for example between 'policy scholarship' and 'policy science' (Fay 1975) or between the 'true intellectual' and 'the rival callings of "opinion maker" or "pundit"' (Hitchens 2008) or 'cameo intellectual' (Olson and Worsham 2004: 6–7). See also Ignatieff (1997), Joffe (2003) and Furedi (2006).

while Burawoy (2005) recognises a role for what he calls 'professional sociology', this is within a framework that casts sociology itself as playing a public intellectual role, indeed a partisan one (Nielsen 2004; Holmwood 2007). In much discussion over this whole period, the role of the public intellectual was viewed as integral to that of the university academic; though other commentators identified a conflict between the two, usually on the grounds that belonging to the academy gets in the way of being an intellectual or of engaging in effective political action (Jacoby 1987; Mies 1991).

As should be clear, the contrast drawn in the literature between intellectuals and technicians/professionals is an evaluative one, with the first privileged over the second. However, the role of the intellectual has not always been regarded as worthwhile or beneficial. Sartre identifies 'one fundamental reproach' that is often directed against intellectuals, one which brings together a number of common themes:

> *the intellectual is someone who meddles in what is not his business* and claims to question both received truths and the accepted behaviour inspired by them, in the name of a global conception of man and of society. (1974: 230)

In other words, intellectuals are deplored in some quarters because they 'stray outside their field of competence' and 'abuse their celebrity or their authority to do violence to public opinion, by concealing the unbridgeable gulf that separates their scientific knowledge from their *political* appreciation'. This sort of criticism has generally come from the political Right, most intellectuals being identified and identifying themselves as 'of the Left'.[3] However, criticism of the notion of 'the intellectual' from the Left is not unknown. For example, according to the French Marxist, Paul Nizan, a friend of Sartre, what was needed in the 1930s was not philosophers or intellectuals, but rather 'the professional revolutionary as described by Lenin' (Nizan 1972: 137; see also Schalk 1979: 67; Redfern 1972: 42). Here professionalism, of a particular kind, is valued over being an intellectual.

My interest in this chapter will be, first of all, to explore what it means to describe the social scientist as an intellectual, since that term can imply a variety of very different roles or social functions.[4] I will outline these and provide some historical illustrations from the classic period after the emergence of the concept in the Dreyfus Affair in France around the beginning of the twentieth century. Towards the end of the chapter I will argue that there are severe restrictions on the kind of intellectual that social scientists ought to be, and that the concept of profession is an equally important way of conceptualising their role, as contrasted with that of the technician, which seems to be an increasingly influential view of the social scientist in some powerful quarters today.

---

[3] In older scholarly discussions of intellectuals this link with the political Left is by no means always preserved, reflecting in part the wide range of ways in which the realm of the intellectuals or the intelligentsia has been defined. See, for example, de Huszar (1960), Joll (1961), Shils (1972) and Brym (1980). See also Posner's (2003) illuminating economic analysis of academics as intellectuals.

[4] For discussions that exemplify the shifting dimensions and contrasts involved in use of the term 'intellectual', see for example Coser (1965: vii–xiii) and Melzer (2003: 4). See Eyerman et al. (1987) for a useful brief account of discussions of the concept of intellectual or the intelligentsia in the twentieth century, one that balances my emphasis on the French case in this chapter.

In debates about the role of the intellectual in France during the twentieth century, we can identify at least five rather different models. The first of these – as producer of knowledge (or of literature or art) – underpins the others, in the sense that belonging to an 'intellectual' occupation is regarded as a necessary but not a sufficient condition for the others. A second notion of the intellectual was exemplified in the Dreyfus Affair: someone belonging to an 'intellectual' occupation who acts as a public witness to and defender of universal values. Later, this model was criticised, especially by those who argued that intellectuals must be directly engaged with political movements aimed at bringing about progressive social change. From this point of view, it is necessary to be an 'enlisted' or organic intellectual.[5] Around the same time, there were also those who insisted that while intellectuals should be committed to a particular political cause, they ought not to subordinate themselves to any party or other organisation – they should act as independent, public intellectuals. An influential French example here is, of course, Sartre. Finally, in the second half of the twentieth century, there was a reaction against all these previous models. The role of the intellectual was now to be more 'specific': for instance concerned with supporting some oppressed or marginalised group involved in a particular struggle, and aimed at subverting the discourses that are integral to currently dominant 'regimes of truth'. This model is to be found, for example, in the work of Foucault and Lyotard.

THE INTELLECTUAL AS SPECIALISED PRODUCER OF KNOWLEDGE

At this point, I will give relatively little attention to this first interpretation of what it means to be an intellectual, but will return to it later. According to this definition, an intellectual is simply a member of an occupation that has 'intellectual' work as its core element. Durkheim (1969: 19) defines this type of work as 'using understanding to extend understanding, that is to say to enrich it with knowledge, ideas, and new sensations'. The set of occupations included here can be interpreted broadly, for example perhaps even including all occupations involving mental rather than primarily manual labour.[6] Alternatively, it may be interpreted much more narrowly; for example as including only writers, artists, scholars and scientists. My primary interest here, of course, is to explore the implications

[5]'Enlisted' is an attempt to translate the French word *embrigadé* following Landsberg's (1937) discussion of 'embrigadement'; see Schalk (1979: 23). However, although not used by French intellectuals of the time, I will use Gramsci's term 'organic intellectual' to label this particular form of engagement, since it is now widely used. See Joll (1977: ch. 9).

[6]This is not, of course, an entirely straightforward distinction. For a classic, Marxist discussion see Sohn-Rethel (1978). See also Sartre (1974), who characterises the occupations from which intellectuals come in capitalist society as those of 'technicians' or 'specialists' of 'practical knowledge'. He provides the following enumeration: 'scientists, engineers, doctors, lawyers, jurists, academics and so on' (p. 232). Curiously, his own occupation, which was perhaps best described as 'freelance writer', is not explicitly mentioned here, and does not seem to fit the definition. For a discussion of some relevant variations and changes in 'intellectual' occupations in the twentieth century, see Westoby (1987).

of different models of the intellectual for one particular occupation: that of the academic social scientist. And I will simply assume that this occupation counts as an 'intellectual' pursuit.

A major point about this first model is that, however broadly or narrowly its scope is defined, nothing is implied beyond commitment to and pursuit of an intellectual task. There is no suggestion that, in order to be a true intellectual, it is necessary to play a public role, or to have any concern with how the knowledge one produces might be used, beyond perhaps seeking to ensure that it is not seriously misrepresented.[7] By contrast, each of the other models demands more than this. Another key point is that, on this first model, the purpose of intellectual work is generally defined as the development and distribution of knowledge, understanding, sensibility, etc., rather than the pursuit of practical or political goals. The other models of the intellectual depart from this first one too.

THE INTELLECTUAL AS PUBLIC WITNESS FOR UNIVERSAL VALUES

As I have noted, the term 'intellectual', used as a noun, came to prominence through the Dreyfus Affair in France during the 1890s, in which influential writers, scholars, artists, scientists and others spoke out publicly against the conviction on charges of treason of the Jewish army officer Captain Alfred Dreyfus. The novelist Emile Zola's open letter to the President of the French Republic, entitled *J'Accuse*, came to be seen as the exemplary act of the intellectual. In it, he denounced the injustice that had occurred, blaming it on clericalism and anti-Semitism.[8] This was followed by a petition, which a large number of writers, artists, scientists, and philosophers signed (including social scientists such as Durkheim). This petition came to be known as the 'Manifesto of the Intellectuals', 'intellectual' being a term of abuse used by their opponents. By taking this stand, Zola and the other Dreyfusards attracted the wrath of a substantial portion of the French public, as well as that of the Army and the Government, though at the same time they also gained much support among the Republican Left. The Affair plunged France into deep turmoil because it symbolised fundamental political and religious divisions within the country. Zola was tried and sentenced, and went into temporary exile in England. Dreyfus was pardoned after four years in prison, and Zola died in 1902 under suspicious circumstances.[9]

Of course, there had been intellectuals, in some sense of that term, before the late nineteenth century. Julien Benda makes this explicit in his book, *The Treachery of the Intellectuals* (Benda 1928). It is significant that its French title uses the word *clerc*, and

---

[7]There are, of course, other ways in which members of 'intellectual' occupations may be required to participate in the public sphere, notably to defend those economic and political conditions that enable them to pursue their work effectively.

[8]In fact, Zola wrote several open letters and much else besides on the Affair. For these documents, see Zola (1996).

[9]For accounts of the Affair, and of the various interpretations of it, see Kedward (1965) and Bredin (1986).

Benda includes clerics among the examples he discusses.[10] In fact, he sees secular intellectuals as largely taking over the function performed by religious predecessors; and, as the title of his book indicates, he believes that some modern intellectuals have betrayed that vocation. In large part, his book was an attack on influential French anti-Dreyfusard intellectuals, and those he saw as their mentors (both French and German), who had not only supported nationalist causes but also subordinated their intellectual work to these.

So, this second model starts from the assumption that *in pursuing their vocations* intellectuals should serve universal or spiritual values, so that their work is not limited by local or petty concerns. Of course, living in particular societies, intellectuals will sometimes need to protect their own interests. However, from the point of view of this second concept of the intellectual, doing this need not be a self-interested matter, because their work is treated as symbolising universal or higher interests. Furthermore, it is believed that all intellectuals should be committed to the full range of universal or spiritual values, with these regarded as forming a unified whole. Finally, an essential component of this second model is that on some occasions intellectuals must intervene to support a cause, or remedy an injustice. In short, while the intellectual's primary task remains the pursuit of intellectual activities, he or she is also seen as playing not only an important symbolic but also sometimes an active role in the wider society, as the champion of higher values. The engagement in politics involved is occasional, and the authority of such intellectuals when they do intervene derives precisely from the nature of their primary work, which is seen as guaranteeing not just their wisdom but also their disinterestedness. They are 'above politics'.

Benda's book is probably the most influential presentation of this second version of the intellectual's role, and it also exemplifies many of its ambiguities. He draws a sharp distinction between material and spiritual concerns, intellectual work focusing on the latter. Intellectuals are:

> all those whose activity essentially is *not* the pursuit of practical aims, all those who seek their joy in the practice of an art or a science or metaphysical specu-lation, in short in the possession of non-material advantages, and hence in a certain manner say: 'My kingdom is not of this world'. (p. 43)

This formulation gives a hint of the extent to which Benda's position is a secularised version of Judaeo-Christian ideas. And the political role he assigns to the intellectual is analogous in some ways to that of Old Testament prophets; though it should be noted that his conception of 'the spiritual' is framed in terms of Greek rationalism rather than of Judaism or Christianity. He argues that, given the nature of human beings (after the Fall, as it were), most are preoccupied with their own material

---

[10]I have translated '*trahison*' as 'treachery', rather than 'treason' or 'betrayal', since this seems best to capture what is involved. 'Treason' implies a relationship analogous to loyalty to a monarch or nation-state, which is not implied by Benda's discussion. The objection to 'betrayal' is simply grammatical: to speak of 'the betrayal of the intellectuals' is ambiguous as to whether the intellectuals are the betrayers or the betrayed. On the meaning of the term '*clerc*' see Nichols (1965: 104–8). An analogue, though not a close one, to Benda's use of this term is Coleridge's idea of the clerisy, see Coleridge (1830). For an account of Benda's life and thought, see Niess (1956).

concerns and selfish interests, but that there are some among them, the intellectuals, who still place spiritual values above these petty matters. Drawing on the Greek distinction between *theoria* and *praxis*, intellectual work is portrayed as contemplation of the divine (or a secular equivalent of this) (Lobkowicz 1967). In effect, the role of intellectuals is to serve as the conscience of humanity.[11]

It is against this background that Benda identifies the 'treachery' of some intellectuals, and its consequences. He argues that in the nineteenth century, initially in Germany but later in France as well, there were those who betrayed their vocation by using their knowledge and skills to celebrate and promote the particular and practical rather than the universal and spiritual. Examples he mentions include Fichte, Hegel, Nietzsche, Treitschke, Barrès, Péguy, Maurras, and Sorel. According to Benda, damage is done here to the intellectual work itself, which becomes partisan and thereby debased. But, equally important is the resulting transformation of politics from a relatively pragmatic matter into more ideological forms. It is now gripped by passionate involvements focused on questions of religious, national, or class identity. He comments: 'Today, I notice, that every political passion is furnished with a whole network of strongly woven doctrines, the sole object of which is to show the supreme value of its action from every point of view, while the result is a redoubling of its strength as a passion' (p. 26). The age, he says, is that of 'the intellectual organisation of political hatreds' (p. 27). And, as already noted, he sees this as resulting from, or as being strongly associated with, the fact that some intellectuals, rather than standing above politics and acting as witnesses for universal values, had subordinated themselves to it. 'Today', he remarks, 'the clerc has made himself minister of war' (p. 107).

Benda sees this betrayal of the vocation of the intellectual as closely related to the rise of democracy. It is not entirely clear what he has in mind here, but the implication may be that democracy encourages intellectuals to address popular audiences; and that in doing this they necessarily begin to give attention to the material and particularistic concerns of those audiences, instead of retaining their autonomy and their spiritual vocation.[12] In an interesting sense, reinforcing the quasi-religious character of Benda's perspective, this betrayal of the intellectual role amounts to a second Fall by some of those few human beings who had previously managed to keep contact with spiritual concerns. And, like the first Fall, according to Benda, it resulted from their succumbing to the temptations of the material world.

Benda sees the proper role of intellectuals as keeping alive the possibility of an alternative form of life, and moderating the excesses of evil in the world. Unlike some of those who stress engagement, to be discussed later, he does not regard true intellectuals as waiting in the wings ready to become philosopher–kings or 'legislators' of an ideal society (Bauman 1987). At one point Benda comments:

---

[11]The influence of religious models on secular thought is a central feature of the development of French intellectual culture; see Wernick (1984: 133). For an illuminating discussion of the differences, and similarities, between the ancient Greek model of the philosopher and the modern intellectual, see Melzer (2003).

[12]This is not an explanation that fits the case of the 'German mandarins', who vociferously and actively supported the war effort in 1914, since most of them were and continued to be strongly opposed to democracy, which they identified with 'the West', in other words with Britain, France, and the United States; see Ringer (1969).

Must I repeat that I am not deploring the fact that the cults of honor and courage should be preached to human beings; I am deploring the fact that they are preached *by the 'clerks'*. Civilisation [...] seems to me possible only if humanity consents to a division of functions, if side by side with those who carry out the lay passions and extol the virtues serviceable to them there exists a class of men who depreciate these virtues and glorify the advantages which are beyond the material. (1928:139)

Later, he makes the point even more strongly:

It will be seen that I entirely disassociate myself from those who want the 'clerk' to govern the world, and who wish with Renan for the 'reign of the philosophers'; for it seems to me that human affairs can only adopt the religions of the true 'clerk' under penalty of becoming divine, i.e. of perishing as a human'. (p. 192)

Furthermore, Benda believed not only that intellectuals could never govern but also that it was becoming increasingly difficult to be an intellectual in the modern world, because of the way in which politics had become ideological, largely under the influence of democracy and the treachery of many intellectuals (p. 159).

What Benda condemns most of all, however, is the abandonment by some intellectuals of the commitment to truth *in their work itself*:

In historical science especially, they honor the intelligence which labors under the guidance of political interests, and they are completely disdainful of all efforts toward 'objectivity'. Elsewhere they assert that the intelligence to be venerated is that which limits its activities within the bounds of national interests and social order, while the intelligence which allows itself to be guided by the desire for truth alone, apart from any concern with the demands of society, is merely a 'savage and brutal' activity, which 'dishonors the highest of human faculties'. Let me also point out their devotion to the doctrine (Bergson, Sorel) which says that science has a purely utilitarian origin – the necessity of man to dominate matter, 'knowledge is adaptation'; and their scorn for the beautiful Greek conception which made science bloom from the desire to play, the perfect type of disinterested activity. And then they teach men to accept an error which is of service to them (the 'myth') as an undertaking which does them honor, while it is shameful to admit a truth which harms them. In other words, as Nietzsche, Barrès, Sorel plainly put it, sensibility to truth in itself apart from any practical aim is a somewhat contemptible form of mind. (pp. 152–4)

At the same time, in line with classical rationalism, as well as with the Judaeo-Christian tradition and some Enlightenment thinkers, Benda sees truth as belonging to a set of universal values that make up a spiritual unity. It is this coherent world of the spirit that he believes ought both to guide the intellectual's work and to govern any political stands taken. And it is this, above all, which he believes that many modern intellectuals have betrayed.

There are, however, difficulties in maintaining a distinction between legitimate and illegitimate political roles here. For example, Benda defended his support for France in the First World War on the grounds that his country represented universal values against German particularism. And the same justification was available in the case of his opposition to Italian fascism and German national socialism. But it is difficult not to suspect that elements of patriotism and self-interest were also involved. And, if this suspicion is correct, perhaps one should see the political intervention on the part of intellectuals allowed by Benda in a tragic light: as a process in which even the genuine intellectuals are dragged down into the political mire as a result of the initial betrayal of their colleagues.

In these terms, modern intellectuals are perhaps faced with a dilemma. On the one hand, to be true to their role they must speak out against ideological forms of politics because these deny universal values and threaten the very existence of true intellectuals by removing any scope for independence. On the other hand, in seeking to counter this trend the intellectual enters politics, and in order to be successful in this realm will be tempted to, and perhaps must sometimes, act in ways that deny universal values. In this fashion the true intellectual may also seem to, and indeed may in practice actually, betray her or his vocation.

In Benda's work, then, we have a model of the intellectual as properly standing above the worlds of politics and practice, in the sense of being concerned with spiritual, that is universal, values. Intellectuals should not seek to rule the world, or attempt the hopeless (and perhaps even undesirable) task of trying to make ordinary people pursue spiritual instead of material values. The intellectual's role, instead, is the pursuit of truth; which is of value in itself and is closely associated with other values, such as justice. And an intellectual's dedication in following this life functions as a salutary reminder to others that there are higher things than everyday concerns. Furthermore, this is reinforced by interventions in particular situations to denounce falsehoods and injustices, the Dreyfus Affair being a prime example.

The following assumptions seem to be involved in the notion of the intellectual as witness to universal values:

- Intellectuals are engaged in activities associated with high culture, and they have authority because of the knowledge, skills, sensibilities, etc., deriving from these.
- They are committed to truth, and because truth is widely believed to be closely associated with the value of justice, intellectuals are regarded as the upholders of universal values more generally. In these terms, they are seen as the conscience of humanity.
- In their public interventions, they speak and write about events and issues that are of general concern, and do so in terms of a comprehensive view of the world. This is often contrasted with the parochialism of ordinary people, with the partisanship of politicians and/or with the narrow viewpoint of the technician or the professional.

- Intellectuals have autonomy from temporal power and/or have the courage to speak out fearlessly whatever the consequences. To a large extent, this is inherited from the role of the cleric, who was seen as God's representative on earth.[13]

The other models of the role of the intellectual that I will examine retain some elements of this position but reject others, challenging their factual accuracy as a description of those playing the role of intellectual, and questioning the ethical or political value given to key parts of this first definition of the role.

THE ORGANIC INTELLECTUAL

Under this third model, the intellectual enters into a direct and sustained commitment to some particular political or practical project, and her or his work is designed to further or protect it. One version of this is the intellectual as philosopher–king, or legislator, which Bauman sees as the aspiration of most intellectuals until recent postmodern times (Bauman 1987).[14] A rather different version, on which I will concentrate, is the 'enlisted', party, or organic intellectual.

In the 1930s, the younger generation of French intellectuals reacted against the politics of the Third Republic, and the model of the intellectual (exemplified by Benda), which they saw as associated with it (see Schalk 1979). They believed this model to be false in several ways: it was defeatist, denying the possibility of what must be attempted, namely a transformation of society; it cut ideas and reflection off from life, and thereby produced an anaemic intellectual culture; and it was elitist in presenting the intellectual as superior to the masses. Thus the idea of a spiritual world that stands above politics was rejected by many of them, along with the associated view that intellectuals are or can be non-political. These ideas were illusions, it was argued, since intellectual work always has political motives, implications and effects – whether these are disclosed or not, and whether or not the intellectuals concerned are aware of them. Furthermore, the critics insisted, such ideas are illusions that serve a reactionary political role. On this basis, it was argued that intellectuals must engage self-consciously with the world of politics and promote progressive social change directly through their work. Furthermore, this necessarily involves taking sides with some political groups against others: no neutral or detached position is possible.

---

[13]Of course, in practice the Christian Church was a powerful force in medieval society. The Orthodox and Catholic churches have continued to be, and some protestant groups also gained considerable secular power, so that this otherworldly view of the clerics is misleading as regards much of the history of the West and beyond.

[14]On how Saint-Simon and Comte envisaged social scientists as legislators, see Gattone (2006). He also examines some twentieth-century social scientists who played the role of public intellectual, in one way or another. For an illuminating discussion of intellectuals who sought to take on leadership roles in politics, see Joll (1961). In particular, Joll discusses the case of Léon Blum, who became French Prime Minister in 1936 and was a major target of criticism for the organic intellectuals I am about to discuss.

The instability and indecisiveness of politics under the Third Republic formed the background to this reconstruction of the role of the intellectual in France. Power had switched from Right to Left and back again, without much progress being made in any direction. Cobban sums up the problem from the point of view of the Left as follows:

> [The misfortune of the radicals and socialists] during the inter-war period was that each time they achieved an electoral victory – in 1924, 1932 and 1936 – the swing against the right occurred, naturally enough, when its policies, or world conditions, had brought France to the eve of a grave economic crisis. The left was thus repeatedly presented with the need for taking decisions which it either could not take, or which, if taken, almost inevitably destroyed its naturally weak cohesion. (1990: 138)

Furthermore, instability on the French Left was generated by the question of the appropriate attitude towards communism, and in particular towards the Soviet Union (see Caute 1964; Judt 1986). Many saw the Russian Revolution as the next phase of worldwide transformation that had begun in France in 1789. Others regarded communism as a form of Russian imperialism.

Another critical factor in stimulating the move towards engagement was, of course, the rise of fascism in Italy and Germany. The effect of this was complex. On the one hand, it represented an immediate external threat, especially from Germany. Franco-German relations were already strained as a result of the First World War and the failure of Germany to pay war reparations, and this fuelled resentment that could be traced back to the Franco-Prussian War of 1870, when France had been forced to pay a large indemnity to the Prussians. On the other hand, to many eyes the kind of decisive politics that Mussolini and Hitler represented contrasted favourably with the compromise and indecisiveness of French coalition politics. Indeed, many of the criticisms made of the Third Republic paralleled those that had been directed at Weimar democracy. Thus, both communism and fascism seemed to represent a new kind of politics, one that refused the separation between ideals and life that was characteristic of established philosophical and political views in France. For many of the new generation of French intellectuals, the only genuine choice seemed to be between these two options, and they went in both directions. Indeed, some of those who later became influential figures on the Left had been involved with fascist groups in their early years (see Redfern 1972: 113).

A book by Paul Nizan exemplified the new mood (Nizan 1932/1972). In many respects *Les Chiens de Garde* was a direct reply to *La Trahison des Clercs*. In the book Nizan takes over the idea of betrayal, but his interpretation is very different from that of Benda. The 'guard dogs' of his title are intellectuals who have carried on their work in a purportedly pure fashion, claiming to be above politics, and have thereby done nothing to bring about justice:

> We are living in a time when the philosophers are abstaining. They are living a scandalous life of absenteeism. There is scandalous divergence, a scandalous gap between what Philosophy propounds and what happens to men in spite of all its promises; at the very moment when it is repeating those promises Philosophy

is in full flight. It is never to be found where its services might be needed. It does, or rather appears to, abdicate. It might be more accurate to speak of desertion, of treason. (Nizan 1972: 28)

Where Benda had regarded intellectual work as of universal human value for its own sake, what was all-important for Nizan were its effects, its practical usefulness. He comments that 'philosophy resembles medicine; there is thought which cures and thought which does not' (cited in Schalk 1979: 58). He demanded a transformation of philosophy that would put it to work in realising the goals to which intellectuals such as Benda claimed to be committed. So, from Nizan's point of view, there is no escape from partisanship. As Redfern comments about Nizan's book: 'The tone is one of: Stand up and be counted. Whose side are you on?' (Redfern 1972: 36).

In some places Nizan's argument goes beyond the idea that influential Third Republic intellectuals are guilty of an abdication of responsibility: he denounces them for actually supporting the status quo. Indeed, he argues that they serve exactly the same purposes as do generals, politicians and the like (Schalk 1979: 65). The 'professors' are simply involved in a more subtle form of domination. Here, he turns Benda's concept of the 'clerc' against him, arguing that the university has taken over the role of the church as the 'spiritual lever of the state'.[15] For Nizan, this is the real betrayal by intellectuals. To be true to their vocation, he argues, they must challenge an unjust society; and they must do this through participating in collective political action, since this is the only means by which such a challenge is likely to be successful.

In some respects, Nizan's views are a development of Benda's position: he resolves the ambiguity within that position by going one step further than Benda was prepared to do in terms of political involvement. However, any emphasis on continuity would be misleading. Nizan's argument implies a fundamental change in underlying assumptions. As we saw, Benda distinguished between material and spiritual worlds, and he believed that this contrast should be reflected in the relationship between an intellectual elite and the mass of ordinary people. Moreover, he regarded these distinctions as inevitable, and believed that the different functions performed by the elite and those outside it were complementary. By contrast, Nizan regards this differentiation of function as an aspect of human alienation. It means not only that ordinary people are being deprived of access to intellectual culture but also that the intellectuals themselves have become a distorted form of humanity, cut off from other aspects of life.

Simone de Beauvoir summed up the spirit of the group of students to which Nizan belonged at university as follows:

They jabbed a pin in every inflated idealism, laughed high-minded souls to scorn – in fact, every kind of soulfulness, the 'inner life' […] they set out to prove that men were not rarefied spirits but bodies of flesh and bone, racked by physical needs and crudely engaged in a brutal adventure that was life. (de Beauvoir 1974: 336, quoted in McCarthy 1985: 193)

---

[15]In this respect, Nizan's views parallel Gramsci's (1971) account of the role of 'traditional intellectuals', who present themselves as neutral but whose work nevertheless supports the interests of the ruling class.

As this makes clear, Nizan and his fellow students drew on those forms of life philosophy, both German and French, which had been influential in the late nineteenth and early twentieth centuries, many of which were seen by Benda as examples of intellectual betrayal.[16] However, it was Marxism that provided the main framework on which Nizan relied. From his point of view, what was required was a social transformation that would not only overcome social class differences but also produce a new form of humanity in which intellectual functions would be reintegrated with other aspects of human life. It was in this context that he demanded of intellectuals that they 'renounce themselves', that they 'wish for the annihilation of their own nature' (quoted in Schalk 1979: 64).

An equally important difference between Nizan and Benda was that, whereas for the latter the dangerous trends that were taking place in the 1930s represented a second Fall which had to be resisted to prevent the disappearance of the spiritual aspect of life, for Nizan what was happening was that capitalism was nearing its end and a new society could be created. It was therefore the duty of intellectuals to do whatever was necessary in this struggle to bring about change, since this would lead to the realisation of those values to which they are, or ought to be, committed.

Nizan seems to have reached his radical views about the role of the intellectual as a result of taking a year out from his studies at the École Normale Supérieure to live in Aden, then a British colony, where he worked as tutor to the son of a leading French businessman. Schalk comments: 'he saw capitalist society there in all its nakedness, he saw undisguised colonialist oppression', and as a result 'he understood Europe better, where the social evils were hidden beneath a veneer of cultural and personal freedom' (Schalk 1979: 55). However, Schalk argues that it was not until Nizan returned home that this political reaction was felt: there was little evidence of it in his correspondence when he was away. At the same time, his 'flight' to Aden, and the response it produced in him, were to some degree a result of the alienation he had previously felt in Paris, an alienation (as we have seen) that was shared with others of his generation.

After his return from Aden, Nizan joined the Communist Party, seeing this as the only available vehicle for the realisation of universal values. In fact, he became a full-time official (Schalk 1979: 54). He believed it was necessary for the intellectual to accept party discipline, to toe the Party line even when he or she disagreed with it (indeed, he himself had doubts about the formation of the Popular Front, the communists joining with Blum's socialists in order to gain entry to government). Here Nizan, like Gramsci and Lukacs, accepted the idea that the Party in some sense embodies a larger truth than any individual member of it can grasp, including (and perhaps especially) those who are intellectuals. Commitment to the Party was therefore the overriding virtue. However, history played a bitter trick on Nizan. Like others, he had seen the communists as the only effective opposition to the fascists. The result was that he could not swallow the Nazi–Soviet pact of 1939. In response, he resigned from the Party, joined the French Army, and did not live to see the Pact revoked, being killed in battle soon after going to the front. Worse still, he was

---

[16]On life philosophy at this time, see Ringer (1969: 336–9). To varying degrees, it drew on Rousseau, the counter-Enlightenment, and Romanticism.

denounced by the Communist Party as a national traitor, on the basis of information that was never disclosed and which was almost certainly false.

At university Nizan and Sartre were close friends, often jokingly referred to as 'Nitre'.[17] Indeed, it has often been noted that in many respects Nizan was a role model for the later Sartre. However, their careers followed very different paths. Sartre became the most prominent French example of the fourth model of the intellectual I will discuss here.

THE PUBLIC INTELLECTUAL

Before the Second World War, Sartre was far less interested and involved in politics than his friend, and this perhaps stemmed from a belief that an authentic life depended more on individual will and decision than on the transformation of society through politics; indeed, from his point of view the latter was seen as involving inauthenticity. He wrote: 'that such a close friend should be a revolutionary struck me as totally grotesque' (Hayman 1986: 248–9). Sartre was resistant to recognition of any constraints on human freedom. To acknowledge them was to accept the status quo, instead of resisting it. However, the fate of Nizan and the experience of the Occupation had a profound effect on Sartre.

First of all, and most importantly, these events convinced him of the need for intellectuals to play a public political role, and his own growing fame as a philosopher and novelist enabled him to do this. Moreover, he recognised the part played by the Communist Party in the Resistance, and the contribution of the Soviet Union in defeating Nazi Germany. This laid the basis for Sartre's belief after the Second World War that the Party was the best hope for political progress. Perhaps even more importantly, like others, he saw it as a strategic bulwark for France against the spreading influence of American capitalism. At the same time, he never became a member of the Party, despite sometimes acting on its behalf, and he retained an ambivalent attitude towards it. Its treatment of Nizan, and of other intellectuals, no doubt fuelled his distrust of it; and, along with his existentialist commitment to maintaining his own freedom, this probably discouraged any inclination to join it. Indeed, Sartre's views about the Party fluctuated over time, perhaps paralleled by changes in attitude towards the memory of Nizan. McCarthy (1985: 200) comments that 'Nizan is too much of a communist to please the 1948 Sartre [of *What is Literature?*] and too much of an ex-communist to please the 1952 Sartre [of *The Communists and the Peace*]'. Later, of course, Sartre denounced the communist stance on Algeria and other issues, eventually supporting the Maoists.

So, in the post-war period Sartre came increasingly to emphasise the importance of political engagement by the intellectual, but he also insisted on the need for intellectuals to have political autonomy. And he lived out the tensions that this involved, for example in his role as editor of *Les Temps Modernes*. In writing *What is Literature?* Sartre argued for a committed form of writing but also distanced this from the Stalinism of

---

[17]On the relationship between the two, see McCarthy (1985). Apparently, they were sometimes mistaken for one another.

the French Communist Party, with its claim to infallible insight into history and its attempts to control Leftist intellectuals. Sartre comments: 'we will not join the watchdogs of the Communist Party' (quoted in McCarthy 1985: 200), thereby transforming Nizan's use of 'watchdogs' or 'guard dogs' in a highly significant fashion. In *What is Literature?* Sartre argues that writing should be aimed at a concrete liberation of readers from their alienation, and simultaneously of the writer from her or his own alienation: 'We want the man and the artist to work their salvation together, we want the work to be at the same time an act; we want it to be explicitly conceived as a weapon in the struggle that men wage against evil' (Sartre 1948a: 233). The aim is to reveal the truth about the world so that people may take full responsibility for it and set about changing it. And this involves partisanship: 'the writer's duty is to take sides against all injustices, wherever they may come from' (p. 211). Here, the Party is neither assigned a central role in bringing about emancipation, nor ruled out as a source of injustice.

At the heart of Sartre's early philosophy was the idea that human beings make themselves (existence precedes essence), and that therefore they are responsible for what they become. However, equally important, especially for his later views, was the universalism that he inherited from Kant, and which is not to be found in what are often taken to be the main sources of existentialism: Kierkegaard and Nietzsche. For Sartre, the individual is not only responsible for her or himself but for everyone (Sartre 1948b). In making any choice, Sartre argues, we are in some sense choosing for everyone else and must be conscious of that fact. In effect, he insists that nothing can be good for a particular individual that is not good for all human beings. From this he concludes that it is the responsibility of any individual to transform the world through her or his actions, thereby making it one in which everyone can live an authentic life. As in the case of Nizan, Benda's distinction between the spiritual and material worlds has been abandoned.

Sartre saw intellectuals as playing a key role in revolutionary struggle because they occupied a distinctive position within Western societies: 'that which defines an intellectual in our society is [...] the profound contradiction between the universality which bourgeois society is obliged to allow to his scholarship, and the restricted ideological and political domain in which he is forced to apply it'. And, later in the same article, he comments: 'the intellectual is the man whose own contradictions lead him, if he grasps the contradictions, to take the position of the oppressed – because, in principle, universality is on that side' (Sartre 1974: 52).[18] Indeed, Sartre seems to see the intellectual as having a distinctive radical function in relation to oppositional groups, serving as a crucial bulwark against reformism:

> In the struggle between the irrational particular and the universal, no compromise is possible: it cannot consist in anything other than the *radical* destruction of the particular. Thus, every time there is a choice to be made in a question of parties or other political formations, the intellectual is led to choose the most radical in order to regain the universal. (1974: 52)

---

[18] The argument that intellectuals, of some kinds at least, occupy a contradictory social class position, and that this shapes their consciousness in significant ways, is not uncommon. See, for example, Brooks and Gagnon (1988: 6–7 and *passim*). See also Brym (1980).

In short, 'the intellectual is faced with the difficult and contradictory task of affirming principles in the service of people who, like himself, want universality, but who may not be aware of the extent to which deviation can compromise the future' (p. 55). Here, it seems that the intellectual has the potential to be more politically 'advanced' than the party or ordinary people, in other words to be the spearhead of change. This is why it is essential that the intellectual retains the autonomy that allows criticism even of purportedly revolutionary parties or movements. And this was very much the critical role that Sartre himself played in his interventions in French politics (see Aronson 1980: Part 4).

Sartre (1972) views intellectuals as emerging from the numbers of what he calls the 'technicians of practical knowledge', and as a 'monstrous product of a monstrous society' (p. 247):

> If he is a professor or a scientist, he does *know* certain things even if he cannot derive them from true principles. But as an intellectual, he is searching for other things: the restrictions, violent or subtle, of universality by particularism, and the envelopment of truth by myth have made him essentially an *investigator*. He investigates *himself* first of all in order to transform the contradictory being assigned to him into a harmonious totality. But this cannot be his only object, since to find his inner secret and resolve his organic contradiction, he must proceed to apply the rigorous methods he uses as a specialist technician of practical knowledge to the society of which he is a product – to its ideology, its structures, its options and its praxis. (p. 247)

It is worth noting that what is proposed here seems to fit the case of the social scientist, even better than that of the philosopher or the novelist.

There are interesting similarities and differences between the public intellectual, as exemplified by Sartre, and the two previous models I have discussed. While Sartre rejects the idea that intellectuals inhabit a quite distinct realm above ordinary life, he nevertheless regards them as occupying a unique position within bourgeois society that gives them the capacity to be in the vanguard of progressive change. They are able to see and to understand what is required, presumably on the basis of a coherent, comprehensive social philosophy, and are not constrained by the practical considerations that are likely to turn others in reformist rather than revolutionary directions.

It is perhaps worth stressing that the notion of the public intellectual is by no means restricted to revolutionary politics. There are important parallels, for example, between the role of Sartre in mid-twentieth-century French society and that of John Stuart Mill in nineteenth-century England (see Collini 1991). However, this model does tend to be associated with a view of society as capable of linear or dialectical progress, by contrast with the rather more pessimistic view underpinning the orientation of the intellectual as witness. There is a claim to superior vision, partly on the basis of knowledge and understanding produced via intellectual work, and this is taken to derive from a comprehensive perspective that indicates the nature of the past, what is progressive in the present, and the sort of future towards the achievement of which all energy must be directed. The key task of the intellectual, aside from developing the theoretical perspective necessary, is to make political interventions via public debates, designed to propel the society forwards.[19]

A rather different model of the public intellectual can also be found in the same generation as Nizan and Sartre, indeed he was among the same group of friends at the École Normale Supérieure in the 1930s. Raymond Aron combined his role as a social scientist with that of political commentator, being variously described as a 'committed observer' (Aron 1983; Colquohn 1986) or a 'peripheral insider' (Judt 2003). For Aron this meant drawing on his wide sociological, historical and philosophical knowledge so as to mediate between political principles and practical issues. But he drew a sharp distinction between his scholarly work and political commentary: the former was to be governed by value neutrality, whereas the latter could be guided by his own political values and pragmatic judgements. He engaged in both kinds of work throughout his life, and each informed the other.[20] While, in practice, Aron probably had rather more influence on mainstream French politics than did Sartre, he was a less prominent figure on the intellectual scene and for much of his life he was denounced in Leftist intellectual circles as right wing, though it would be more accurate to describe his political position as that of a moderate liberal. By comparison with Nizan and Sartre, he was much more circumspect about the prospects for radical change, and was not prepared to sacrifice liberty for equality. He saw politics as necessarily involving difficult choices in which something was always lost in return for whatever was gained, even though overall gain was sometimes possible. In some respects, Aron represents a bridge to the final model of the intellectual I will discuss, even though his political role and orientation were as different from Foucault's and Lyotard's as from Sartre's (see Jennings 1997).

THE SPECIFIC INTELLECTUAL

In France from the 1960s onwards, there was a general process of disengagement from the Communist Party on the part of French intellectuals. However, the positive attitude towards Marxism persisted, even after the blend of existentialism and Marxism that Sartre had promoted went out of favour. For example, drawing on the growing influence of structuralism, Althusser reinvigorated French Marxism, and in doing so shaped the attitudes of a substantial number of young intellectuals who were active within and outside of the Communist Party. However, in the aftermath of the events of 1968, it was not just the Party that came to be rejected by some on the Left but Marxism as well. This was reinforced by belated recognition of the realities of life in the Soviet Union and its treatment of dissidents. Publication in France of Solzhenitsyn's book *The Gulag Archipelago* played a key role here. The idea of the intellectual as siding with a party that would bring about a revolution to realise

---

[19]Among a younger generation in France, Bourdieu was arguably another example of this model, though his conception of the universal was different from that of Sartre: see Lane (2006: 6–7 and ch. 7).

[20]There is a parallel here with the case of Max Weber, who was an important influence on Aron.

universal values came to be rejected, and so too did the model of the public intellectual as exemplified by Sartre. Abandoned here was any assumption that the Communist Party, or intellectuals, enjoyed superior insight into the true and the good, and into how these values could and should be realised. Also challenged was the idea that there can be a coherent, comprehensive theory that can tell us about the nature of society, what is wrong with it, and where it ought to be going. Such ideologies came to be dismissed as themselves totalitarian and oppressive in character.

One source of these trends, within Marxism itself, was the Maoist movement that flourished especially among Althusser's students. A key strand here was an emphasis on the need for political activists to carry out investigations to find out the views of the groups they were seeking to assist and the character of the local situation in which political action was to take place (see Bourg 2007: ch. 5). This fed directly into the notion of the 'specific intellectual' (Foucault 1980: 125–33; Jennings 1997: 75–6). Like the two previous models, the specific intellectual is unavoidably politically committed, but he or she no longer claims to represent universal values or to have a more comprehensive and deeper understanding of the world than others. Nor is he or she committed to an organisation that claims to play a universal, politically progressive role.

The most explicit and influential account of this model was provided by Foucault (Foucault and Deleuze 1977; Foucault 1980). Like others who came to be labelled as post-structuralists, he rejected 'totalising' theories; though, of course, to avoid inconsistency his rejection of this is always put forward as only a partial and local rejection. Interestingly, Foucault appeals to the example of those among the technical intelligentsia who had reacted against the ways that their knowledge was being used, in particular Robert Oppenheimer and other physicists protesting against nuclear weapons. However, he reinterprets this model significantly. For Foucault, the specific intellectual's responsibility is to put her or his specialist knowledge and skills to work in order to assist the struggles of those resisting 'disciplinary power'. More than this, though, the aim is 'to make visible the mechanisms of repressive power which operate in a hidden manner' and to show how these work through 'the regime of truth that is so essential to the structure and functioning of our society' (quoted in Jennings 1997: 76). Here, power is no longer conceived simply in terms of its exercise by a capitalist class over subordinate classes, but rather as an all-pervasive force that takes a variety of forms in different contexts, and can only be resisted in those contexts.

To understand what is involved here we need to sketch in the main themes of Foucault's later work. He gives this the label 'genealogy', taken from Nietzsche, by which he means a descriptive form of philosophical history in which the aim is to document the political struggles, the exclusions and suppressions, out of which emerged current social practices and the forms of knowledge associated with them. In this enterprise he specifically rules out any kind of essentialism or teleology, so that history is not presented as a story of gradual success, of necessary realisation of true human nature, or for that matter of inevitable decline. The task is simply to document the emergence of modern social practices and forms of social knowledge in particular domains: psychiatry, penology, medicine, etc. In each case he recounts the way in which disciplinary power has come to pervade the social fabric, this both enabling (indeed *constituting*) human subjectivities and also constraining what is possible. In modern societies, through surveillance and treatment, the population is disciplined, indeed is trained to discipline itself.

According to Foucault, a key role is played here by science, and especially by the psychological and social sciences. From this point of view, power and knowledge are intimately linked, each serving as the condition for the other. Nevertheless, on the margins there are to be found popular forms of knowledge, and subaltern groups acting as carriers for these, that resist disciplinary power. The task of the specific intellectual, or at least the task Foucault set himself in this role, is to put specialised knowledge and skills at the disposal of these subordinated groups, and to use their subjugated forms of knowledge as a means of understanding the role of disciplinary power in modern societies.[21] The aim was to interrogate and unsettle what is taken for granted as a result of disciplinary power. As May (1994: 6) puts it, the task is 'to address particular strategies of oppression, offer particular historical and philosophical analyses, and, on occasion, recommend particular types of resistance', in the course of standing 'in solidarity with those whose situation forces them to struggle' (p. 7). But, in addition, behind this there seems to be the idea that in doing this the path for change can be opened up. This is not, and cannot be, change to a new society whose character has been anticipated by the intellectuals or by anyone else. Nor is it one whose value can be evaluated independently, since like any regime of truth it sets its own terms of evaluation.

As well as in his writing, Foucault exemplified this new definition of the intellectual's role through the assistance he gave to various groups, for example in helping to establish *Mèdicens Sans Frontiers*, and above all in setting up the *Groupe d'information sur les prisons* (GIP). His work with GIP, assisting his partner Daniel Defert, exemplified the role of the specific intellectual. He emphasised his subordinate position, being concerned primarily with enabling prisoners to speak about conditions in prison, through responses to questionnaires distributed via families and interviews, using his status as a well-known intellectual to publicise their case (Bourg 2007: ch. 5).

Another version of the specific intellectual can be found in the writings of Lyotard.[22] Here too there is a rejection of Marxism on the grounds that it relies upon a totalising theory, a grand meta-narrative, that claims to represent the world and human experience. Instead, he emphasises the extra-discursive force of desire and the heterogeneity of experience that is suppressed in attempts to represent it. What is required, instead, is continually to bear witness to what escapes any account, with modernist forms of art and literature being exemplars of how this is to be achieved

---

[21]There are analogies here with Kristeva's (1986) argument that the intellectual should be 'dissident', seeking to destabilise the 'master discourses' of the dominant social order. However, her position and that of the 'new philosophers' is in other respects closer to the intellectual as public witness: there was often a return here to the idea that the world is politically irredeemable (see Bourg 2007: Part 4).

[22]However, it should be noted that he rejects the label 'intellectual' in favour of 'philosopher', the latter referring to an artist/philosopher engaged in a form of politics that involves exercising reflective judgement or critical intelligence in pursuit of justice. What is involved here is 'a philosophical politics apart from the politics of "intellectuals" and "politicians"' (Lyotard 1988: xiii).

(see Drolet 1994). While this may seem similar to Benda's conception of the intellectual serving as public witness, Lyotard emphasised that it necessitated engagement in politics – art is not locked away in some separate realm. Rather, it has a crucial political function in life. Here, of course, the role of the artist is valorised against that of the traditional philosopher, and perhaps even more against that of the scholar or scientist.

The relevant question raised by Lyotard for the intellectual is: 'how is one to write, speak, or act politically without presuming an authority, [and thereby] implicitly practicing [a] kind of totalitarian injustice?' (Readings 1993: xvi). He rejects what he takes to be the Enlightenment's promise of a redemptive politics that will realise heaven on earth. At the same time, contrary to Adorno, there is no mourning for what has been lost or for what cannot be gained. Politics is resistance to that which denies the contingency, uncertainty, heterogeneity, and particularity of phenomena, including of human beings. Proposed here is a kind of 'post-structuralist anarchism' (May 1994) that inherits the 'antinomianism' (Bourg 2007: ch. 1) of May 1968. What lies beyond, or cannot be 'captured' in terms of, a particular discourse is valorised, so that the function of the specific intellectual comes to be seen as under-labouring for a contingent historical process:

> For Lyotard, politics [...] is an activity that frees events, and the manner in which they are conceived from *all* 'prejudice' or forms of transcendental logic. [It] thereby exposes the *living* specificity of events, the revelation of their unpresentable aura. It offers the release of the free flow of the sublime. (Drolet 1994: 265)

What is distinctive about the specific intellectual is that criticism is not driven by some single, coherent set of ideals, by some comprehensive worldview implying a conception of the ideal society and how it can be brought into existence, by commitment to some particular political project, or even by sheer opposition to the status quo. [23] A major element is a high degree of scepticism, a concern always with how particular beliefs or institutions came into being, and with what they exclude or repress. The role of the intellectual in these terms is purely formal or instrumental in character: it is to facilitate a process that is held to be productive or therapeutic, but without the intellectual knowing what the outcome of the process will or should be. The aim is to challenge current institutions and ways of thinking, so as to open the way for something else. [24]

---

[23] A somewhat similar model to the specific intellectual was exemplified by editors such as Pierre Nora and Olivier Mongin, of *Le Débat* and *Esprit* respectively, where the politics is closer to a traditional French democratic liberalism. Here, the task of the intellectual is formulated as providing 'clarification': see Jennings (1997: 78–9).

[24] Bourg (2007: 265–72) describes the influence of Maurice Clavel and his religious preoccupation with 'the passage from human efforts that end in nihilism to "something else"'. Echoes of this can be found in Foucault and other influential French writers in the 1970s and 1980s. In some respects there is a parallel here with the role of Socrates in Athens (Bourg 2007: 94 and 274–5). One interpretation of the latter's role is that he claimed no knowledge, at least beyond knowing that he knew nothing, thereby being a precursor of the sceptics. On this view, the aim of his engagement in dialogue was to show people that they do not, and cannot, know what they think they know;

DISCUSSION

This chapter has identified several conceptions of the intellectual that are clearly at odds with one another. So, when it is insisted that social scientists must act as intellectuals, not merely as professionals or technicians, we need to be clear about what kind of intellectual is intended, and about the grounds for adopting one model rather than another. Furthermore, there are important questions to be raised about each of the models. These relate to: the idea of commitment to universal values; the nature of the knowledge that intellectuals produce and have; and the issue of the subordination of intellectual work to other purposes.

THE INTELLECTUAL AND UNIVERSAL VALUES

At least two of the models I have discussed assume that 'intellectual' occupations have a distinctive commitment to universal values, and that this enables them to play a unique role in the wider society. This is central to the idea of the intellectual as witness, as well as to that of the public intellectual. However, questions have been raised both about whether there is any such distinctive commitment and about the very notion of universal values.

It can hardly be denied that occupations vary in their goals and values, the means they employ, their institutional conditions, the sort of mentality they encourage, and so on. It is less clear, though, whether there is a set of 'intellectual' occupations that share distinctive features in these respects, in such a way as to prepare their members to act as public witnesses to universal values, or more broadly to play a role in public debates about social and political issues. Indeed, we might argue that the reason why particular writers, artists, academics, and so on took such an important part in the Dreyfus Affair was, first of all, because they were in a position to do so: they were celebrities, their names were well known and respected at the time, so that what they said about the issue would be publicised and given attention. Moreover, not all members of 'intellectual' occupations at that time would have been in a position to do this, so that it is only *some* members of intellectual occupations who are uniquely placed to play this role. On this basis, we might argue that *which* occupations supply public commentators on social and political issues is to some extent a matter of historical contingency, depending upon who becomes widely known and respected or admired within a society. In *The Old Regime and the French Revolution* (1856), De Toqueville notes the distinctive rise to this position of French writers during the course of the eighteenth century (see de Huszar 1960: 11–18). Their influence still continues today

---

and perhaps thereby to bring them to that state of tranquillity or authenticity deriving from a recognition of unavoidable ignorance. There are, of course, other interpretations of the aims of Socratic dialogue: see Seeskin (1987) and Kahn (1996). One interpretation (see Gonzales 1998: Introduction) argues that Plato, following Socrates, used the dialogue form because what he was trying to convey was a non-propositional form of knowledge. This is a position which has affinities to the idea, characteristic of some versions of post-structuralism and postmodernism, including Lyotard's work, that what is most important is what cannot be expressed in discourse.

in that society, though it is less than in the past, and there has been criticism of the way in which participation in 'media politics' changed the role of the French intellectual in the last decades of the twentieth century (Debray 1981; Lecourt 2001). There today, and even more so in other societies, we find film actors, television presenters, rock musicians, doctors, sportspeople, business leaders, and others making influential comments on social and political issues. In other words, members of occupations that would not normally be, or previously have been, labelled as intellectual have gained sufficient celebrity for their voices to be amplified via the mass media.[25]

Aside from this, there is the question of whether those in 'intellectual' occupations playing a public role have tended to take a stance that champions universal values. Even on Benda's own account, it is clear that this has by no means always been true; many 'betrayed' those values – indeed, there were 'intellectuals' on the other side of the struggle over Dreyfus, just as today there are intellectuals who champion the interests of particular religions against others, nationalist causes of various kinds, and so on.

There are also questions about how far those pursuing 'intellectual' occupations are committed through their work to *the whole range* of universal values. The assumption that those engaged in scholarly work, in writing imaginative literature, or in producing art works are uniquely in contact with, or have a distinctive commitment to, *all three* universal values is open to serious question. Most concepts of 'the intellectual' pick out a set of occupations that, it is claimed, are concerned with the production of objects (texts, paintings, sculptures, etc.) designed to embody the true, the good, and the beautiful.[26] However, even if we concede that scientists are committed to discovering the truth, and that artists are concerned with producing beautiful objects, claims that have themselves been questioned, we might ask in what sense scientists are distinctively committed to beauty, and artists to truth. There are, of course, arguments to the effect that scientists judge theories in terms of criteria like elegance, but in this context those criteria are regarded as means of deciding likely truth; and what is taken to be elegant is often very different from the ideas that have guided artists. Moreover, artistic notions of beauty themselves differ greatly over time and across cultural contexts. Similar problems arise with the idea that artists seek to represent the truth through the objects they produce. What is meant by 'truth' here is likely to be very different from what scientists mean by that term. There are, of course, novelists who seek to represent some aspect of the world, highlight a feature of human nature, or document some particular situation in a factual manner. And many novelists research particular historical events or social situations so as to maximise accuracy in what they write. But their purposes still usually

---

[25]This partly reflects the spread of literacy and the rise of mass media that allow the widespread transmission of oral statements, but also a transformation in the form of statement that is acceptable. It may be insisted, of course, that, despite playing this role, such people are not intellectuals, but this highlights the problem of definition, of how we draw the boundary around the category of intellectual occupations; whether membership of such an occupation is taken to be a defining, or at least a necessary, requirement; whether engaging in public commentary or campaigning is itself sufficient; and whether the stances taken must have a particular cultural and/or political character. The meaning given to 'an intellectual' drifts across these various criteria in context-sensitive ways.

[26]There are some problems with the relationship between art and beauty, for example to do with the category of the sublime, but I am ignoring these here. I am treating 'beauty' as equivalent to the aesthetically ideal.

differ from those of scientists; and, more importantly, they involve a significant move away from any concern with producing 'beautiful' texts.

Up to now, I have left the third universal value, the good, out of account. Most scientists, novelists and artists would probably claim that their work is aimed at producing good. But this would also be true of those pursuing many other, 'non-intellectual' occupations. So, even more than with the other values, we might ask whether those involved in intellectual occupations have a distinctive or more direct relationship to this one. Does a nurse looking after a large number of patients on a hospital ward who subsequently becomes an academic doing research on nursing thereby move into a closer relationship to the good? It might be argued that all human beings have a direct concern with the good, and perhaps also with the other universal values, so that any claim to a unique relationship on the part of particular occupations is open to question, or is at least a matter of degree.

In addition, there are problems with the concept of universal values itself. One concerns the relationship among those values normally included in this category. Far from these values forming a coherent, harmonious whole, they are often in conflict with one another (Berlin 1990; Larmore 1987; Gray 1995). Another problem concerns the interpretation of particular values. The idea that intellectuals are committed to universal values carries the implication that what is true, beautiful, and good can be determined in the abstract, rather than being a matter of situated judgement in which local considerations (about which members of 'intellectual' occupations cannot usually claim distinctive expertise) must be taken into account. Yet there are reasons for doubting the idea that universal principles can be applied without local knowledge.

The most obviously problematic value here is the good. One way of trying to give it general meaning, in relation to actions, would be in terms of a specification of human rights. However, there are trenchant opponents of the notion of rights, from Bentham to Fish. And where Bentham (see Dinwiddy 1989) offers an alternative, universal means of determining the good, which has itself been subject to considerable debate, namely utilitarianism, Fish (1994) and others argue that the very idea of some abstract means of determining the good is misconceived. Instead, all value judgements are necessarily situated, and context-sensitive. Indeed, 'the good' amounts to little more than a placeholder for a whole variety of 'goods' – justice, freedom, happiness, etc. – that provide conflicting criteria for evaluating particular actions and situations. Nor does the problem stop there, since there are alternative interpretations of these more specific values. Justice, for example, can be defined in terms of desert or distributive equality, each of which can itself be judged in different ways (Foster et al. 1996: 44–50).

All this raises questions about the capacity of intellectuals to make authoritative public interventions about socio-political issues that are not closely related to their own areas of experience; and, of course, where the relationship between these *is* close they are likely to be seen, quite rightly, as interested parties. There is also the question of whether the notion of 'universal values', as typically operationalised, has not come to stand for a particular set of situated value judgements, of a broadly Leftist kind, so that, in effect, the term has an ideological function. Moreover, since there is not a harmonious relationship among 'universal' values, and given that they are always subject to contextual interpretation, in the public sphere intellectuals will often find themselves on different sides in disputes, rather than always occupying a single vanguard of progressive change. We need to recognise not only that there were writers and academics on the other side in the Dreyfus Affair, but also that these anti-Dreyfusards were not simply committed to their own self-interest, but rather to local values. Indeed, a central component of the anti-Enlightenment philosophical ideas to which some of them were attached was an explicit rejection of the concept of universal humanity in favour of more concrete specific identities, a point famously summed up by that old reactionary de Maistre: 'I have seen, in my life, Frenchmen, Italians, Russians [...] but as for *man*, I declare that I have never met him in my life; if he exists, he is unknown to me' (1862: 88). Without sharing the values of the anti-Drefusards, we can recognise that a central intellectual trend in the course of the twentieth century, exemplified in much writing that is placed under the heading of 'postmodernism', was growing distrust of claims to universality, indeed rejection of the very idea of universal values, in favour of insisting that all valuations reflect local commitments.[27]

Here, then, is another problem for the idea that intellectuals are uniquely connected to universal values and the assumption that this renders their public interventions beneficial. Seeing deviation on the part of intellectuals from 'universal values' as treachery or betrayal presumes too much about their relationship to those values, about the affinity among these, and about how each value should be interpreted in specific situations.

Similar problems arise, albeit in a different way, in the case of the organic intellectual. This also relies upon the idea of commitment to a coherent set of universal values, this time believed to be embodied in a broader social movement, or in an organised party. In its Marxist form, the model of the organic intellectual assumes that the working-class movement and/or the Communist Party is committed to universal human values and is the unique vehicle for their realisation. Later versions, for example among feminists, changed the vehicle but not, as it were, the fuel. But we need to ask why some particular agency – the proletariat, the Party, women, marginalised groups of various kinds – is held to have a distinctive relationship to universal values, why it is believed that these values cohere, and why it is assumed that interpretation of them can rise above the specific situations in which these organisations and groups are involved. The most common rationale takes the form of a historicist meta-narrative, as in the case of Marxism, but it is hard to see how this can avoid being highly speculative and therefore a matter of faith rather than of cogency.

THE PROBLEM OF KNOWLEDGE

The idea that intellectuals are uniquely positioned to intervene on a wide range of public issues, in order to highlight what is wrong, and what should be done, also assumes that they have access to the factual knowledge required for this. It is by no

---

[27]Interestingly, the notion of universal values and rights came to be revived in France by the 'new philosophers', who formed part of a reaction among French intellectuals 'against the Left' in the 1970s (Christofferson 2004).

means clear that this is a reasonable assumption in the case of artists and novelists, or even of natural scientists. Much depends on the level and kinds of knowledge that are assumed to be necessary. It could be argued that social scientists are better placed than others to have the required knowledge, but there are some questions even about this. One concerns the range of knowledge to which any particular social scientist will have access. The products of social science are today so great in number that no-one can have knowledge of more than a very small proportion of the literature. Furthermore, it is still true that, to a large extent, most social scientists belong to particular disciplines – economics, sociology, political science, etc. – and that these cross-cut interest in any particular policy issue, with the result that an individual social scientist is likely to have knowledge only about some specific aspects of each issue.[28]

A second difficulty here is that a requirement for intervening effectively in any public debate is information about what happened in the particular case concerned, and social scientists will often have less access to this than some others. What they *will* probably have is knowledge about general tendencies, and perhaps also about other similar cases that have been studied. While these resources are of value, they are no substitute for local knowledge. Those who are participants in the case may know much about the people and circumstances involved, what was and was not done, etc. Social scientists may, of course, be able to access this information, though it could be argued that investigative journalists will often be better placed to do this. My point here is simply to qualify any assumption that the social scientist is uniquely placed in relation to *all* the kinds of factual knowledge required.

Of course, a central element of the argument for the role of both the public and the organic intellectual is the idea that he or she has unique access to, or is able to produce, a comprehensive socio-historical perspective, in terms of which the more specific kinds of information just discussed, as well as evidence from empirical social research, must be located if a true understanding of any specific situation is to be gained. And there is, surely, something to be said for the idea that particular bits of information cannot on their own enable us to understand what is going on and why. Indeed, consciously or unconsciously, in practice we cannot avoid placing items of information within *some* wider framework of assumptions, for example about the nature of the society concerned, about societies more generally, about human nature, about particular types and groups of people, etc. It is important to be aware of this process, and to guard against reliance upon false background assumptions. Moreover, it might be argued that social scientists, or those engaged in intellectual activities more generally, have skills that enable them critically to assess such assumptions, and thereby to produce more adequate understandings of particular situations.

However, we need to remember that some of those background assumptions will relate to the priority of particular value principles, in determining what is and is not relevant, or what is central and what peripheral. And it is unclear why we should assume that intellectuals have any distinctive expertise in making such decisions, even if they are better placed than others to identify the nature of the assumptions and their implications. The problems discussed in the previous section, particularly about

---

[28]This problem is even worse once we recognise that these disciplines are divided by conflicting approaches.

conflicts among values and the judgements involved in interpreting their meaning in particular situations, are relevant here. Any failure to respect the limits of social scientific expertise in this respect amounts to scientism (Hammersley 2008b; 2009b).

Broader questions can be raised about the idea that there is a single comprehensive perspective, uniquely available to social scientists, that provides the framework for understanding all specific issues. The onus is on those who believe that there *is* such a framework to justify the claim, since it goes against the increasingly specialised character of both natural and social science, and the fragmentation now to be found *within* the latter field. Previously influential arguments along these lines have faced cogent criticism. In the case of Marxism, as noted earlier, what is involved is reliance upon a very questionable, and now largely discredited, meta-narrative (the grand narrative par excellence) in which human values (including truth) are progressively, albeit dialectically, realised over the course of history, with the working class and/or the vanguard party playing a crucial, guiding role. Similar problems arise with the various meta-narratives offered in support of feminist standpoint theories (see Chapter 4). In the case of Sartre, the appeal was to his own philosophy, a form of Marxism reinterpreted through phenomenological and existentialist presuppositions, but this was subjected to criticism from all sides (see Blakeley 1968; Aronson 1977; Gorz 1977; Aronson 1987). Some sociologists see their discipline as providing this sort of perspective, on the model of Mills' 'sociological imagination' or Gouldner's 'reflexive sociology' (see, for instance, Brewer 2003; Hollands and Stanley 2009). Yet any comprehensive, academic theory of this kind is inevitably largely speculative in character, and amounts to a failure to maintain the distinction between a disciplinary orientation and what is required for practical decision-making (Hammersley 1999).

The problems I have discussed in this section apply especially to the organic intellectual and the public intellectual models. In the case of the specific intellectual, of course, any idea of a comprehensive perspective is rejected, on both cognitive and political grounds. The notion of specialist knowledge and skills on the part of the intellectual is retained, but this seems to be in tension with the idea that marginalised groups have access to subordinated forms of knowledge whose public expression can serve as a lever to unhinge the dominant regime of truth (see Bourg 2007). Foucault claims, for instance, that 'the masses no longer need [the intellectual] to gain knowledge: they know perfectly well, without illusion, they know far better than he and they are certainly capable of expressing themselves' (Foucault and Deleuze 1977: 207). So, no meta-narrative is involved here, and especially no conception of what form an alternative society might or should take. Moreover, it seems that very little distinctive knowledge on the part of the intellectual her or himself is assumed. Even more than with the public witness, what is required for the role appears, primarily, to be celebrity status. There is, nevertheless, an unavoidable assumption that the outcome produced through the intervention of the specific intellectual will be desirable, even though judgement about this is regarded as undecidable. The grounds for this judgement, as well as for validation of the knowledge of marginalised groups, are unclear. Subordination or marginalisation surely does not give just anyone automatic access to privileged knowledge of social reality, even if it provides access to experience and specific items of knowledge that are hard to acquire in other ways.

Moreover, these processes can generate their own forms of bias, as Lenin and others pointed out.[29]

THE SUBORDINATION OF ACADEMIC WORK

Finally, there are questions about the relationship between intellectual work and any public role played by the intellectual. In the case of the intellectual as witness, the pursuit of academic social science is seen as continuing alongside occasional interventions in the public sphere, so that what is involved is likely to be limited to the opportunity costs of spending time on one activity rather than another. However, as soon as we move to the organic intellectual and the public intellectual, any distinction between intellectual work and the wider role starts to be eroded. To a large extent, the task becomes to do research that can make an immediate public or practical contribution. And, very often, this involves trying to meet two sets of conflicting requirements. Commenting on the case of C. Wright Mills, Howard Becker writes:

> His research, even in such major works as *White Collar* and *The Power Elite* [...] seldom displayed the tight coupling of assertion and evidence the sociological world of his time required of 'real research'. Horowitz's [1983] analysis of these works makes clear how cavalier Mills could be in putting together empirical reality and his own ideas. He was often led, by the prospect of rhetorical flourish or a fine-sounding phrase, to assert what the materials he had at hand did not warrant. (1994: 181)[30]

Moreover, the role of the public intellectual is often thought to require a transformation of both work and life. For example, late on in his career, Sartre portrayed 'the intellectual proper' as 'a provisional halt in the steady transformation of a technician of practical knowledge into a radicalized companion of the masses'. What is required is 'that he takes a new distance from his profession, in other words from his social being, and understands that no political denunciation can compensate for the fact that in his social being he remains objectively an enemy of the people' (Sartre 1974: 227). Here, it seems that, for Sartre, any distinction between the role of the public intellectual and intellectual work must be abandoned.

The boundary between these is eliminated even more explicitly in the case of the organic intellectual. Potentially, the demands of serving a particular organisation or movement extend to all aspects of life, including any specifically intellectual work. Furthermore, the conception of how knowledge is produced that is built into this model is at odds with that embedded in most fields of academic enquiry. In place of

---

[29]The reference here is to Lenin's notion of 'trade union consciousness' (Lenin 1947). In much the same way Althusser challenged the spontaneous ideology generated by ordinary activities. See Althusser (1990).

[30]See also Horowitz's (1994: 534) argument that Mills 'chose politics as a vocation', in fact 'as an ideology', over 'sociology as a calling' or a science.

the idea that knowledge is gained through a specialised process of investigation, it is insisted that true knowledge comes largely through direct engagement in political or practical activity. While intellectuals bring important knowledge and skills, they can only gain the capacity to make a unique contribution by participating in the movement and the party – by learning both from ordinary people and from the political struggle.

Another implication is that research is now to be directed to problems that are of concern to the movement or organisation being served, rather than selected according to what is important within an academic discipline. In other words, the overwhelming priority is practical rather than academic research (Hammersley 2002a: ch. 6). But we must ask what the consequences of this are likely to be for the sustained development of knowledge. While practical enquiry can provide some basic sorts of information, it is much less likely to be capable of producing sound explanations and theories. There is also the issue of bias. An organic relationship between a researcher and a movement or organisation is likely to increase the danger that the background assumptions and preferences of the researcher will introduce error – because questioning those assumptions and preferences will not just be an individual but also a collective matter, and because strong organisational interests may be involved. Tolerance for unwelcome information, or for questioning fundamental assumptions, is likely to be low on the part of those engaged in political struggle or other kinds of demanding practical work. Furthermore, from this is likely to arise pressure to over- or under-interpret evidence so as to serve the interests of the organisation. The goal of promoting those interests is likely to override the researcher's proper commitment to discovering the truth about the issue concerned. Examples of these problems are legion.

The *publicising* of 'inconvenient' information is also likely to be discouraged, if not banned. Here, findings may be either kept secret for use by the movement or organisation, or turned into propaganda. The principle that the findings of research will be communicated to a research community that involves no restriction on entry as regards political allegiance is an essential component of academic enquiry, precisely because it facilitates the production of sound knowledge. Deviating from this does not guarantee error, but it greatly increases its likelihood.

There are serious doubts, then, about the capacity of the organic intellectual to generate reliable explanatory and theoretical knowledge. Of course, in its Marxist version there is a theory that claims to show that, in fact, it is *only* through the political success of the working class that true knowledge can be gained. It is argued that no bias occurs here because this class embodies a historical process that is directed towards realising the value of truth, along with other universal values. But, as already noted, this meta-narrative has now been largely abandoned, for good reasons, and without it the viability of this organic mode of knowledge production, or at least its superiority over academic enquiry, lacks plausibility. Much the same is true of other meta-narratives of the same kind, such as those associated with feminist standpoint theory.

The case of the specific intellectual is less straightforward. Much depends upon whether it is conceived as a whole way of life or as just one role that can be pursued alongside academic work. In practice, both Foucault and Lyotard seem to have carried on with their own projects. However, we should note that there is incompatibility at the theoretical level. As we saw, part of the rationale for the specific intellectual, in Foucault's version, treats particular marginalised groups as privileged possessors of knowledge. The implication of this is that those who are not in such a position, which would presumably include most researchers, do not have access to knowledge directly themselves. From this point of view, if it is to avoid being totalitarian, academic work can amount to no more than amplifying the voices of the marginalised – though, of course, the published work of both Foucault and Lyotard goes well beyond this. Moreover, it is not clear what the rationale could be for this social epistemology. The closest parallel is standpoint theory, whether in its Marxist or feminist form, but this is underpinned by rationales explaining why knowledge is differentially distributed – of a kind that are specifically rejected by Foucault and Lyotard. In the absence of a rationale, it is hard to see how this version of the specific intellectual can be justified. Implicated here are issues about how marginalisation and oppression are to be judged, and by whom; and about how we identify those marginal groups whose interests should be served from others. Members of far-Right organisations can claim to be marginalised, and perhaps even oppressed, in many Western societies, but this in itself surely does not warrant providing them with intellectual support. Furthermore, within any marginalised group there is unlikely to be a consensus on most issues, so that questions will arise about which views should and should not be amplified.

There is another aspect of arguments for the specific intellectual that is at odds with the principles of academic enquiry. This is that knowledge is treated as a tool – its value lies in what it can be used to do (Foucault and Deleuze 1977: 208). Arguably, the importance of subordinated knowledges for Foucault is not dependent upon whether or not they are actually true – in effect, that whole issue has been put in suspension. Instead, their value lies in the fact that they can challenge the dominant regime of truth. The underlying ethic here is presumably some notion of permanent revolution, a fundamental abhorrence of all forms of institutionalisation, or perhaps there is also the notion that destroying existing structures will allow the emergence of a form of life in which desire achieves unconstrained expression in 'the cultivation of joyful passions' (Bourg 2007: 152). Bourg's history of the turn to ethics in France since 1968 reveals the problems with this, for example in dealing with the issues of rape and adult–child sexual relations. So, too, does Foucault's positive attitude towards the Iranian Revolution (see Afary and Anderson 2005).[31]

Further questions relate more specifically to Foucault's concept of 'regimes of truth' and Lyotard's reworking of the idea of language games, and their shared assumption that instances of these phenomena are incommensurable, in the sense that there can be no grounds for evaluating them in relation to one another. Advocacy of the idea of the specific intellectual often involves a strong dose of scepticism: the task is to

---

[31]Lindbergh (1940: 17) adopted a rather similar attitude towards the rise of communism and fascism in the 1930s. She writes: 'Something, one feels, is pushing up through the crust of custom. One does not know what – some new conception of humanity and its place on the earth. I believe that it is, in its essence, good; but because we are blind we cannot see it, and because we are slow to change, it must force its way through the heavy crust violently – in eruptions. Some of these eruptions take terrible forms, unrecognizable and evil forms.' She draws a parallel with the French Revolution (pp. 19–21).

challenge all claims to authoritative knowledge, and perhaps especially those that purport to be based upon scientific, including social scientific, evidence. For this reason too it is hard to see how or why the social scientist acting as a specific intellectual would continue with academic research.

CONCLUSION

In this chapter I have examined five rather different models of the intellectual, drawing on examples from France in the twentieth century, with the aim of clarifying what it might mean for the social scientist to be an intellectual, rather than a professional or a technician. The first model identifies a particular kind of occupation as 'intellectual' in character, so that anyone pursuing it could be counted in this category. The other four models, which were the main focus of discussion, start from this definition but add a public or practical dimension to the role, with the intellectual participating in the public sphere in one way or another and/or working to serve the interests of a particular political cause. I have argued that these more ambitious definitions of the role involve significant problems when applied to academic enquiry in social science, and more generally. Some of these concern the extent to which people engaged in intellectual occupations are likely to be as well-prepared for the extended role as is claimed. Others are about the dangers involved in subordinating academic work to this broader remit. These dangers are particularly great in the case of the organic intellectual and the public intellectual, though the other two models are not without difficulties.

I am not suggesting, of course, that social scientists can or should play no role in the public sphere, or have no relationships with policy makers, politicians, political activists, and others. Indeed, they have an obligation to disseminate their findings, and to correct any factual misrepresentations of these in the public sphere. In my view, they also have a responsibility to make clear what the limits are to the authority of social scientific knowledge: that it can provide factual knowledge of particular kinds that are more likely to be true than those from other sources, but that it cannot supply all the factual knowledge that would be necessary to make sound policy decisions or practical judgements, nor validate the value principles on which such decisions or judgements depend. At the present time, in my view what is expected of social science by outsiders frequently exceeds what it is capable of producing; even worse, many social scientists routinely make claims on the basis of their research that exceed its warrant (Foster et al. 1996, Hammersley 2006b).

Of course, *as citizens, policy advisers, professional educators, practitioners of one sort or another, etc.*, social scientists can perform a wider range of functions than those mentioned above. In doing so, they will inevitably draw upon knowledge and skills that they have developed or acquired as part of their work. And for this reason they have a distinctive and important contribution to make; even though they are by no means the only people whose occupational background facilitates performance of such roles. However, in all circumstances, they should make clear under which auspices they are speaking, and the boundaries around this, including the limits that operate on the authority of research. In this respect, my position is similar to that of Aron.

It is worth noting that there are at least two rather different aspects to discussions about whether the social scientist should be an intellectual, rather than a professional or a technician. One is the extent to which research amounts to applying specific knowledge and techniques designed to answer fixed types of question, or whether it must involve the exercise of wisdom, creativity, and discretion in deciding what to investigate, how best to pursue enquiry, and what conclusions can be drawn. In its technical form, research can be contracted by some outside agency, or commanded within a bureaucracy, but it is often argued that because it is not 'merely' technical in character academic enquiry requires that researchers be free 'to follow their enquiries wherever these lead' and without deadlines. The goal is to produce a body of general knowledge that is of value in itself, a resource that is available for anyone to use, as contrasted with specific information that is tied to the needs or demands of particular stakeholders. Also sometimes included here is the contrast between living *off* the knowledge and skills one has, and living *for* ideas (see, for example, Coser 1965: viii). This is a contrast between extrinsic and intrinsic motivation, between an instrumental orientation concerned with satisfying external demands, and a passion to discover new knowledge that is valued for its own sake.

This first contrast is an important part of the classic discussions of the nature of sociology by Mills and Gouldner, referred to at the beginning of this chapter. Both deplore the way in which some social scientists are apparently becoming technicians, in the sense that they 'take' rather than 'make' the problems that they address. In other words, they are given a problem to solve by others, and they accept the terms in which it has been defined, and deploy their technical expertise in doing this. It is argued that, instead of this, they should be intellectuals who select which problems to investigate and reformulate them as and when necessary, in light not just of what is learned during the course of investigation but also of a broad understanding of society, culture, and history. Also opposed here is the tendency to think of research in terms of the *application* of techniques; what is required instead is a more theoretical and thoughtful approach.

It is important to note that this first aspect of the contrast parallels an important difference between the professional and the technician (see Shils 1997). A key feature long claimed by professional occupations has been the independence to determine how the functions to which they are devoted will be performed, with individual practitioners themselves exercising considerable discretion in their work. Furthermore, there is resistance to the idea that professional 'good practice' can be specified in terms of explicit rules, or the adoption of specified methods for dealing with predefined problems. Equally important, the ideal mode of occupational organisation has generally been seen as collegiate in character, rather than those organisational structures characteristic of either market relations or bureaucracy. Indeed, this ideal had an influence even when professions operated within commercial firms or within the public sector; though this influence declined over time as a result of neo-liberalism and the 'new public management'. As I noted in the Introduction, these trends are also undermining the academic ideal within universities.

As we have seen, however, Mills, Gouldner, and others who call for social scientists to be intellectuals mean rather more than can be included under the heading of professionalism, and would reject that model for other reasons too (Hammersley 2009a). They believe that social researchers should take on a wider role, of the kinds I have discussed in this chapter. Indeed, their discussions have a close affinity with a broader debate about the extent to which 'the intellectual' has been destroyed by incorporation into universities (Jacoby 1987; but also see Robbins 1993). As I have noted, this may simply amount to taking on an additional role alongside the occupational one, and even here the combination may be unstable, but in the case of the organic and the public intellectual a transformation of the academic orientation is demanded. While Mills, Gouldner, and those following their lead, such as Burawoy, believe that this will enhance, not destroy, academic social science, for the reasons presented in this chapter and elsewhere in this book I think they are mistaken.[32]

In effect, calls for social scientists to be intellectuals, in this extended sense, amount to attempts to resist the very process of social differentiation that has been identified, by most sociological accounts, as central to the development of large, modern societies. The justification for this differentiation is that considerable expertise can be developed through specialisation. Of course, there are also associated costs: in adopting a narrower view, technicians and professionals may fail to see 'the big picture'; and therefore fail to act in ways that are ethically or politically required by this; though the idea that there is a single 'big picture' has been discredited. Needless to say, they may also exploit their expertise, and the licence and mandate associated with this, for their own purposes. But what these costs point to is a dilemma, a problem that cannot be resolved or transcended. The best way of dealing with it, in my view, is to recognise that there are times when technicians or professionals must suspend the practice of their occupation and act instead in some other role. But to demand that they play a wider role all the time, whether alongside or instead of their primary occupation, amounts to foregoing the benefits of specialisation.

As I argued in the Introduction and in Chapter 1, it does seem to me that academic social science is a kind of work that cannot be reduced to a technical model. While there may be types of information about social affairs that can be produced in this way, and these will often be of value, most of the explanatory tasks that academic social scientists tackle are not amenable to this approach. The professional is undoubtedly a better model than the technician, and I believe that this must involve the capacity to draw on a wide range of knowledge, not only that associated with a single discipline or segment of a discipline. In *that* sense, academic social scientists must also be intellectuals. However, for them to redefine their role so as to become organic, public, or even specific intellectuals amounts to a betrayal of their professional vocation, and may also involve an abuse of the authority that is associated with it. One such redefinition requires that social scientists adopt a 'critical' stance, and in the next chapter I will explore the ambiguities at the heart of this.

---

[32]Burawoy distinguishes between public and critical sociology, differentiating both from professional and applied varieties. However, as Holmwood (2007: 47) points out, he treats critical sociology as foundational, and it is far from clear that what he outlines is a stable division of labour among types of sociology.

3

SHOULD SOCIAL SCIENCE BE CRITICAL?

[…] science must begin with myths, and with the criticism of myths; neither with the collection of observations, nor with the invention of experiments. (Popper 1963: 50)

They who are to be judges must also be performers. (Aristotle *Politics*, 8.6)

If you're out to beat a dog, you're sure to find a stick. (Yiddish proverb, see Ayalti 1949: 47)

In social research, the word 'critical' has become a term of praise, an honorific title used by writers to commend their work or the particular approach they adopt. Thus, we have 'critical theory', 'critical rationalism', 'critical realism', 'critical social research', 'critical discourse analysis', 'critical anthropology', 'critical action research', 'critical policy research', 'critical ethnography', etc. Conversely, the work of opponents is sometimes dismissed as 'uncritical'. But what does it mean to be 'critical' or 'uncritical'?

Traditionally, within research, the most basic form of criticism is the assessment of knowledge claims in terms of their likely validity. This is something that researchers engage in privately as regards their own work, since enquiry is composed of alternating creative and critical phases, as well as in reading relevant literature. However, criticism also takes more collective, and public, forms: it is part of the operation of research communities, where colleagues openly assess one another's findings in terms of their likely validity.

This meaning of being 'critical' – critical assessment of the likely validity of knowledge claims which are designed to contribute to a disciplinary field – is central to some uses of the adjective, notably 'critical rationalism' (see Albert 1985). However, it is not the main meaning of the term within social science today. The scope of criticism, as regards its targets, its grounds, and the nature of the critical act, has become much broader. Thus, to be critical, as a researcher, is now often held to involve assessing public policies, institutions, and forms of social practice, not just knowledge claims made by fellow researchers; and doing this in terms of practical values, such as social welfare, social justice, or economic efficiency. Furthermore, the critical act has been expanded to include analysing the fundamental assumptions and social contexts associated with what is being assessed, and perhaps also necessarily taking an oppositional stance towards it. In line with this usage, accusations of being 'uncritical' usually refer to an alleged failure to engage in these broader forms of criticism, on the grounds for example that this amounts to supporting the socio-political status quo.

An important source of this wider interpretation of what 'critical' means is, of course, Marxism and perhaps especially the 'critical theory' of the Frankfurt School. Marxists developed – or sought to transcend – the idea, central to the Enlightenment, that our understanding of the world is distorted or biased by social factors. Marx drew on Hegel in seeing *all* ideas as products of social development, with true ideas pointing to, or only attainable at, the end of history. And, within Marxism, the critical assessment of knowledge claims came to be closely tied to criticism of prevailing social arrangements, in two respects. First, criticism of society could be seen as itself contributing to the achievement of knowledge, to the extent that it succeeded in progressing society towards the point where truth is 'realised'; in the complementary senses of being made real and of becoming transparently obvious (Cohen 1982). Secondly, ideas were to be judged as much in terms of their origin, and their social function, as by their cognitive validity. Or, rather, validity was now conceptualised as socio-historically relational – as intrinsically connected to social function – because it is located within the context of a teleological meta-narrative that pointed to the eventual realisation of absolute truth. In this way, a strong instrumental element was injected into the notion of validity. The most important result of all this, for my purposes here, was that the boundary between intellectual and political criticism tended to be erased (see Prokopczyk 1980).

Another significant contribution, especially of Frankfurt critical theory, was a radical development of the Kantian notion of critique. As a consequence of this, criticism of knowledge claims became a matter of not simply assessing them against evidence, but of understanding the whole framework of assumptions in which they operated, and identifying the limits to that framework's validity or value. For early critical theorists this meant challenging the ideological character of prevailing modes of thought, these being seen as representing in ideational form the material constraints of the mode of social organisation with which they were associated (Horkheimer 1972). And an important consequence of this is erasure of another boundary: that between scientific and philosophical criticism, both of these are simultaneously being merged with political criticism.[1]

These changes in the meaning of the term 'critical' generated by Marxism and Critical Theory encouraged the view that the social scientist is necessarily a politically engaged intellectual; in other words, the conclusion that research should be, and in some senses cannot avoid being, political. This involved abandoning the idea, to be found for example in Julien Benda's book *La Trahison des Clercs* (1928), that

[1]For useful accounts of these aspects of the development of Marxism and Critical Theory, see Lichtheim (1971) and Bottomore (1975).

intellectuals ought to have an otherworldly concern with knowledge, literature, music, or art, their political participation being limited to making occasional public pronouncements in order to support universal ideals. Instead, for example along the lines sketched out by Gramsci, they were to be viewed as partisans, and as only authentic when acting as organic intellectuals linked to material (that is, to political) forces.[2]

Benda's book is a useful guide here because it brings out some of the complexities in notions of the role of the intellectual (Nichols 1965 and 1978) and provides essential background to more recent conceptions of that role (see Jennings 1997; see also Chapter 2 of this book). It was prompted by his horror at the way in which some German and French intellectuals in the late nineteenth and early twentieth centuries had become partisans for nationalism. There were two elements of his opposition to this. First, nationalism is particularistic; in other words, it stands opposed to universal ideals, whereas it is the responsibility of intellectuals to symbolise and preserve those ideals.[3] Secondly, these intellectuals had deserted their proper preoccupation with thinking, writing and creating ideal objects. They had subordinated themselves – and thereby the value of thought, morality, etc., for which they were responsible – to the dirty business of politics.

I think it is fair to say that Benda was ambivalent towards Marxism; and it is not difficult to see why. On the one hand, he applauded its commitment to universal ideals. Indeed, in the 1920s and 1930s it offered some of the most powerful opposition to right-wing nationalist movements in Europe. On the other hand, it insisted on the need for intellectuals to be politically engaged, so as to realise those ideals. Furthermore, as part of this it seemed to have become tied to more particularistic interests: those of party functionaries and indeed those of the Soviet Union (see Caute 1964). At the very least, from Benda's point of view, it thereby infringed the autonomy of intellectuals, and often seemed to demand behaviour that ran contrary to universal principles in the name of successful political action.[4] I suspect that, unlike Marxists, Benda believed that universal ideals could never be fully realised; but he also recognised that the new right-wing nationalism and its associated 'intellectuals' were a threat to the very existence of a world that would tolerate intellectuals in his sense of that term – those who are engaged in autonomous intellectual work and thereby bear witness to universal ideals in a profane world. While few social scientists today would adopt a position close to that of Benda, echoes of it remain; and the neo-Weberian view adopted in this book shares some features in common with it.

Aside from the influence of Marxism, there are some other, more recent, influences that have broadened what it means to be critical in the context of the social sciences and social research. One of these is second-wave feminism. This also frequently treats research as necessarily political, and as properly engaged in the pursuit of political goals. Like Marxism, some versions of feminist research rely on a historicist meta-narrative. Other feminists renounce this, under the influence of various ideas labelled

---

[2] A more appropriate contrast with Benda would be Nizan, see Chapter 2 and Schalk (1979). However, Gramsci's writings have been much more influential on Anglo-American social science.

[3] It should be said, though, that like many French writers at the time he tended to see France as the embodiment of universal values.

[4] See Lukes (1985) on the problem of ends and means in Marxism.

with that much-used floating signifier 'postmodernism'. Despite the differences within and between them, both feminism and postmodernism have led to further erasure of the boundaries between research, on the one hand, and both politics and philosophy, on the other. A distinctive contribution of postmodernism, and of those forms of feminism influenced by it, has been widespread abandonment of – or at least increased suspicion of – the very notion of truth as correspondence or representation. Thus, postmodernism undercuts what I treated earlier as the core meaning of the term 'critical' in a research context: collective assessment of the validity of their knowledge claims by researchers. It subjects to sceptical criticism any framework that could indicate what would count as more or less convincing evidence, and which sets up boundaries between researchers and non-researchers. Its logical implication is rejection of all knowledge claims – on the grounds that none can be judged as valid, or as more valid than others – or the treatment of *all* beliefs as knowledge.

One effect of postmodernism has been that, to a large extent, the main target of critique has become the knowledge claims of scientists and social researchers themselves, with these being judged in political or ethical, rather than cognitive, terms. This reflects the extent to which some postmodernists see the world, and especially contemporary society, as textual in character; and/or their belief that the appeal to science, rationality, and knowledge has become the principal means of social legitimation, the currently dominant expression of Power. For them, the primary task is to challenge the scientific 'regime of truth'; and especially its alleged denial of validity to any other forms of knowledge; indeed, to champion those that have been marginalised.

While with Hegel and Marx sceptical arguments were kept in bounds by a historically emerging philosophical framework, one that was held to be eventually capable of objectively comprehending the true and the good (see Forster 1989), no such principled restriction of scepticism is available within postmodernism. Here, it can only be restrained in an ad hoc fashion, producing what Woolgar and Pawluch (1985) refer to as ontological gerrymandering. There is a performative contradiction here.[5]

In one currently influential hybrid form, combining scepticism with a commitment to the ideal of 'equality' (see, for examples, Gitlin et al. 1989; Griffiths 1998), the effect of postmodernism is to encourage unfettered criticism of the socio-political 'status quo' as involving social injustice, and especially of the ideas deemed to 'rationalise' this injustice. It involves showing how these ideas reflect economic and political circumstances and interests, and it deploys arguments against them that draw on epistemological scepticism. Yet postmodernism – like existentialism and structuralism before it – does not provide us with any rational basis for committing ourselves to particular ideals. The sceptical arguments associated with it undercut all claims of rational commitment to practical ideals, just as much as they do claims about truth. In this respect, postmodernism seems to ratify, and perhaps thereby reinforce, what Marcuse (1964) referred to as the one-dimensional character of modern society. Indeed, some versions recognise the implication that any criticism is itself necessarily part of, indeed a product of, society. In the face of the performative contradiction

---

[5]Woolgar and Pawluch do not interpret ontological gerrymandering as a defect, but rather as an ineradicable feature of producing accounts. For the charge of performative contradiction, see Habermas (1985) and Dews (1987).

intrinsic to this kind of postmodernism, those influenced by it often restrict the purpose of criticism to disruption or subversion, in the manner of 'negative critique'. Given belief in the textually constituted character of reality, and/or in the essentially legitimatory function of appeals to knowledge, they see a key role for what Ball, paraphrasing Eco, calls 'semiotic guerrilla warfare' (Ball 1995: 268).

These, then, are the trends of thought which have broadened and changed the meaning of 'critical', as it has been used in the context of social research in the past 20 or 30 years. In these terms, the researcher's task is to act as a public intellectual or social critic; either constructively or simply in order to subvert the claims of other 'experts'. Elsewhere, I have argued that the central assumptions of this position are unconvincing: while research is political in some senses, it is not and should not be in others. In particular, it is not inevitably, and ought not to be, directed towards political goals. Its only immediate purpose should be the production of knowledge. Moreover, the sceptical arguments against knowledge as representation, which are now widely influential, are unsound. The defects of 'critical' and postmodernist positions are obscured by their use of words such as 'political' and 'truth' in ways that move implicitly among quite different senses; and by a failure to recognise the implications of a consistent and exhaustive application of the arguments of epistemological scepticism (see Hammersley 1992a: ch. 6; 1995; 1998b; 2000a).

Given the importance of retaining the distinction between research and politics, in subsequent sections I will look separately at the kinds of criticism that are appropriate in these two contexts, and thereby try to identify their proper limits. I should make clear that this is an exercise in research methodology, or perhaps even in the political philosophy of research. In other words, it is *not* a description of the form that criticism actually takes in the domains of research and politics, but an argument about what is legitimate in each area. It is an argument which is a development from Weber's position on objectivity and academic freedom (see Weber 1949; 1974).

THE ROLE OF CRITICISM IN RESEARCH

Starting from the assumption that the sole immediate goal of enquiry is the production of knowledge, criticism within research should be primarily concerned with whether this goal has been achieved; and, secondarily, with whether it has been pursued effectively. There are other considerations involved in assessing research, of course; such as whether it has been carried out in a way that does not unjustifiably breach the rights of those studied, whether the latter have been harmed, what the consequences of publishing the findings might be, etc. However, these do not relate to its immediate goal. Indeed, the central, though not exclusive, ethical requirement placed on the researcher is commitment to the effective pursuit, and publication, of knowledge.

Such a view of enquiry carries a number of specific implications for the form that criticism ought to take in a research context. First of all, it makes clear that criticism is a means not an end: it is a means to the collective discovery of truths, or at least to the elimination of errors. This distinguishes it from much criticism in other spheres.

For instance, it differs from the kind of criticism that forms part of advocacy in law courts. Thus, while the function of the legal process is to discover the truth, and thereby to produce a just verdict, the task of the individual barrister (in the English system) is simply to argue the case of her or his client in the most effective way possible within the rules of court procedure. Evidence at odds with that case will be challenged, while that supporting it will not be. The division of labour between barrister, on the one hand, and judge and jury, on the other, is taken to be the best mechanism for achieving the institutional goal of discovering truth and attaining justice.

This contrasts with what happens in research. While advocacy, like criticism, plays a part here, it is very much a subordinate one. The researcher's task in writing a research report is to present a line of argument in the most persuasive way that is legitimate, but it should also be a line of argument that he or she believes to be true. Moreover, researchers are expected to judge counter-arguments in a different manner from lawyers: not in terms of how these can best be rebutted, but according to whether they do indeed throw doubt on the original knowledge claims. And researchers are required to change their views if the evidence becomes convincing that these are wrong. Similarly, critics are expected to put forward criticisms that are based on reasonable doubts about the validity of what is claimed, not to engage in criticism for the sake of it, or in order to discredit the researcher or the line of argument being pursued. And they are to respond to any defence presented by the researcher not in terms of how best to undermine it, but according to whether it resolves the problems they previously identified and/or raises any further ones. Most importantly, there is no fixed division of labour: researchers whose work is criticised will on other occasions be critics; and those who are critics will at other times put forward positive knowledge claims. The task of critic is rotated.

A second implication of the fact that the sole immediate goal of research is to produce knowledge is that legitimate criticism is restricted primarily to critical assessment of *knowledge claims* put forward as contributions to disciplinary knowledge. In other words, the *aim* of research is not to subject state policies, social institutions, occupational practices, or even the views and assumptions of powerful political actors, to critical assessment. Of course, research findings may run counter to ideas that are widely held to be true and/or that underpin policies and institutions. But this is a by-product; it is not the *aim* of research to challenge these ideas.[6] On the interpretation I am putting forward here, it is not part of the task of the researcher to be a social critic; so in this sense research *should* be uncritical.

It is also important that criticism does not come to focus primarily on the *character* or *competence* of other researchers, or on the way they have pursued their work, rather

[6]Here there is a parallel between criticism and bias, as discussed by Becker (1967). He notes that researchers cannot avoid being accused of bias: there are social contexts where this will happen, however successful a researcher actually is in avoiding bias. This is because research findings have implications for powerful interests that will defend themselves by trying to discredit the research. (On Becker's argument, and how it is frequently misinterpreted, see Hammersley 2000a: ch. 3). In the same way, even where researchers operate on the basis I have outlined, they will often be accused of engaging in political criticism. This is because research findings are frequently relevant to factual assumptions involved in judgements about policy and practice, and because the distinction between the factual and value components of those judgements is often ignored.

than on the knowledge claims they have put forward. Indeed, any critic should begin from the assumption that the researcher whose work is being assessed was properly committed to the collective task of discovering the truth. And this assumption should only be abandoned on the basis of overwhelming evidence to the contrary, in terms of expressed principle and/or practice. Of course, this runs against the trend encouraged by Marxism, Critical Theory, much feminism, and postmodernism. From these points of view, since researchers are members of society, their accounts must be assumed to reflect their social characteristics and circumstances; most important of all, it is assumed that the validity of their accounts should be judged in this light. The position I am taking here does not deny the likely effects of such characteristics and circumstances, but it does deny that they are reliable indicators of validity or invalidity. To believe otherwise is to commit the genetic fallacy.[7]

In summary, among researchers, criticism ought to take the form of critical assessment focused on specific knowledge claims that are designed to contribute to the body of research knowledge. And those claims should be judged solely in terms of whether they seem likely to be true given the evidence available. The task is a collective one of discovering likely errors, and moving towards more and more sound knowledge. In this, as already indicated, there is no fixed division of labour between advocate and critic. Rather, these roles are rotated continually; and neither should be performed single-mindedly, but always with a view to the larger task of producing knowledge of the relevant kind. Furthermore, it follows from this that criticism should *not* be concerned with the apparent political or practical implications of a knowledge claim. Nor should it be assumed that these implications were the primary motive of the person putting the claim forward. In other words, the focus of assessment should be the validity of research findings, not the integrity, identity, political orientation, or alleged interests of the researcher.[8] Only if there is very substantial evidence that the researcher has not been oriented mainly to the production of knowledge should the influence of these factors be subject to examination.

In addition, critical assessment in the context of social enquiry should not employ the arguments of epistemological sceptics unless these can be shown to be specifically relevant to the problem being addressed. Above all, such arguments must not be used selectively in an ad hoc way. One test here can be found in Wittgenstein's book *On Certainty* (1969). An implication of his discussion is that if we are tempted to doubt something we should consider what other beliefs that level of doubt would force us to relinquish. This is a way of operationalising the notion of reasonable doubt in the face of forms of epistemological scepticism which, if applied consistently, would force us to doubt things that there is no good reason to question, including some which the very act of doubting relies upon.

It is important to underline that, while epistemological scepticism must be rejected if research is to be possible, nevertheless the arguments put forward by researchers will often be seen by outsiders precisely as doubting the obvious. As Merton argued,

---

[7]For a discussion of this in the context of Karl Mannheim's sociology of knowledge, see Hartung (1970: 698–701). Of course, some of the main sources on which Mannheim drew were Hegel and Marx.

[8]For a similar argument in the context of feminism, see Patai (1994).

science of all kinds is governed by a norm of organised scepticism (1973b: chs 12–13), yet this is very different from epistemological scepticism. Only knowledge claims that are judged, by most researchers in a field, to be above a high threshold of likely truth can be treated as established knowledge. This is the cutting edge of scientific research as a knowledge production process.[9]

My outline of the proper nature of academic criticism is, of course, at odds with influential views in current social research methodology; in particular, those outlined in the first section of this chapter. Yet there is still widespread *practical* commitment to these principles, even on the part of those who explicitly adopt a 'critical' or postmodernist orientation – especially where they identify deviance on the part of others. I take this to be evidence that this conception of criticism is intrinsic to the character of academic enquiry as an activity; it is essential because it serves to maximise the chances of detecting errors, and discovering truths, of a factual kind. Any deviation from this form of criticism – including that encouraged by Marxism, Critical Theory, some feminism, and postmodernism – is likely to undermine the production of sound knowledge (see Hammersley 2000a).

In the next section I want to look at the idea of the researcher as critic from a different perspective: in terms of the proper role of criticism in the context of politics and practical affairs.

CRITICISM IN POLITICS AND PRACTICAL MATTERS

The idea of the researcher as social critic assumes the desirability of criticism in political and practical contexts. And in some versions it involves an application to those contexts of assumptions about the desirability of criticism which arise from the field of research. An influential example, I suggest, is the account of the public sphere put forward by Habermas (Habermas 1989; Holub 1991). He places a very high value on the role of criticism in public discussion of policy and practice, seeing this as an essential device for coming to recognise what is true and what should be done. This amounts to what has been referred to as a discursive conception of democracy (see Dryzek 1990; Gutmann and Thompson 1996).

However, arguments for the positive role of criticism in politics are not necessarily tied to this particular concept of democracy, they can be more general. For example, they are an important part of the liberal case for a multi-party political system and for a free press. Criticism of prevailing policies and practices is believed to be healthy because it leads to their flaws being discovered; and it is assumed that these will be more easily seen by those who do not have a commitment to the policy or practice concerned. Equally important, criticism may reveal that a policy or practice favours some section of the population at the expense of another. It is expected that those who do not have the interests of the beneficiaries at heart will be able to recognise the bias better than those who do; and that they will also be less willing to overlook

---

[9]Hammersley 1995: ch4. I am assuming a distinction between scientific and practical research here, see Hammersley (2000b).

it. From this point of view, criticism serves to keep governments true to espoused public principles: it counters their tendency to believe their own propaganda and to serve only their own, or their supporters', interests.

Much the same argument for the role of criticism is sometimes used in relation to occupational practitioners of various kinds. It is argued that external criticism forces them to examine their own behaviour against high standards, and to rectify any shortfall. Furthermore, it may require them to take seriously a wider range of considerations than their narrow professional perspective encourages. Here, too, criticism is seen as countering an inherent tendency to inertia and self-interest.

Moreover, in all these cases the value of criticism is viewed as lying in more than just its immediate effect. The idea is that those who are subjected to criticism will internalise the process, and become more routinely self-critical in relevant ways; and that this will improve their work. In other words, they will become more reflective, and thereby more effective, policy makers and practitioners. Of course, it is often argued that continued external criticism will nevertheless still be necessary – because of the tendencies in the opposite direction, towards conservatism, that are inherent in the institutionalisation of policy making and practice.

What I want to suggest here is that while criticism can and no doubt often does play a desirable role in relation to policy making and practice in these ways, its effects will not always be beneficial; so here too there must be informal constraints on it. The views outlined above, if taken to justify unrestrained criticism, as they often are, imply that it keeps policy makers or practitioners on a straight, narrow, and upwardly leading path; or, in more radical versions, that it forces them to jump the chasm to a higher level, or to a different kind, of policy or practice. But this involves a crucial and questionable assumption. It presupposes that, at least over the medium term, criticism points in a single direction, and that this is towards improvement or desirable change. There are some good, though by no means unchallenged, reasons for believing that this is true for empirical enquiry. Indeed, I have suggested that this idea is a constitutive assumption of research as an activity. However, there is little justification for this assumption in the case of public criticism of policies and practices.

The main reason is that while in the context of research the ground for criticism is restricted to cognitive validity, this is not the case with political or practical criticism. Policies and practices need to be judged in terms of their desirability, not just according to the validity of the assumptions on which they are based. And the problem is that there are *multiple* value principles in terms of which desirability can be assessed; principles which are frequently not in harmony with one another in their implications for particular cases. This means that very often there are not unique best solutions available for political or practical problems. Policy makers and practitioners usually have to make some trade-off among different values.[10] As a result of such dilemmas, whatever the direction in which policy or

---

[10]One dilemma, much discussed in the literature of political philosophy but frequently forgotten in other spheres, is that between liberty and equality. On value pluralism in the influential work of Berlin, see Gray (1995: ch. 2). There are also competing principles to be found under the heading of equity, see Hammersley (1997).

practice goes, there will always be scope for criticism, and often from *multiple* angles.

An added problem is that there is always considerable room for questioning the *factual* assumptions on which policies and practices rely. Very often these relate to what is feasible, and to what consequences are likely to follow from various courses of action, including the reactions of relevant other agents.[11] The endless scope for possible doubt about validity is a potential problem in the research context, but it can be resolved there in practical terms by the mode of orientation I outlined in the previous section. However, this mode of orientation is not enforceable, or even appropriate in principle, in the political sphere. Here, we cannot assume that individuals or groups, and even less their representatives, will be simply committed to determining what factual assumptions are correct, or even to finding what is the most desirable policy or practice in universalistic terms.[12] Worse still, there are reasons why such an orientation would not even be reasonable on their part.

One of these arises from the very fact that there will often *not* be a single unique solution to the question of what is in the common interest. In this situation it may be justifiable for those involved in public discussion to press for the option which serves their own interests best, among those which could also be held to serve the common interest. This is reinforced by a second point, which is that our ethical intuitions are not exhausted by universalistic commitments: whether in terms of achieving the greatest good or of conforming to universalisable principles (approaches which are themselves not always compatible in their implications). While these commitments have considerable force, we also recognise obligations that are particularistic, that are distinctive to us because of who we are (see Larmore 1987). The most obvious ones are those towards family and friends, but there are analogous obligations towards work colleagues and fellow members of a profession, obligations which arise especially sharply in relation to the rights and wrongs of 'whistle blowing'.

Thus, differences in view among the individuals and groups involved in policy decisions cannot be regarded as solely a product of error, ignorance, or ulterior motive. Rather, in part, they will reflect the diversity of value principles that can be brought to bear on an issue; the socially located obligations of the different parties; and the differential knowledge and reasonable inferences available to them. Thus, even in ideal circumstances, differences in view often will not be resolvable through critical discussion directed towards discovering the right course of action. Rather, what may be required is negotiation – and perhaps even some manipulation or coercion – if any decision is to be reached.

One implication of this is that, in the political realm especially, what others propose must be approached not simply in terms of whether it is true, or is of value, but also according to what it is designed to achieve, and who they are. Other participants in public debate can be assumed to have practical goals which they are pursuing. This is not to say that what they say and do should be treated simply as an expression of

---

[11]For an elaboration of the uncertain relationship between research-based factual knowledge and practical decision making, see Hammersley (2002a).

[12]This is recognised by Rawls in his use of the device of 'the original position' in thinking about the nature of social justice (Rawls 1971).

their interests. Indeed, this cannot be true, since interests are not facts which determine views but are themselves value interpretations (see Hindess 1987). Nevertheless, to one degree or another, participants in the public sphere are engaged in strategic action directed towards achieving, preserving, or opposing policy and practice of particular kinds, and this must be taken into account in dealing with them. Thus, a critical approach in the political sphere may need to take the form of sustained opposition to others who are pursuing policies that are designed to realise a different set of values from those to which one is committed; not just critical appraisal of the particular proposals they make. In this respect, too, the nature of the critical act is likely to be rather different from the form it ought to take in the context of research.

Another important point is that, even when sound in terms of validity, public criticism may have negative consequences. It may serve to discourage a course of action which, from most points of view, would be preferable to available alternatives. A commonly recognised aspect of this is that ideas about the best can drive out the good, and leave us with what is worse. This is especially true where criticism is focused on a single value issue; since policy and practice usually have to take account of a whole range of issues simultaneously, very often trading some of these off against others. Where policy makers and practitioners are highly responsive to criticism, the result is often a kind of seesaw effect over time: on one occasion they will be accused of a particular failing and will seek to avoid that; on the next, they will be accused of its opposite and will respond accordingly; and so on, back and forth. In such contexts, responsiveness to criticism may not be a good thing, beyond a threshold. Social workers dealing with allegations of child abuse might be a case in point.

A further issue, one that is of much more significance in the field of policy and practice than in that of research, is that dealing with criticism involves costs: time, energy, and other resources are applied that could have been deployed in other ways. In addition, criticism may delay a decision being made among the options available, and this too can have negative consequences. There are associated general costs as well: continual criticism tends to undermine public trust in those criticised, and opens the way to demands for 'transparent' accountability: the impossible requirement that everything be made fully explicit, and thereby open to immediate judgement by everyone.[13] A further effect is erosion of the confidence of policy makers and practitioners in their own ability to make judgements, and this may encourage them to limit decisions to those that minimise the risk of criticism from powerful constituencies.

So, it cannot be assumed that public criticism of policies or practices will have desirable consequences; in the way that it *can* be assumed that criticism of the appropriate kind in the context of research generally will, at least over the longer term. This is a difference of degree rather than an absolute one, but it is important nonetheless. In research, criticism may lead to the wrong judgement about the validity of a knowledge claim. But there is no limit on the period of time over which knowledge claims can be assessed. Even those that become widely accepted within a research community may later be opened up to question again, and perhaps even rejected. While the procedure for detecting error is by no means perfect, over the

---

[13]For further discussion of this, see Hammersley (2002a).

long run it should approximate to full effectiveness. By contrast, in the fields of policy making and practice, decisions *do* have to be made at particular points in time, perhaps irrevocably; in addition, circumstances change so that what was the right decision in the past for dealing with some problem may soon no longer be.

What is implied by all this is that those engaging in criticism in the public sphere must take into account not just the soundness of their arguments but also the likely consequences of their making this particular criticism at this particular time, since these consequences cannot be *assumed* to be beneficial. In this respect, criticism of policies and practices in the public sphere is a political act in a way that criticism of knowledge claims in the context of research is not; and the implication I am drawing is that it must be restrained by prudence.

Now it seems to me that this is a necessary constraint that is frequently overlooked, or denied, by those who see the researcher as a social critic or public intellectual. One reason for this may be that they assume a teleological notion of progress, whether of a Marxist kind or of the sort built into notions of 'modernisation' associated with the 'new public management' that is currently influential in many Western states. These positions presuppose that there is directionality built into criticism of policy and practice in the same way that there is with criticism of research findings. However, as I have made clear, this is not the case. Another reason why the need for prudence may be overlooked by researchers acting as social critics is that they intellectualise the nature of discussion in the public sphere, in the manner of Habermas. Postmodernists have, of course, recently been in the forefront of criticising both these positions. Yet they too tend to neglect the need for prudence in political criticism, under the influence of an apocalyptic notion of historical discontinuity. As noted earlier, for some of them the task of criticism is to disrupt the status quo, the assumption often being that this will allow entrance of 'the Other' to create the possibility of a new age whose character is incommensurable with that of the present. This is a perspective which positively encourages political irresponsibility, through a valorisation of 'transgression'.[14]

One factor generating this neglect of prudence may arise from a difference in social organisation between academic and public spheres. As we saw, in the context of research there is rotation between critics and those engaged in the task of developing positive knowledge claims; and this plays an important role in limiting criticism to those matters that are open to reasonable doubt. By contrast, there is usually little rotation between researchers engaged in criticism of public policies or extant practices and those who make policy decisions or enact practices of the relevant kinds. As a result, there is no analogous limiting process operating on the social criticisms that researchers make. Instead, there is a tendency towards commitment politics, rather than to a political orientation aimed at pragmatic effectiveness.[15]

---

[14]Something like this seems to be the position of Foucault, Deleuze, and Lyotard, and of many on the far Left in France post-1968, see Bourg (2007). For a discussion which shows how this kind of ultra-Leftism came out of Marxism, see Foucault and Deleuze (1977). On Foucault, see also Dews (1986). For Lyotard's position, see Readings (1993).

[15]This tendency has been at the heart of conflict between party intellectuals and the parties to which they are affiliated: see Caute (1964). Relevant here is Weber's distinction between an ethic of conviction and an ethic of responsibility: see Bruun (1972: 255–73).

There may even be a sense, then, in which researchers have a trained incapacity for acting as social and political critics; though we should recognise that Utopian criticism can sometimes have the desirable effect of challenging the tendency for a pragmatic orientation to become narrow and fixed. Of course, there are also reasons why researchers could be well suited to the role of critic. Above all, they usually have better access to knowledge of relevant research evidence than others, and the cognitive skills developed in the course of their work may also be a distinctive benefit. Thus, I am not suggesting that those who are researchers cannot also play the role of public intellectuals engaged in social criticism. Rather, my argument has been that these are separate roles; that there are limits on what is appropriate criticism in the spheres of both research and politics; *and that these limits are different in the two cases.*

I would also add that there is a danger when researchers play the role of public intellectual that research is given greater weight as a source of evidence than it should be, as against evidence from practical experience. Moreover, researchers' participation in that role may also encourage the idea that research can, by itself, tell us what is desirable and undesirable, and what should be done; thereby obscuring the value judgements involved in policy and practice. And there is little justification for the idea – central to the model of the intellectual promoted by Benda and many other writers – that those engaged in intellectual pursuits have a unique commitment to universal values. We should perhaps view this as, in large part, an occupational ideology.

Social researchers have a public responsibility to make clear what can, and *cannot,* reasonably be concluded from their findings; and this involves exercising in public the kind of organised scepticism that is an integral part of their work as researchers. This operates as a necessary brake on the tendency for public discussion to ignore dependence upon assumptions which may be open to serious question. It also restrains the tendency to overlook implicit reliance on value principles; in other words, the temptation to deal with policy or practical issues as if these were simply factual matters, when they are not. However, in the public sphere, neither the responsibility nor the authority of social scientists extends any further than this.

CONCLUSION

In this chapter, I began by outlining what I take to be the core meaning of the term 'critical' in the context of research: the assessment, according to their validity, of knowledge claims put forward by researchers. I noted how the meaning of this term shifted among social scientists over the second half of the twentieth century. This occurred, to a large extent, under the influence of Marxism and Critical Theory. These movements erased the distinctions between intellectual and socio-political criticism, and between empirical research and philosophical critique. And such erasures were later reinforced by the influence of feminism and postmodernism, in particular through a downplaying and/or rejection of commitment to the ideal of truth as representation.

I argued that these developments are at odds with the proper nature of criticism in enquiry. There, criticism must play a subordinate role in the task of discovering truths, or eliminating errors, from what is taken to be research-based knowledge. In order to do this it should focus primarily on the validity of candidate research findings, and must be carried out in a situation where there is trust that all concerned are committed primarily to the production of knowledge. Thus, disagreement must be met not with rebuttal, but with an attempt to find common ground from which a convincing argument for or against the validity of the contested claim can be made.

In the final section of the chapter I argued that in the public sphere too criticism should respect certain limits, but that these are different from those appropriate in the context of research. Here there is no restriction on the *range* of targets of criticism. Similarly, the *grounds* for criticism are wider, including desirability, not just cognitive validity. And, finally, the critical act may involve taking an oppositional stance, not just critical assessment of individual arguments on their merits. However, whereas in research no restraint is required on criticism as regards its assumed political implications or consequences, this is not true in the realms of policy and practice. Here, prudence must play a much more important role in decisions about what to criticise, and when.

I suggested that this latter point is often overlooked by researchers who see their task as that of social critic: that they misapply to public discussion the irrelevance of prudence in the sphere of research; just as they frequently misapply the wider scope of political and practical criticism to the situation of research.

It is essential that researchers and others recognise both the authority of research *and* the limits to that authority. At present, there seems to be little clarity about those limits. And this is signalled by the way in which the adjective 'critical' has been used. The extension of the meaning of that term which I have discussed here – and the associated erasure of the boundaries between scientific, philosophical, and political criticism – exceeds those limits.

The effect of such a bloated concept of criticism on researchers is to undermine the kind of discussion that is required if sound knowledge is to be produced with any consistency. Meanwhile, in the political field unrestrained criticism – albeit not only by researchers but also by politicians, pressure groups, and the media – is one of the main factors generating cynicism and demands for 'transparent' accountability, thereby making wise policy making and practice difficult if not impossible. Ironically, this opens up greater scope for researchers to act as social critics, and thereby increases the likelihood that these two roles will be confused.

4

OBJECTIVITY AS AN INTELLECTUAL VIRTUE

> Objectivity is not a matter of value disconnection, it is a matter of evaluative appropriateness. It calls for proceeding in such a way that the values appropriate to the context at hand are taken account of in a rationally defensible way. (Rescher 1997: 172–3)

In recent times, the word 'objectivity', like 'truth' and 'reality', has come to be interpreted by some social scientists as referring to a fiction, and is treated by most commentators with great caution or avoided altogether. The uncertain status of the word is some-times signalled by its being placed within inverted commas. While these do not *always* indicate sneering rejection (Haack 1998: 117), they are usually intended to distance the writer from any implication that what the word refers to actually exists, or at least to suggest that there is doubt about it.[1] In this chapter I want to examine the reasons why objectivity is found problematic, and I will also try to develop a clearer under-standing of what function the concept might usefully serve in the context of social enquiry.

UNCERTAINTY ABOUT OBJECTIVITY

There are several reasons for current scepticism about objectivity. Part of the problem is that the words 'objective' and 'subjective' can be interpreted in a variety of ways, and these need to be distinguished. Daston and Galison (2007: 29–35) have outlined their complex semantic history, suggesting that, over time, they have reversed their

---

[1] In short, they operate as 'scare quotes'. Note that my putting quotation marks around 'objectivity' in this chapter does not conform to this usage; instead, it signals when I am *mentioning* not *using* the word.

meanings.[2] They were introduced into scholastic philosophy in the fourteenth century, at which point 'objective' meant 'things as they appear to consciousness' (in other words, objects of thought) whereas 'subjective' meant 'things as they are in themselves' (in other terms, subjects with attributes). Kant modified this usage, so that 'objective' came to refer to the 'forms of sensibility' that structure our perceptions, by contrast with the subjective, that is the empirical, content that is poured into these vessels by the *Ding an sich*, thereby generating our perceptions and cognitions. Post-Kantian usage involved a further twist: 'objective' came to refer to what belongs to nature or to reality independently of our subjective experience of it. In these terms, a judgement can be said to be objective if it corresponds to an external object, and as subjective if it does not. The other side of the same conception of objectivity is the assumption that there is an objective, 'external' world in the sense that things exist and have the character they do irrespective of our beliefs or wishes about them; and, confusingly, there may also be an 'internal' subjective world in which things exist in this sense too. Daston and Galison go on to document different versions of this new conception of objectivity, one appealing to the idea of truth-to-nature, another to the possibility of mechanical reproduction, a third to trained judgement – and these are almost as different from one another as they are from scholastic usage.[3]

Given this confusing history, it is perhaps not surprising that the concept of objectivity should be found troublesome today. Within the context of social science, we can identify several by no means isomorphic contrasts that often participate in how the terms 'subjective' and 'objective' are intended, or interpreted, on particular occasions:

1 Mental versus physical
2 Internal as against external
3 Private rather than public
4 Implicit versus explicit
5 Judgement as against mechanical procedure
6 Idiosyncratic rather than shared
7 Variable versus stable or fixed
8 Particular rather than universal
9 Dependent as against independent
10 Relative rather than absolute
11 Erroneous versus true

In much usage these various distinctions are blended together. There is also sometimes a failure to distinguish between objectivity as achievement and objectivity as ideal or goal. It is one thing to say that we can and should try to be objective, quite another to say that we can ever *be* objective, or know that we have objective knowledge.

---

[2]Anscombe (1965: 158–9) had pointed this out earlier. Collier (2003: 133) links this to a shift from ontology to epistemology within Western philosophy. See Dear (1992: 620–1) for a detailed explication of the original meanings of these terms and how 'objectivity' came to mean disinterestedness. See also Zagorin (2001).

[3]See also Farrell's (1996) illuminating account of changing conceptions of subjectivity in the history of philosophy, and the theological background to this.

The tendency to blur these various senses reflects the continuing influence, both positive and negative, of a particular conception of objectivity that emerged most influentially during the early twentieth century, and that has come to be questioned by many social scientists today. This is frequently given the label 'positivist' – but this term has become very misleading, because of the range of (almost entirely negative) ways in which it is now used. For this reason, it seems better to employ a different label, and the one I will use here is 'objectivism'.[4]

OBJECTIVISM AND ITS ERRORS

Objectivism treats the word 'objectivity' as having a single composite sense, in which all the different meanings listed earlier are combined. In particular, the substantive senses of 'subjective' and 'objective' – referring to the mental versus the physical, the inner versus the outer, etc. – are generally treated as isomorphic with the epistemological sense of these two terms – as referring to the false and the true. Objectivism amounts to a distinctive conception of the nature of scientific enquiry, how it should be pursued, and what it produces. Its starting point is the idea that we are often led into error by false preconceptions and preferences that result in our tending to see or find what we expected or wished rather than what is true. In short, subjective factors of various kinds are treated as leading to our conclusions being subjective rather than objective, in the sense that they reflect our errors rather than the world. Subjectivity is believed to bias enquiry, deflecting us from the truth that we would otherwise discover. From this it is concluded that we must engage in enquiry in a manner that is unaffected by our personal and social characteristics (prior beliefs, values, preferences, attitudes, personality traits, etc.), or at least one that minimises their influence.

Several strategies are proposed for avoiding subjective error. One is that we should restrict ourselves to what is directly observable, and what can be inferred logically or via calculation from such given data. Of course, there is an important sense in which nothing is directly observable, so this tends to turn into the idea that researchers should rely only upon the sort of capabilities that every human being has, or that anyone could be easily trained to employ, rather than on specialised forms of intuition or connoisseurship.[5] More broadly, there is the notion that we must commit ourselves to a research design that specifies in procedural terms what will be done through all stages of the process of enquiry; not just in data collection, but also in drawing conclusions from the data. And this plan must then be followed as closely as possible. Thereby, it is argued, the enquiry process can be standardised and rendered

---

[4]This too has been employed in different ways, but it has not been debased to the same extent as 'positivism'. Bernstein (1983: 8) defines it as the false conviction that there is 'some permanent, ahistorical matrix or framework to which we can ultimately appeal in determining the nature of rationality, knowledge, truth, reality, goodness, or rightness', while Ratner (2002) defines it in a positive manner, also at odds with my usage here, tracing it back to Dilthey.

[5]This idea can be traced back at least to the writings of Francis Bacon: see Gaukroger (2001).

transparent, eliminating the effects of idiosyncratic, subjective factors, an ideal that is sometimes referred to as procedural objectivity (Eisner 1992; see also Newell 1986).

Such proceduralisation is viewed by objectivists not only as of value in itself, in that it minimises error deriving from subjectivity, but also as facilitating the use of checks on the accuracy of observation and inference, so that one investigator's findings can be compared with those of others. Of course, such comparisons had long been recognised as a means of assessing validity, but objectivism claims that if researchers use quite different approaches from one another, reflecting their personal characteristics, then it is impossible to determine who is right and what the source of any discrepancy is. By contrast, if multiple investigators use the same method, their findings will be comparable.

In one version of objectivism, the very use of procedures designed to eliminate subjectivity is taken as itself constituting objectivity, and as defining what counts as objective, or scientific, knowledge. In other words, from this point of view, knowledge or truth is simply whatever conclusions are reached via such proceduralised enquiry. This nominalist version was influential in some strands of US psychology and sociology during the second quarter of the twentieth century, under the influence of Bridgman's operationism and interpretations of logical positivism. However, there is another version of objectivism that treats proceduralised enquiry as achieving objectivity because, by eliminating subjective factors, it allows the objective voice of the world to speak through the research. In other words, it enables us truly to capture the make-up of the world, as consisting of distinct objects belonging to types that have essential characteristics defined by law-like relations. This might be labelled realist objectivism. While the distinction between this and its nominalist counterpart is of analytic importance, it is sometimes hard to draw, and is probably of little significance in practice.

Serious problems have been identified with objectivism. These can be outlined as follows:

1   While it is true that we may be led astray by subjective factors (whether conceived of as mental, inner, inexplicit, particular, or whatever), it is also the case that we are inevitably dependent upon personal knowledge, capabilities, and motivations in producing any evidence or conclusions. For instance, we cannot avoid relying upon our senses in making observations, and these are in important respects subjective, culturally constituted, and cannot be separated from expectations or habits. Nor is it possible to reduce them entirely to the following of explicit procedures (Polanyi 1958). Much the same applies to the processes of inference involved in producing evidence and drawing conclusions from it. Here, we cannot operate entirely in the manner of a calculating machine: assumptions, ampliative inference, and imagination are all necessarily involved.

2   It is also important to recognise that research depends upon subjective commitments of various kinds. Even in the case of objectivism, researchers must be committed to following procedures carefully, and this is a personal characteristic as well as a social one. I will argue later that research necessarily depends upon a range of epistemic virtues, of which objectivity (of a certain kind) is itself one.

3   It may be true that evidence coming from the use of ordinary everyday perceptual capabilities is less open to potential error than that which relies upon specialised knowledge and skills; or, at least, that it is easier to check the results. However, this does not mean that reliance solely on those capabilities is more likely to lead to sound knowledge of the kind desired. What needs to be observed may not be accessible to ordinary capabilities, so that the questions we are addressing cannot be resolved by appeal to evidence of this sort. Similarly, drawing the kind of conclusions required, in a sound manner, will usually depend upon specialised knowledge and skills.

4   Subjective factors are not the only source, and certainly not the only cause, of error in observation and reasoning. For example, we may accurately note how the sun rises in the sky each morning, but to describe it as moving over the earth is still an error. Similarly, we may correctly document the similarities between two pieces of rock and infer, on the basis of their easily observable characteristics, that they must have been produced by a common causal process when, in fact, one rock is igneous while the other is a product of sedimentation. In other words, we may employ careful observation and uncontroversial modes of inference yet still reach false conclusions. It could even be that the questions we are asking are based on false assumptions: the effect we are seeking to explain may not exist, our hypotheses may be misconceived, and so on.

5   It is never possible to ensure that different researchers will apply a procedure in exactly the same way, however closely it is specified. This is particularly true in social research because here much depends upon how the people being studied respond to the procedures employed: it is not just the behaviour of the researcher that must be standardised but theirs too. Moreover, it is in the nature of human social interaction that the actions of each side will be shaped by the other. Objectivism seeks to ensure that all subjects or respondents in a study are presented with the same stimulus field, but since what they experience will depend partly on their background expectations, cultural habits, interactions with the researcher, and so on, it is always likely that what they *actually* experience will be rather different from what was *intended*, and may vary considerably. For example, even if experimental subjects are presented with the same instructions, they may interpret them in discrepant ways, and behave differently as a result; whereas, had they interpreted them in the same way, their behaviour would have been the same. Similarly, two subjects may interpret the instructions differently and as a result produce the same type of response, whereas, had they interpreted the instructions in the same way, their behaviour would have been different.

6   Following a procedure will not *always* improve the quality of the observation or reasoning. This is because any procedure relies upon assumptions and these could be false. Furthermore, applying a procedure may rule out the use of some personal capability that is essential if the required type of observation is to be made, or if error arising from use of the procedure in particular circumstances is to be detected. Procedures and guidelines can serve a useful function in reminding us of what needs to be taken into account, but they can also

result in our failing to notice what could be important in particular cases. There are issues too about what is and is not measurable by means of fixed procedures, which relate to the nature of the world being investigated. Some have argued that social phenomena are complex, in the technical sense that they are systems subject to influence by a potentially unlimited number of variables, and 'the influence of particular factors is variable according to the relationships that they enjoy with others at any moment in time' (Radford 2007: 2). This seems likely to subvert reliance on procedures.

7 For all the reasons outlined above, the fact that two or more observers using the same procedure agree in their observations, or that two or more analysts using the same procedure come to the same conclusion in working with the same data, does not in itself indicate that their reports are true, even where they have operated independently of one another. Instead, their work may be affected by errors, including those built into the procedure itself, that lead them in the same, false direction.

There are also problems that arise specifically with what I have called realist objectivism. This portrays knowledge as in some sense re-presenting, reflecting, or reproducing reality, in such a way that there is a correspondence between the account produced and the object(s) to which it relates. There is a danger of being misled by metaphor here. In the face of visual metaphors of picturing, or even those of mapping or modelling, it is essential to remember that any body of knowledge consists of answers to some set of questions, and that many different questions can be asked about any specific set of objects, producing different knowledge about them. While there cannot be contradictory knowledge about the same set of objects, there can certainly be a very wide range of knowledge claims made about them. This suggests that it is false to assume that we are dealing with a world made up of objects, each having a finite set of features that can be exhaustively 're-presented'. What objects are identified and what features they have will depend partly on the questions we ask about the world. This seems to rule out the sort of ontology assumed by realist objectivism.

While it is probably true that most social scientists have never adhered completely to objectivism, much methodological thought and research practice has been strongly affected by it. Indeed, it continues to have some influence even today – especially among quantitative researchers and in the context of research methods training courses. At the same time, the problems with objectivism have led many social scientists, especially qualitative researchers, to reject it completely. Indeed, a few have attacked, or abandoned, the concept of objectivity itself, while others have sought fundamentally to reconstruct it. I will look at their arguments in the next section.

REACTIONS AGAINST OBJECTIVITY

Radical critics of objectivity sometimes start from what they take to be systematic error operating across social science. For example, Hawkesworth writes: 'A significant proportion of feminist scholarship involves detailed refutations of erroneous claims about women produced in conformity with prevailing disciplinary standards of objectivity' (1994: 152). Much the same sort of claim has been made by other radical critics, focusing on other sorts of bias; relating to social class divisions, ethnicity, sexual orientation, and so on. These critics have tended to focus their attack upon particular elements of objectivism that they believe have served to disguise bias. For example, they have sometimes seen objectivity as requiring that research be entirely value-free, that it not be dependent upon or influenced by any value commitments at all. On this basis they argue that objectivity is impossible, and that any claim to have achieved it is ideological. Similarly, critics often take objectivity to require the elimination from research of all passion and personal involvement. In these terms, it is presented as requiring researchers to turn themselves into robots without feeling. And, given that this is undesirable, objectivity is rejected for this reason too. A related criticism is that objectivity implies that researchers must separate themselves from all inherited assumptions, from the particular circumstances in which they are located, and/or from their other background characteristics, so as to adopt a universalistic 'view from nowhere'. Again, the impossibility and/or undesirability of this is used as a basis for denouncing any commitment to objectivity.

It is important to recognise that what is being rejected here is objectivism, and that by no means all interpretations of 'objectivity' make these impossible or undesirable demands upon researchers. For example, in its original Weberian form the notion of value-freedom was more sophisticated than its critics usually recognise. Weber acknowledged that there are constitutive values guiding research, notably truth, that other values are involved in defining relevant phenomena for investigation, and that bias deriving from non-epistemic value commitments is a persistent danger (see Keat and Urry 1975: ch. 9; Bruun 2007). Similarly, objectivity does not necessarily require the suppression of all passion or personal involvement in research, or the pretence that it is possible to step outside of one's social location and background assumptions.

However, some attacks on objectivity are even more fundamental. They challenge the very concepts of truth, knowledge, and error on which it relies, amounting to a sceptical rejection of traditional notions of enquiry.

ABANDONING OBJECTIVITY

Some critics reject objectivity because they deny the very possibility and desirability of knowledge, as conventionally understood. Also involved here may be the idea that objectivity amounts to a form of inauthenticity, an attempt (inevitably futile) to produce knowledge that does not reflect the distinctive personal characteristics, or unique social location, of the investigator. What is required, instead, it is argued, is that any account be openly presented as a *construction*, rather than claiming to represent the object(s) to which it refers. Moreover, it should be a construction that explicitly acknowledges the fact that it draws on particular resources in particular circumstances, for particular purposes. What is also demanded is recognition that there can always be other, and conflicting, accounts; with choice among these being in an important sense undecidable or arbitrary.

This sceptical approach denies that it is possible for us to escape the influence of our social identities and locations, or desirable for us to try to do this, *and insists that this undermines the commitment to produce knowledge*. It is argued that the idea of gaining knowledge of phenomena that are independent of our beliefs about them is an illusion; and that any attempt to do this is therefore naive or deceitful. Furthermore, not only are all claims to knowledge necessarily constructions or socio-historical products, but so too are all means of assessing these. In place of the possibility of knowledge, we are faced with irreconcilable *claims* to knowledge. And it is suggested that the only grounds for evaluating these, at best, are ethical, political, or aesthetic.[6]

While this kind of scepticism is currently quite influential, under labels such as 'relativism' and 'postmodernism', we should note that it is unsustainable in practical terms: we cannot live without relying on something like the traditional concepts of knowledge and truth. Doubting something always depends upon taking something else for granted. Moreover, while actively generating doubt about what we take for granted may occasionally be of value, so as to remind ourselves of the fallibility of whatever we believe we know, this does not require denying the very possibility of knowledge. And the idea that knowledge claims can and should be assessed in ethical, political, or aesthetic terms amounts to a failure to follow through the logic of sceptical arguments. These apply in much the same corrosive way to claims about what is good or right – in ethical, political, or aesthetic terms – as to claims about what sorts of thing exist in the world, what characteristics and powers they have, and so on.

RADICAL RECONSTRUCTIONS OF OBJECTIVITY

Other critics of objectivity, rather than abandoning the concept, have set out radically to reconstruct it. I will outline two broad approaches of this kind here, though there are different versions of each, and these are sometimes combined.

(a) It is quite common today, especially among qualitative researchers, for a commitment to reflexivity to be seen as, in effect, a substitute for objectivity. What is meant by 'reflexivity' here is the attempt to make explicit all the assumptions, value commitments, feelings, etc., which went into or which underpin one's research, how it originated and progressed, etc., so that readers can understand how the conclusions were reached.[7] This idea was anticipated by Myrdal (1969) in *Objectivity in Social Research*, though it seems unlikely that he envisaged it as implying the sort of autobiographical excavation it has sometimes induced on the part of qualitative researchers, culminating for example in various forms of auto-ethnography (Ellis and Bochner 2000). Interestingly, what is involved here is an ideal of transparency that is shared with procedural objectivity. Moreover, the commitment to reflexivity often seems to involve two forms that parallel the two versions of objectivism. There are some who see reflexivity as a process of research auditing (Lincoln and Guba 1985; Schwandt and

---

[6]For some background to this, see Hammersley (2008a).

[7]There are many different interpretations of the term 'reflexivity'; see Lynch (2000) and Hammersley (2004c).

Halpern 1988; Erlandson et al. 1993). Here, reflexivity is an instrumental requirement designed to allow error to be recognised and rectified. It is argued that, for the findings of research to be trustworthy, it must be possible for an auditor to retrace the path of the researcher, checking the premises on which each step of the analysis depended. By contrast, in what is now probably the most influential version, reflexive transparency is treated as of value in itself, rather than being designed to allow readers to determine whether researchers 'went wrong' in reaching the conclusions they did; even less is the idea that it will allow readers to replicate the study. From this point of view, all accounts of the world are relative to, or are reflections or expressions of, how they were produced, most notably who was involved in producing them; and therefore may be seen as incomparable. Given this, it is taken to be incumbent upon social scientists to display this fact, and to show the particular manner in which their own accounts were generated.

While there is something to be learned from both these notions of reflexivity, each encounters serious difficulties. Financial audits themselves are by no means unproblematic, but in comparison with the assessment of research they are very straightforward procedures indeed. Assessing the validity of research findings involves making judgements about their plausibility and credibility (Hammersley 1998a); it is not merely a matter of ensuring that the required information has been provided and that it 'adds up'. Moreover, there is a great deal of room for disagreement in judgements about the cogency of arguments and evidence. One reason for this is that research is not founded on data whose meaning and validity are given. Moreover, the concept of research auditing seems to rely on the idea that enquiry involves inference from data to conclusions in a relatively linear way, so that each step in the process can be checked. This does not match how research is actually, or could be, done. Indeed, it is not clear that readers need the sort of detailed background information, about the researcher and the research process, that this notion of reflexivity requires.

The constructionist version of reflexivity amounts to relativism, of a personalist kind: the notion of validity or truth is transposed into a form of personal authenticity. Contradictory accounts of the world are to be tolerated, so long as their proponents are tolerant of others' accounts; in other words, so long as they refrain from claiming that their own views are true in any sense beyond 'honestly believed'. Indeed, it is implied that there is no other ground for judging the value of accounts of the world than in terms of their degree of reflexivity, including their recognition of their own constructed and particularistic character. The notion of social science as the systematic development of knowledge is abandoned here (see Eisenhart 1998). It is also important to note that this kind of reflexivity is an unending, indeed an unachievable, task. This is partly because there is no limit to what could be included in a reflexive account, as regards personal background, cultural history, or epistemological assumptions. There is also the problem that, presumably, any reflexive account must itself be explicated if it is to facilitate full reflexivity, this explication in its turn also requiring reflexive explication, and so on *indefinitely*.

(b) A rather different strategy for radically reconstructing objectivity is what has come to be labelled 'standpoint theory' or 'standpoint epistemology'. Standpoint theorists reject the idea, central to objectivism, though not to all older conceptions of objectivity, that the background perspectives and orientations of the researcher are necessarily a source of error that must be eliminated or suppressed. Indeed, it is argued that a particular social location or identity within society can facilitate discovery of the truth about it, and may even be essential to this. At the same time, other locations or identities are viewed as involving serious epistemic blockages. In other words, it is claimed that those occupying a particular type of social position have privileged access to the truth, while the truth is obscured from others. Moreover, this is often taken to include normative as well as factual truths: that is, knowledge about how the world ought to be, what is wrong with how things are, and what ought to be done.

An influential model for standpoint theory is Marx's claim that, once the capitalist system has become established, the working class are in a uniquely privileged position to understand its mode of operation. Here, Marx is sometimes portrayed as relying upon a philosophical meta-narrative similar to that of Hegel, who had portrayed history as a process of dialectical progress towards true knowledge, and the realisation of all human ideals. In the Marxist version of this, 'the self-understanding of the proletariat is simultaneously the objective understanding of the nature of society' (Lukács 1971: 149).

Various other arguments have been employed by Marxists to bolster, or substitute for, this metaphysical meta-narrative. One of these appeals to a notion of cultural lag: it is claimed that the ideas of any dominant class were necessarily accurate when they were forged in the struggle for power but later become obsolete because of changed circumstances. Alongside this, it is also sometimes argued that once in power a class no longer has a motive to understand society; indeed, it may even be motivated to misrecognise the character of the society, in order to rationalise its own dominance. In short, it will seek to deny or explain away unpleasant truths about the social relations over which it presides. By contrast, so the argument goes, the subordinate class has a strong motive to understand the real nature of society in order to gain power for itself, and it will have no motive for refusing to recognise the defects of existing society. Indeed, members of it are likely to develop a 'double consciousness', both recognising the true nature of the society and the official myths about it.[8]

The most influential recent exponents of standpoint theory have been among feminists (see Harding 2004). They have argued that because women are subjected to oppression and/or are marginalised within patriarchal societies, they are better able than men to understand the nature of those societies: in particular, to recognise forms of sexist prejudice and discrimination, and how these emanate from the very nature of the social formation.

There are some serious problems with standpoint epistemology, and it has been subjected to criticism by some Marxists and feminists (see, for example, Bar On 1993). The first issue concerns whether the warrant or rationale for epistemic privilege on the part of the subordinated or marginalised group is true. The Marxian–Hegelian meta-narrative is open to doubt; indeed, it is less than clear what would count as strong evidence for or against it. The other sorts of warrant, relying on a social psychology of oppressor and oppressed, are less problematic in principle, but they tend to be put forward without much evidence supporting them. And, while they have some plausibility, as with many such theories, there are competing arguments that are

---

[8]For discussion of standpoint theory and the notion of marginality, see Pels (2004).

equally convincing. For example, even if we adopt the simplistic assumption that society is composed of a single set of oppressor and oppressed groups, it could plausibly be argued that the oppressors must have gained considerable knowledge about the nature of the society in the course of gaining power that is not available to the oppressed, and whose value could be durable. Moreover, they may have substantial motivation to seek further knowledge and understanding in order to sustain, and perhaps even expand, that power. What seems likely is that the two groups may have access to rather different sorts of knowledge, but this in itself does not epistemically privilege one side or the other in any general sense. Similarly, while the marginalised may escape the effects of the dominant ideology, this does not guarantee that they will therefore 'see reality clearly'. Knowledge is not produced by gaining direct contact with the world, through immediate perception. Rather, cognitive work is required that draws on cultural resources. Whether or not any particular marginalised group, or sections among them, have access to the necessary resources and are able to engage in this cognitive work is an open question. Furthermore, it is not beyond the bounds of possibility that they may generate their own ideology or myth in order to reconcile themselves to their position, as Nietzsche argued had been the case in the development of Christianity as a 'slave morality'. From this point of view, it would be unwise to privilege just any set of ideas that is at odds with mainstream views in Western societies, especially when these may include fundamentalist religions and nationalist creeds of various kinds.

A second problem with standpoint epistemology concerns how any particular standpoint theory is to be subjected to assessment. Crudely speaking, there are two options here, one of which undermines standpoint theory while the other is circular, and therefore cannot provide support. The first tries to assess the warrant for epistemically privileging one category of person on the basis of the evidence available, without assuming that any one evaluator of that evidence is better placed to do this by dint of social identity or location. However, even if this evaluation were to support the particular standpoint theory, there is an important sense in which it would have also undermined it. This is because it amounts to founding standpoint theory on, or justifying it in terms of, a competing epistemology. So the question would arise: if we can determine whether or not a particular standpoint theory is true or false without relying upon the standpoint of the well-placed evaluator, why would we need to rely upon a distinctive standpoint for evaluating substantive claims to knowledge? The other option would, of course, be to evaluate a particular standpoint theory on the basis of that theory's assumptions about who is epistemically privileged. But this is circular and therefore potentially undermines any claim to validity.

The final problem concerns how we are to identify who belongs to the epistemically privileged category of person.[9] Once again, because of circularity, this cannot be resolved by reliance upon the standpoint theory itself, but must be decided in more mainstream epistemological terms. However, if the latter serves for this purpose, why not for others? Even putting this aside, there is the possibility, recognised by many standpoint theorists, that some members of the epistemically privileged category

---

[9]This is what Pels (2004) calls 'the spokesperson problem'.

may have 'inauthentic' perspectives, for example because their views have been shaped by the dominant ideology or by sectional interests. Examples would include women who reject feminism. The problem here concerns how any judgement of inauthenticity can be justified, given that anyone placed by one commentator on the wrong side of the membership line could themselves draw the line in a different place; and it is unclear how there could be any non-arbitrary resolution to this dispute. Another problem of a similar kind arises from the way in which the boundaries of different categories of oppressed or marginalised groups intersect. If multiple types of oppression or marginalisation are accepted – for example, centring on gender, social class, sexual orientation, 'race'/ethnicity, and disability – then how are these to be weighed in relation to one another in determining who speaks with epistemic privilege and who does not, or whose voice is more true and whose is less so? Again this looks like an irresolvable problem within the terms of standpoint epistemology.

It is worth noting that the various alternatives to objectivism I have discussed are incompatible with one another. Reflexive auditing and standpoint theory retain the concepts of truth and knowledge, whereas postmodernist scepticism and constructionist reflexivity do not.[10] At the same time, the first two positions involve quite different notions from one another about what is necessary for sound knowledge to be produced. Nevertheless, elements of these approaches – especially constructionist reflexivity and standpoint theory – are sometimes combined. An example is Harding's notion of 'strong objectivity' (Harding 1991; 1992; 1993; 1995). She argues that evaluation criteria must take into account both who is putting forward the knowledge claim, and its implications for what is taken to be the goal of enquiry, which extends beyond the production of knowledge to bringing about emancipation. She criticises, what she sees as, the weak objectivity that has operated within natural and social science, claiming that it has failed to challenge the patriarchal, and other oppressive, assumptions that she believes pervade Western societies, and social research itself. So Harding argues that greater reflexivity is required than weak objectivity generates: much more of the background assumptions and institutional structures of social scientific work must be exposed to scrutiny. She claims that conventional forms of both natural and social science are shot through with the ideological assumptions that come naturally to the white, middle-class men who predominate among researchers. It is the task of strong objectivity to challenge these. Moreover, she regards engagement with the perspectives of those who are oppressed or marginalised as essential for stimulating this process. It is not that their concerns or views should be accepted at face value, but rather that they are in the best position to identify the normalising assumptions that operate within mainstream society, and that bias conventional research.

It is worth noting how Harding's position relates to the criticisms of the two approaches outlined above. The notion of strong objectivity places limits on reflexivity, since what needs to be exposed is defined by a comprehensive social theory about the current nature of Western society and its social divisions – and about the sorts of bias that these are likely to generate. So, there is no longer the problem that achieving reflexivity is an unending task. As regards standpoint theory, she avoids the criticism that adopting the perspective of the oppressed or marginalised may involve taking

---

[10]Though, arguably, *in practice* they cannot avoid reliance upon them (Porpora 2004).

over false assumptions on their part, since she recognises that epistemic privilege cannot be treated as automatically leading to the truth. However, serious problems remain with her position. The most important concerns the epistemic status of the comprehensive social theory about social and epistemic inequalities on which she relies. She simply takes its validity for granted, yet many social scientists would dispute it. And here she cannot escape the fundamental dilemma of standpoint epistemology: to try to justify that theory by appeal to the epistemic privilege of the marginalised or oppressed would be circular, and it is not clear on what else it could be based without undermining it.

RECONCEPTUALISING OBJECTIVITY

In my view, neither objectivism nor currently influential reactions against it provide us with a satisfactory basis for the concept of objectivity, though there is much to be learned from them all. We need a more subtle approach that identifies what is wrong with, and also what was right with, objectivism. The solution that objectivism proposes – and even its diagnosis of the problem – may have been wrong, but it was nevertheless a response to a genuine concern. This is about the threats to validity that stem from the background assumptions, preferences, commitments, etc., of the researcher. At the same time, it no longer makes sense to try to preserve a coherent sense of the word 'objective' as simultaneously applying to the enquirer, the mode of enquiry, the conclusions reached, and the phenomena to which those conclusions relate. A more specific meaning must be given to the term.[11]

As a starting point, we should focus on the core idea – common to objectivism, audit reflexivity, and standpoint theory – that error can derive from the individual and social characteristics of the researcher, and that there are ways of minimising this threat. Of course, we do not need to, and should not, assume that research can operate without reliance upon personal or socio-cultural capabilities and motivations. Similarly, we should not assume that preconceptions and preferences always lead to error, and never help us to understand the truth. Rather, the focus of any concept of objectivity must be on protecting the research process from the *negative* effects of these 'subjective' characteristics. At the same time, contra to standpoint theory and Harding's 'strong objectivity', we cannot rely on a prior, supposedly comprehensive theory to tell us where sources of error might lie and whom they will affect. There is no well-validated theory of this kind available, and none may be possible. Rather, we should draw on the full range of ideas about how errors *could be* generated, from whatever directions. And we must assess their likelihood in particular cases, and take precautions against and check them, as far as is possible.

In order to make any progress in reconceptualising objectivity, we probably need to differentiate among the ways in which error arising from 'subjectivity' can appear,

---

[11]As part of this, we will have not only to distinguish objectivity from other epistemic virtues, but also to sort out its terminological relations with near synonyms such as 'detachment' and 'neutrality'; see Montefiore (1975). See also Lacey (1999), who distinguishes between neutrality and impartiality.

and treat it as designed to counter just one of these. I propose that it is treated as concerned with error resulting from preferences, and the preconceptions associated with them, that derive from substantive commitments *that are external to the pursuit of knowledge*.[12] In these terms, objectivity amounts to continually being on one's guard against errors caused by preferences and preconceptions deriving from this source, what might be called 'motivated bias'.

Motivated bias arises, primarily, from the fact that all researchers have other identities and roles, which are concerned with different sorts of goal from research itself. Moreover, there will be overlap in areas of concern between research and these other roles. One effect is that researchers may believe that they already know the answers to questions that are, from a research point of view, still open to doubt; or they may be too easily persuaded of some things and too resistant to considering or accepting others. In other words, there may be a tendency to opt for or against particular possibilities because of false prior assumptions or preferences (for example, because of inferences from evaluative views about particular people, places, situations, etc.); or there may be a temptation to fill in gaps in data in ways that are false or at least speculative. Similarly, there may be attitudes towards the likely truth of particular knowledge claims that derive from what are taken to be the latter's political or practical implications and consequences. Moreover, these tendencies may be increased by a sense of urgency or disquiet, for example by anger over injustice or fear of change.

Each of the various roles that we play in our lives involves not only distinctive goals but also relevancies and assumptions about the nature of pertinent aspects of the world, why they are how they are, how they ought to be, and so on. In performing any one role we foreground what is taken to be appropriate and necessary to it and background the rest. While we cannot and probably should not completely suppress what is relevant to other roles, at the same time the assumptions and preferences associated with these can interfere negatively with how effectively we play what is our main role on any particular occasion. A commitment to objectivity is designed to minimise such negative interference, and the notion applies to other roles as well as that of researcher. For example, in selecting candidates for admission to an educational institution, recruiting people to employment, or ranking patients in terms of priority for medical treatment, there is usually a requirement of objectivity. Objectivity, in this general sense, requires that all, *and only*, the considerations relevant to the task must be taken into account. Any other matters, however significant they may be from the point of

---

[12]I have identified the type of error associated with objectivity elsewhere as one form of culpable, systematic error that can be termed 'motivated bias' (see Hammersley and Gomm 2000). It is worth noting that there are preconceptions and preferences that can lead us astray that are generated *by* the research process even though they are not intrinsic to it. These include a researcher's public and/or private attachment to the truth of some knowledge claim or to the value of some method or source of data, the desire to find an interesting pattern or some clear answer to the research question, and so on. One aspect of this – bias deriving from theoretical commitments – was the preoccupation of seventeenth-century natural philosophers: see Daston (1994).

view of other roles, or in terms of our own personal convictions, should be put on one side or downplayed.[13]

So, in place of the very broad interpretation of 'objectivity' associated with objectivism, I suggest that we interpret the meaning of the term more narrowly. Given this, there are several sorts of 'subjective' error that lie outside the scope of objectivity as I have defined it here. One is error that derives from the failings of our perceptual and cognitive capabilities, or from misuse of them. Also excluded is what we might call wilful bias (see Hammersley and Gomm 2000). This is the knowing committal, or risking, of systematic error in the service of some goal other than the production of knowledge, whether this is the propagandist misusing or even inventing evidence in order to support some cause, or the lawyer deploying genuine evidence to make the best case possible for a preconceived conclusion. In the context of research, such wilful bias is, I suggest, best conceptualised as stemming from a lack of proper commitment to enquiry, or at least to its rational pursuit, in favour of commitment to other goals. Of course, I am not suggesting that these other goals, or these ways of pursuing them, are in themselves illegitimate. After all, enquiry can be subordinated to other activities (Hammersley 2002a: ch. 6; 2003a; 2004a). However, a key feature of academic research, in my view, is that it should not be subordinated to any other task.

So, I suggest that we see objectivity as one, among several, epistemic virtues that are essential to research. Other epistemic virtues include a commitment to truth and truthfulness (Williams 2002), intellectual sobriety (a determination to follow a middle way between over-caution or excessive enthusiasm for any particular knowledge claim, form of evidence, or method) and intellectual courage (a willingness to resist fear of the consequences of pursuing enquiry wherever it leads, including personal costs relating to life, livelihood, or reputation) (Montmarquet 1993: 23). Like objectivity, these other epistemic virtues relate to distinctive sorts of threat to the rational pursuit of enquiry and the need to resist them.[14]

CONCLUSION

As with a number of other terms, today the word 'objectivity' is often avoided or even treated with derision. While part of the explanation for this is uncertainty about its meaning, evidenced by its complex semantic history, the major cause, I have suggested, is the considerable influence, and subsequent collapse, of what we might call

---

[13]Of course, there may well be disagreement about *which* considerations should, and should not, be taken into account in any role or decision. And sometimes the narrowness of vision involved in specialised roles is rejected. Arguments that social scientists should act as public intellectuals (see Chapter 2) are a case in point.

[14]There is considerable literature on epistemic virtues, and on virtue epistemology more generally. See Kvanvig (1992), Montmarquet (1993), Zagzebski (1996), Axtell (2000), Brady and Pritchard (2003) and DePaul and Zagzebski (2003). Another line of approach is to draw on Merton's discussion of the scientific ethos, and the literature dealing with this: see Merton (1973b: Part 3), Stehr (1978), Mulkay (1980) and Hollinger (1983).

objectivism. This portrays scientific enquiry as needing to eliminate, or minimise, the effect on the research process of subjective beliefs and practices; in other words, of what is psychological, private, or implicit in character. Suppression of these beliefs and practices is taken to be necessary, from an objectivist point of view, because they are regarded as the main, if not the only, source of error. On this basis, it is required that enquiry follows explicit procedures that *anyone* could use, so that no reliance is placed upon the subjective features of the investigator, and so that the results can be checked via others using the same procedures.

Ideas approximating to objectivism were very influential within social science during the second quarter of the twentieth century, but came under sharp attack later. They are now rejected by many social scientists, and this has sometimes led to a jettisoning of the concept of objectivity itself, as well as to attempts fundamentally to reconstruct it. At the same time, the influence of objectivism has never been entirely extinguished. In this chapter I have tried to clarify some important functional distinctions that objectivism conflates, so as to allow a more satisfactory view of the concept of objectivity. This is necessary, I suggested, because some of what this term refers to is essential to any defensible form of enquiry. I argued that we should think of objectivity as an epistemic virtue that is designed to counter one particular source of potential error: that deriving from preferences and preconceptions associated with commitments that are external to the task of knowledge production – in other words, those that relate to the various goals any researcher has as a person, citizen, etc. Objectivism was wrong to treat the preconceptions deriving from external roles as simply a source of error, and therefore as needing to be suppressed or eliminated: they can stimulate, and even be essential resources in reaching, true answers to factual questions. However, they *can* also be a source of error, and objectivity as an epistemic virtue is concerned with minimising the risk that they will lead us astray in assessing the likely validity of knowledge claims. It involves a conscious attempt to counter any tendency for such external commitments, through the preconceptions and preferences associated with them, to interfere with the rational pursuit of enquiry.

5

TOO GOOD TO BE FALSE? THE ETHICS OF BELIEF

To sum up: it is wrong always, everywhere, and for anyone, to believe anything upon insufficient evidence. (Clifford 1947: 77)

Believe truth! Shun error! – These, we see, are two materially different laws; and by choosing between them we may end by coloring differently our whole intellectual life. We may regard the chase for truth as paramount, and the avoidance of error as secondary, or we may, on the other hand, treat the avoidance of error as more imperative, and let truth take its chance. (James 1897/1995: 260–1)

In 1987, an article entitled 'Too good to be false: an essay in the folklore of social science' was published in the US journal *Sociological Inquiry* (Reed et al. 1987). It received little attention at the time, and has not attracted much since. Yet it carried an important message. Indeed, the reception of this article might be taken to illustrate the obverse of its message: that unappealing conclusions tend to be ignored.

In their article, Reed et al. argue that there is 'a structured impediment to reliable knowledge in the social sciences' (p. 1), in that some findings strike such a chord with researchers that belief in them persists even after serious doubt has been thrown on their validity.[1] The authors use as an example a finding first reported in 1939: a purported correlation between fluctuations in the price of cotton and the number of lynchings of black people in the southern United States, an association which had come to be used by social psychologists as a standard illustration of frustration–aggression theory. The authors point out that, even though serious doubt was soon cast on this statistical association, it continued to be cited in the literature, including in introductory textbooks. Furthermore, a survey among members of the Society for the Psychological Study of Social Issues showed that it was still widely believed.[2] The

---

[1] This is an additional form of bias to the tendency for journals to be more willing to publish positive rather than negative findings – often referred to as the 'file drawer effect' or publication bias.

[2] The correlation, as originally presented, was in any case by no means a straightforward one. In its original formulation it was an association between deviations from trend lines: see Reed et al. (1987: 2).

authors suggest that one way of looking at this is: 'that the story of cotton prices and lynching rates has entered the folklore of social psychology; that it has become a tale told by the elders around the campfires where the young are initiated into the tribe' (p. 2). In other words, this finding had taken on the role of a myth: it was passed on largely by word of mouth or by citation, rather than by people reading the original source, and had been transformed in the process of telling through the introduction of various errors. Later, using a different metaphor (and, given the nature of the example, an unsavoury one), the authors report that 'despite the attempt to drive a stake through its heart' the correlation 'continues to wander, zombie-like, through the social-science literature' (p. 5). They draw a contrast between this process and how findings are supposed to be assessed, and accepted or rejected, as part of normal science. In short, the take-up and citation of research findings is not determined simply by judgements about their validity but by whether they are a 'good story': '"good" less in scientific than in journalistic terms' (p. 8).[3]

Reed et al. hint that the phenomenon they have uncovered is quite common. However, they do not show this, and I cannot establish its prevalence here. Instead, for the purposes of illustration, I will outline a more recent example, this time from the field of education.

THE CASE OF *PYGMALION IN THE CLASSROOM*

It is widely assumed today, within the educational research community and beyond, that teachers' expectations play a major role in influencing children's learning. In support of this, reference has frequently been made to a very well-known study, *Pygmalion in the Classroom* (Rosenthal and Jacobson 1968). This arose out of research that Rosenthal had done on the effects of experimenters' expectations on the outcomes of experiments, which led to the introduction of double-blind procedures to limit this source of error (Rosenthal 1966). Rosenthal and Jacobson assessed pupils in a school using a test of 'basic learning ability', and then informed the teachers that 20% of the pupils would 'spurt' in learning over the coming year, though in fact these pupils had been selected randomly. The pupils were tested again eight months later, and then after a further year. Overall, those children identified as likely to 'spurt' had

---

[3]Whether this is a fair representation of the mission of journalism, I leave aside. Around the same time as Reed et al.'s article was published, Latour drew attention to a similar phenomenon within technology research and natural science, noting how certain pieces of research become black boxes: they are closed off and their findings treated as facts beyond question. However, whereas Reed et al. draw a distinction between 'the scientific facts' and 'what are now accepted as facts by the scientific community' (Reed et al. 1987: 7), Latour treats 'fact' as referring to whatever is accepted as fact: 'by itself a given sentence is neither a fact nor a fiction; it is made so by others, later on. You make it more of a fact if you insert it as a closed, obvious, firm and packaged premise leading to some other less closed, less united consequence' (Latour 1987: 25). In line with much recent work in the sociology of scientific knowledge, he operationalises 'scientific knowledge' as what counts as knowledge within the relevant scientific community. The approach I adopt here will be closer to that of Reed et al., since my concern is with methodology, not with the sociology of social science. On the importance of distinguishing between the two, see Hammersley (2000a: ch. 3).

gained 12 IQ points on the test, while the control group had gained only 8 points, a difference that was statistically significant.

As soon as it appeared, this book gained widespread attention, not just from other researchers but also from educationalists and the wider public. Gage reports that it:

> got more attention in the mass media than any other product of the behavioral sciences in the 1960s. It struck a responsive chord among millions who were looking for an explanation of the educational problems of children from low-income areas – problems intimately connected with our most poignant national concerns. (1971: v)

While the book is now cited less frequently than in the past, this is probably because the idea that differential teachers' expectations have a significant effect on pupils' achievement levels has become largely taken for granted: in Latour's terms it has become a 'black box' (Latour 1987).

Yet even the evidence presented in *Pygmalion in the Classroom* indicates that any effect is patchy. Looking at the results for different grades, eight months after the intervention it was only children in the first and second grades, aged 6–8 years, who showed a statistically significant difference in growth of learning. And a year later it was only fifth graders who showed a statistically significant difference. In both tests, in most grades there was no difference that reached statistical significance. Moreover, serious criticisms of the study had emerged quite quickly after publication, pointing to problems with the statistical analysis, with the original test scores, and with reliance on induced expectations. Gage reports that he viewed the findings as doubtful from the outset:

> I was serving as a discussant in the symposium at the American Psychological Association meetings in 1966 at which [Rosenthal and Jacobson] reported their findings. It seemed implausible to me that the IQ, which had proven so refractory, would yield to the admittedly weak treatment administered in the experiment. In my discussion, I said as much and also cited weaknesses in the design, measurement, and analysis aspects of their experiment. A year later, I was asked to review the manuscript of *Pygmalion in the Classroom* for its pub-lisher. Again, I criticized the work roundly. Then the book appeared. […] [I]t received high praise from almost all reviewers. But most of the reviewers were untrained in psychological measurement and statistical analysis. Technically competent reviewers, like R. L. Thorndike and R. E. Snow, seriously questioned the validity of the Rosenthal-Jacobson data and conclusions. (1971: iv–v)

Subsequently, Elashoff and Snow (1971) carried out a re-analysis of the data that threw serious doubt on the findings. Moreover, later attempts to replicate teacher expectation effects have generally failed, though there has been some support from other types of study.

Rogers, who assessed the body of work available on this issue up to 1982, suggested that – rather than establishing the effects of teachers' expectations convincingly – *Pygmalion in the Classroom* had opened up a new area of research that still required further investigation. He outlines the complex character of the expectancy process, involving at least the following components (Rogers 1982: 2–3):

1   Teachers must actually form impressions of particular pupils and on the basis of these impressions come to establish expectations for future performance levels.
2   The behaviour of the teachers must be in some way affected by their expectations, with or without their awareness.
3   The pupils must at some level notice those aspects of teacher behaviour that are related to the teachers' expectations.
4   The pupils must then in some way respond to their teachers' behaviour so that they [...] come to behave in a manner that more closely matches the expectations of the teachers.[4]

Given the complexity of the processes involved, it is perhaps not surprising that attempts to test the original findings have not offered much confirmation of teacher-expectancy theory, though they have provided evidence for some of the linkages. Rogers' own conclusion is that it is not that 'all teachers have expectations for their pupils which will always determine pupil performance – only that this can some-times happen' (Rogers 1982: 38). Moreover, there is only relatively weak evidence about the conditions under which this occurs.[5]

What is significant from my point of view here is that the critical reaction to Rosenthal and Jacobson's study by well-informed researchers, and the failure of much subsequent work to confirm its validity, did not prevent its central finding becoming widely accepted. Writing in 1982, Rogers tells the following anecdote:

---

[4]In fact, the processes may be even more complex than this suggests. There are at least two further complicating factors. First, expectations will be based on, and may be modified by, subsequent experience. There is a tendency sometimes in discussions of expectation theory to treat expectations as if they simply reflected the orientation of the teacher or were purely arbitrary. Teachers' expectations are likely to be rather different in this respect from researchers' expectations about the outcomes of an experiment. Secondly, the mediating factors that might carry the effects of teachers' expectations could also operate independently of them, and may also affect expectations themselves. For example, differential liking of students on the part of a teacher might have as big an effect or a bigger effect than differential expectations, and may also affect expectations.

[5]Smead also provided a review of the findings on teacher expectancy theory, coming to more or less the same conclusion as Rogers: 'despite an impressive array of significant results, it is difficult to demonstrate conclusively that teacher expectations bias student learning' (Smead 1984: 148). Interestingly, she does not refer to Elashoff and Snow's (1971) reanalysis. By contrast, Weinstein (2002: 46) claims that 'although causal claims cannot be made in correlational studies due to potential uncontrolled variables [...] in both field experiments and naturalistic correlational studies, the evidence is consistent and strong: teacher expectations can influence student academic performance, although not in all contexts'. (For similar assessments, see Brophy 1998.) Weinstein claims that through adopting an ecological approach, the substantial effects of teachers' expectations can be revealed, once account is taken of contextual moderators. However, she notes that 'controversy about the existence and magnitude of this effect still persists', and refers later to 'continued skepticism' (p. 57) among researchers.

A few years ago I was preparing a course for undergraduates that was to examine the teacher-expectancy effect literature. As I had only just been appointed to the university in which I was working, I needed to check the library catalogue to ensure that the texts needed for the course were available. Some very well-used copies of Rosenthal and Jacobson (1968) were there, but no copy of Elashoff and Snow (1971), which is highly critical of the former. The immediate success (in publishers' terms at least) of *Pygmalion in the Classroom* has been claimed to be due to the way in which it said exactly what people at that time wanted to hear. Decisions regarding the purchase of books for the University Library seemed to support this. Incidentally, while I could readily order and obtain extra copies of Rosenthal and Jacobson, the book by Elashoff and Snow was out of print and unavailable! (1982: 23)

One field where the idea that teachers' expectations have a significant effect on pupils' performance has become widely accepted is in studies of the educational performance of ethnic minority pupils. Many researchers have appealed to low expectations on the part of teachers in order to explain lower average levels of educational achievement by some ethnic minorities, at various levels of the education system. However, this work has not provided much evidence specifically in support of teacher expectation theory. Rather than testing the validity of that theory, it has largely taken it for granted. Thus, Foster examined studies of the educational performance of African Caribbean pupils in the UK that rely on this theory, showing that the evidence offered is not convincing, and that there are rival explanations for the lower average level of educational performance of these pupils that are equally, if not more, plausible (Foster 1992). He states his conclusion as follows:

> although there is some evidence to support aspects of this theory of Afro/Caribbean underachievement, the evidence is inadequate to demonstrate the complex causal links within it, and certainly does not support the view that the processes outlined in the theory are common or are a major factor explaining underachievement.

He adds that 'the theory itself is implausible in the light of other evidence we have on the ways teachers perceive and interact with their students, and we must look to other factors to explain the underachievement of Afro/Caribbean students' (Foster 1992: 270). None of the studies Foster discusses matches the rigour with which Rosenthal and Jacobson, or many subsequent researchers whose work is discussed by Rogers, set about the task of testing teacher-expectancy theory. Effective evidence is not presented for more than one or two, at best, of the steps that Rogers identified as involved in the process by which teachers' expectations might shape pupils' educational achievement. However, Foster's cautions have been ignored, or dismissed (see, for example, Gillborn 1996), and the theory continues to be regarded as a highly plausible explanation for the underachievement of some ethnic minority groups.[6]

---

[6] The response to Foster's work was part of a wider dispute; see Hammersley (1995: ch. 4; 2000a: ch. 5).

Having provided a further example, this time from the field of education, of the process that Reed et al. had identified in social psychology, in the next section I want to examine and evaluate the reasons why research findings might be treated in this way. This issue is quite a complicated one, and in addressing it I will draw on a philosophical dispute that has continued since the end of the nineteenth century, triggered by William James's critique of the British mathematician and philosopher W. K. Clifford's arguments about 'the ethics of belief'.[7]

THE ETHICS OF BELIEF

In putting forward his version of pragmatism, William James argued that philosophy could only advance by 'adopting the inductive and empirical method of the natural sciences – that is, by abandoning the claim to logical certainty, and by advancing from one provisional working hypothesis to another'. More importantly for my purposes here, he argued that 'we have as much right to adopt working hypotheses in the religious as in the scientific sphere'. Thus, we are not 'committing an intellectual crime if we base our lives on [religious beliefs]' even though these can be neither proved nor disproved' (Knight 1950: 51).[8] Indeed, 'if by "backing" these hypotheses we can live happier and more effective lives, there is no reason why we should not do so; provided, of course, that we realize that they *are* hypotheses, and do not persecute those who reject them' (Knight 1950: 52). In fact, he goes beyond this idea that there is a 'right-to-believe', arguing that it is right to believe in theism on prudential grounds.[9]

In doing this, James challenged W. K. Clifford's claims about 'The ethics of belief', as presented in an article published in 1877. Clifford had argued that 'it is wrong always, everywhere, and for anyone, to believe anything upon insufficient evidence' (Clifford 1947: 77). And he had used as an example a ship owner who allows his ship to sail even though there are doubts about its seaworthiness. The ship sinks and much

---

[7]This was an aspect of a broader nineteenth-century debate about the implications of science, and especially of evolutionary theory, for religious belief; though Clifford's position draws on Locke's earlier argument that the degree of our assent to a proposition ought to be proportional to the strength of the evidence for it (Locke 1975: Bk IV, ch. XIX; see Price 1969: 131; Bridges 2003). On Clifford's article and the debate it sparked, see Madigan 2008. James's earliest formulations of his argument seem to have been a response to a statement similar to that of Clifford made by T. H. Huxley, Darwin's 'bull-dog'. James was especially concerned about the psychological and social effects of the materialism and positivism that were influential movements in late nineteenth-century Europe, and which were spreading to the United States. Turner (1974) discusses the views of English writers who, like James, found the dominant strain of scientific naturalism too narrow. At the same time, it is important to underline the difference between James's defence of belief and that of, say, Newman; for whom religious belief must be absolute, not a conditional working hypothesis (see Price 1969: Lecture 6).

[8]In this respect, his position was similar to that of Peirce, the founder of pragmatist philosophy: see Anderson (2004).

[9]There is a variety of interpretations of James's argument. For a careful attempt to identify its core, see Wernham (1987). For briefer introductions, see Bird (1986: ch. 9) and Hollinger (1997).

life is lost. Clifford argues not only that the ship owner was responsible for the loss of life, but also that his belief that the vessel was seaworthy would have been unethical even had the ship arrived safely at its destination. While James does not challenge the particular judgement in this example, he does question the general principle that Clifford proposes, insisting that it is right to believe on insufficient evidence in certain circumstances.

James's criticism of 'the ethics of belief' was underpinned by his religious commitment and rejection of Clifford's agnosticism. However, it transcends that context. Many today who do not have any religious belief would nevertheless agree with James, rather than with Clifford. Indeed, Hollinger points out that James's arguments are now widely accepted, and have sometimes been identified as postmodernist *avant la lettre* (Hollinger 1997: 69). They are certainly characteristic of some current philosophy that portrays itself as pragmatist, for example the work of Rorty, as well as more general rejections of positivism and empiricism as too narrow in what they treat as well-formulated knowledge and in the scope they allow for legitimate belief.

However, it is important to notice the restrictions that James places upon 'the right to believe'. He argues that we are only entitled to believe knowledge claims for which there is insufficient evidence where there is no decisive support for some alternative position, and where we are faced with a 'genuine' choice – by which he means one that is 'live', 'momentous', and 'forced'. This is a decision where alternative options are real possibilities, where making some sort of choice cannot be avoided and is consequential, and where one of the options is much more beneficial in what it offers than the others. At the same time, it should be noted that James saw even the value of scientific enquiry very much in terms of its instrumental value, rather than appealing to the value of knowledge for its own sake. In fact, he later went on to define 'truth' as 'what works' in practical terms.[10]

The issues involved in this debate are complex ones. Haack has provided a very useful clarification and development of some of them. She begins by drawing a distinction that neither Clifford nor James makes: between epistemic and ethical justification.[11] She argues that while there is overlap between these, they are not the same. She points out that there are occasions when one is ethically justified in holding to beliefs that one does not regard as epistemically justified; and that the example of belief without epistemic justification which Clifford uses, concerning the ship owner, has features that are not universal, and, moreover, these are ones that in themselves imply unfavourable moral appraisal. She counters his position by arguing that 'my believing, on inadequate evidence, that the apples I just selected are the best on the

---

[10]For an attempt to clarify James's position on truth, see Haack (1984). Wernham (1987: 88) insists that James's pragmatism should be clearly distinguished from his 'will to believe' doctrine, but it seems to me that, while they are distinct, there is a close relationship.

[11]It would perhaps be better to think in terms of a distinction between different kinds of evaluation, rather than of justification. We do not always offer justifications for our beliefs, and the word 'justification' is ambiguous in how it is used today. Sometimes it refers simply to an account offered in an attempt to justify something, on other occasions it is restricted to accounts that are true. The term 'evaluation' avoids these problems: an evaluation may or may not be sound, the question is left open. We can therefore retain 'justification' to refer to an evaluation that we judge to be true.

supermarket, is, like many inconsequential beliefs, harmless', and is therefore not open to serious moral criticism. Interestingly, this is an example which indicates that there are very different conditions than those identified by James where belief on insufficient evidence might be acceptable. Haack also provides an example that is somewhat closer to the conditions specified by James: 'if a patient's believing, on inadequate evidence, that he will recover from his illness significantly improves the chances that he will recover, then he may properly be appraised neutrally from a moral point of view' (Haack 1997: 132).[12]

Haack claims that Clifford's case depends on two false assumptions: 'that mere potential for harm, however remote, is sufficient for unfavourable moral appraisal (provided the subject is responsible for the unjustified belief); and that a subject is always responsible for unjustified believing'. And she insists that 'remote potential for harm is *not* sufficient; if it were, not only drunken driving, but owning a car, would be morally culpable [for road accidents]. And a subject is not always responsible for believing unjustifiedly; the cause, sometimes, is cognitive inadequacy' (Haack 1997: 137).[13]

Despite this criticism of Clifford, Haack concludes that while:

> Like James and unlike Clifford, I do not think it always morally wrong to believe on inadequate evidence. [...] [l]ike Clifford and unlike James [...] I think it is always epistemologically wrong to believe on inadequate evidence – in the sense that believing on inadequate evidence is always epistemologically unjustified. (1997: 138)

Moreover, she argues that when it comes to appraisal of the person as enquirer, rather than of any particular belief, the relation of epistemic to ethical appraisal may be more intimate, pointing to 'the moral importance of *intellectual* integrity' (p. 140). In concluding her article, she quotes C. I. Lewis:

> Almost we may say that one who presents argument is worthy of confidence only if he be first a moral man, a man of integrity [...]. [W]e presume, on the part of those who follow any scientific vocation [...] a sort of tacit oath never to subordinate the motive of objective truth-seeking to any subjective preference or inclination or any expediency or opportunistic consideration. (Lewis 1955: 34; quoted in Haack 1997: 141)

---

[12]Clifford, and perhaps others, would argue that even believing on insufficient evidence what is inconsequential or desirable in its consequences is unethical because it undermines the general commitment to only believing what is epistemically justified. It might also be argued on deontological grounds that this ethical rule should be obeyed whatever the consequences.

[13]What she means by 'cognitive inadequacy' here is lacking the intelligence necessary for the task. Carelessness and self-deception are other possible reasons at least to qualify responsibility for unjustified believing. It is also worth noting that Clifford, James, and in this case Haack, sometimes conflate decisions to believe or not to believe something with decisions about taking particular courses of action; yet these classes of decisions may be different in character in relevant respects.

Haack's argument is surely convincing, but I think there are some respects in which it needs reformulation and further development, at least for my purposes here. For one thing, I think we must distinguish the evaluation of statements in epistemic terms and the evaluation of actions, including belief and declaration of belief, which is necessarily a matter of ethics or prudence. To say that something is wrong is to say that, other things being equal, it should not be done – on either moral or prudential grounds. It seems to me that epistemic considerations can only count, in evaluations of people's believing something or declaring belief in something, *as part of* moral or prudential arguments, rather than standing alone. In that sense Clifford was quite right to talk about the *ethics*, rather than the epistemics, of belief. This is because when we talk of the sufficiency of evidence, we are concerned with what ought to be sufficient *in the circumstances*.[14]

So, I do not believe that there is some fixed epistemic threshold dividing what is and is not sufficient evidence. Haack herself points out that there is a *gradient* of credibility, so that knowledge claims are not simply either credible or not credible.[15] What I want to suggest is that the point on this gradient we adopt as the threshold that beliefs must reach if they are to be treated as sound knowledge will legitimately vary across situations. One consideration here, following Haack rather than James, is consequentiality. Whether or not the apples one chose in the supermarket were the best will, in most circumstances, be inconsequential. And, as a result, the threshold for what would be sufficient evidence for or against this belief being adopted legitimately is likely to be low. We can reasonably take a judgement on whatever evidence is available and the direction in which it points; we are unlikely to spend much time enquiring into the matter to assess whether this evidence is convincing in terms of some higher threshold, and we do not open ourselves up to genuine criticism for not doing so.

The other example that Haack provides is slightly different in character: it suggests that, if there is a great deal to be gained from believing something and little to be lost from being mistaken, then we do not need much in the way of evidence in order to be ethically or prudentially justified in treating that knowledge claim as true. What this points to, in more general terms, is that there are often differential consequences following from the two types of error that can arise in assessing knowledge claims: taking something to be true that is false, in other words a *false positive*; or rejecting something as false that is in fact true, a *false negative*. Now the point is that, in many forms of everyday practice, we often legitimately adjust our threshold of belief acceptance according to the consequentiality of different kinds of error, seeking to

---

[14]Haack sees contextual variability as restricted to ethical, not epistemological, acceptability, whereas I am arguing that there is no fixed threshold of epistemic acceptability: where we draw the line will depend upon ethical and prudential considerations. In doing so, we are assessing whether or not someone was rational in how he or she came to the belief concerned, and the conclusion will depend heavily on the evaluative framework we select and what intellectual and other capacities and characteristics we ascribe to the person concerned.

[15]However, in practice, she seems to adopt a single cut-off point between what is and is not epistemically justified, and, more importantly, one that is standard across activities and that seems to operate at the sort of level appropriate in the context of research.

minimise the most important sort of error sometimes even at the expense of increasing the chances of error of a less consequential kind.

This argument can be taken a further step, to conclude that how we judge the legitimacy of treating something as true or false will depend to a large extent on the role we are playing at the time, on the activity in which we are engaged. As Dorothy Emmet pointed out many years ago, ethical judgements are properly shaped by social role (Emmet 1966). And the same goes, even more obviously, for prudential judgements. In playing particular roles we have distinctive responsibilities, and these mean that some considerations are high priorities, while others are given less significance than they would be by people performing other roles. A classic case is the requirement that a doctor assesses what treatment a patient needs independently of any judgement about the financial costs to the hospital, or to the national exchequer. This does not mean that the best course of medical treatment should always be provided irrespective of cost; but rather that, in determining the hierarchy of possible treatments in terms of their relative desirability, financial considerations should not play a part. If they are to come into consideration, this must be after the hierarchy has already been determined.

Now, I want to suggest that a similarly distinctive ethical framework applies to research, or at least to academic research. Here, the primary aim is to produce a body of sound knowledge.[16] In other words, the function of research is to produce knowledge that is more consistently reliable, in the commonplace sense of that word, than that available from other sources. And this has two implications for how researchers should operate. First, knowledge claims must be judged entirely in terms of how likely they are to be true. Other considerations, for example to do with consequentiality, should not play any role. This means that, by contrast with many other activities, there should be a standard, across-the-board, threshold for accepting or rejecting knowledge claims; it should not vary depending upon the specific context. Secondly, a prudential orientation ought to operate that errs on the side of avoiding false positives, at the possible expense of accepting false negatives.[17] Above all, researchers must be prepared to suspend belief in the validity of knowledge claims if there is insufficient evidence for them. Here, in the context of research, more than anywhere else, the spirit of Clifford's ethics of belief properly applies.

---

[16]This does not seem to be accepted by all researchers, but I have argued the case for this conception of research elsewhere: see, for example, Hammersley (2000a). See also Bridges (1999). It seems that, in large part, Haack is writing about what it is ethical for *researchers* to believe. Indeed, the extract from Lewis that she quotes specifically refers to a 'scientific vocation'. And this is certainly her primary concern in another discussion of these same issues: see Haack (1998: ch. 1). There, she refers to what she calls 'a startling failure, or perhaps refusal' on the part of some of her philosopher colleagues to understand what the life of the mind demands (p. 7). She quotes Rorty describing philosophers who think of themselves as seeking the truth as 'lovably old-fashioned prigs', and declares herself to be just such a one. Perhaps I should declare that I am one too.

[17]This is the heart of what Merton referred to as 'organised scepticism', see Merton (1973a). While she cites his work, Douglas (2009) neglects this aspect of his argument, in the course of claiming that in judging whether or not to accept knowledge claims scientists should take account of the relative costs of false positives and false negatives. See Hammersley (2010b).

Moreover, it seems to me that the evaluation of knowledge claims in the context of academic research has a collective character.[18] What counts is not just a matter of what an individual researcher judges to be true; but rather what *the relevant research community* judges to be true, or *would* judge to be true. The researcher, as researcher, must operate in some sense as an exponent of the ethos of the relevant research community, not simply as an individual. In particular, he or she should not treat as true any assumptions or knowledge claims which are not, or would not be, generally accepted by that community. Researchers can of course believe such claims, and may present them as their own opinions, but the lack of consensus about the validity of these claims within the research community must be made explicit.

My central argument, then, is that, in the context of research, a particular approach to the evaluation of knowledge claims is an ethical priority: the threshold that has to be reached is determined entirely by epistemic considerations, and through a process of dialectical deliberation within the relevant research community. Researchers have a primary ethical responsibility not to put forward findings as more likely to be true than they are on the basis of the available evidence, as judged by that community. The effect of this is that the threshold that is set will be standard, and comparatively high, since this is what is required if research is to produce knowledge that is consistently more reliable than that available from other sources.

What I am suggesting, therefore, is that there is an important difference in the ethics of belief between research and some other contexts. In the latter, what is sufficient evidence varies, depending upon a number of considerations: the relevance of the belief to any past or future action, the consequentiality of that action, the likely practical costs associated with errors of different kinds, and the reversibility of the action involved or the remediability of its effects. Where a belief has little relevance to action, or where the action is inconsequential, the threshold can legitimately be set relatively low. If a belief is relevant to action, and that action is consequential, where a false positive would be more damaging than a false negative, or vice versa, a prudential bias should be set up to minimise the cost. And the direction of that bias will vary according to circumstances. Where an action is reversible, or the effects of it remediable, the threshold may be set quite low, with the idea that we can learn by trial and error, correcting any mistakes before they produce significant costs. By contrast, in the case of research a relatively high and standard threshold should be adopted.

In the next section, I will address some arguments that might seem to count against the view I have presented about how researchers should treat knowledge claims.

SOME CRITICISMS AND QUALIFICATIONS

A first criticism derives from the point, central to Haack's position, that all knowledge claims are fallible. She writes that 'one's judgment that another's belief is unjustified must, because of the perspectival character of judgments of justification, their dependence on one's background beliefs, be acknowledged to be thoroughly fallible'

---

[18]However, this does not mean that it can be centrally organised (see Hammersley 2002a: ch. 5).

(Haack 1997: 138). And it might be concluded from this that all knowledge claims are equally uncertain, so that the very notion of evaluating knowledge claims in terms of their likely truth is unjustifiable.[19] However, the conclusion does not follow from the premises, as Haack makes clear: that all beliefs are fallible does not mean that they are all *equally* likely to be false (see also Haack 2009).

The term 'truth' is sometimes avoided or rejected by social scientists, or encased in scare quotes (or what Haack 1998: 92 refers to as 'sneer quotes'), on the grounds that it implies that we can have knowledge whose validity is absolutely certain. However, this is to take over an indefensible conception of truth from foundationalist epistemology. Moreover, it is impossible to avoid reliance on the concept of truth: it is constitutive of the very activity of enquiry, and essential to the distinction between knowledge and belief.[20] Even the epistemological sceptic relies on a conception of truth, albeit one whose requirements can never be met.

Thus, it is important here to be clear about what is meant by 'fallibilism'. It is not the same as scepticism, interpreted as the idea that we cannot know anything. Scepticism, like foundationalism, relies on a definition of knowledge as 'what is known without any possible doubt'. Fallibilism rejects that definition, treating knowledge as 'what is currently believed with good reason', and recognises degrees of legitimate confidence in the validity of various knowledge claims rather than some absolute distinction between what is and is not known.[21] So, to say that our knowledge is fallible is not to say that it is false, or even that its validity is completely uncertain. It is to say that even if we have justifiable confidence in it, we can never be justified in having absolute confidence in the validity of a knowledge claim; even though some come very close to that limit, and even though some seem to operate as 'hinges' on which various activities depend (see Wittgenstein 1969). So, the fact that our knowledge is always fallible does not undermine commitment to truth as a requirement of enquiry, or the application of Clifford's 'ethics of belief' to the researcher.[22]

A second criticism of the position I have presented might be that in assessing knowledge claims researchers are entitled to rely upon how plausible they find these, in terms of how strongly these claims are implied by what is currently taken to be sound knowledge. Thus, even if the evidence from existing studies does not support a claim, if the latter seems to fit closely with other beliefs that are themselves well-established by research evidence, then it can be accepted as true by those who judge it to be.

While there is some truth in this argument, it is only part of the truth. In assessing the likely validity of any knowledge claim, researchers should take account (and, indeed, cannot avoid taking account) of plausibility in the sense indicated here. The

[19]This is a position that is often attributed to Popper, and not just by his critics but also by some of his supporters: see Miller (1994).

[20]It would be more correct to say 'some of the distinctions between knowledge and belief', see Price (1969: Series I, Lectures 1, 2 and 3). On the unavoidability of truth as a standard of evaluation within research, see Bridges (2003: ch. 6 and *passim*).

[21]In fact, some of those who are routinely labelled, or label themselves, as sceptics are closer to being fallibilists. An example would be Carneades: see the discussion in Schutz (1970: 17–21).

[22]An implication of my argument here is that the ethics of belief is not tied to the rather positivist epistemology to which Clifford seems to have been committed.

process of assessing each finding from a study involves assessing whether it is so plausible on the basis of existing knowledge as not to require any further evidence in support of it. Only if it is insufficiently plausible in this sense is evidence required. Moreover, the evidence will itself have to be assessed in terms of *its* plausibility, as well as its credibility (the likelihood that errors were built into its production).[23]

However, plausibility here means: how strongly does what we currently take to be knowledge imply the validity of this additional knowledge claim? Or, in the case of implausibility, how strongly does this claim conflict with what we currently assume we know? Moreover, in line with the collective character of research as an activity, plausibility judgements, like those concerned with the credibility of evidence, must be made in light of the likely reaction to those judgements of most members of the relevant research community. Only knowledge claims which are likely to be accepted as sufficiently plausible by most of a research community should be treated as if they are true. As noted earlier, where a researcher regards a knowledge claim as true, but it is contested (or likely to be contested) within the relevant research community, he or she must acknowledge this fact by not presenting it as well-established, though this does not rule out its presentation as a matter of personal belief or as a working hypothesis. Nor, of course, does it rule out its presentation along with supporting evidence that is expected to be convincing. What is crucial above all, though, is that such a knowledge claim must not be treated as something that can be relied upon as being true, or presented to lay audiences as fact, in the absence of further convincing evidence.

So, the role of plausibility in the judgement of knowledge claims is already included in the account of how research findings are assessed that I have presented. Moreover, this rules out a researcher, or even large numbers of researchers, accepting findings on the basis that, as individuals, they find them plausible. Yet this, I suggest, is what has happened in the case of teacher expectation theory. It is found plausible by many researchers; but not in contexts where the primary concern has been evaluating its validity. Furthermore, the fact that other researchers have treated it as in need of investigation, and that the studies this has generated have not produced convincing evidence, means that, on the argument I have presented in this chapter, it should not be treated by researchers as well-established knowledge – though, equally, there is no warrant for treating it as false. Its validity is currently uncertain.

A third criticism that might be made of the claim that the ethics of belief is central to the practice of research is the argument that researchers have an at least equal obligation to respect values other than truth. It is sometimes suggested that they must therefore incorporate into judgements about the validity of their conclusions, or combine with these, a concern with the latter's political implications or the practical consequences of presenting those conclusions. Some social researchers advocate this position, and we must assume that it shapes their research practice. However, as I have argued elsewhere, it increases the potential for error in research findings (Hammersley

---

[23]Most research findings will not be sufficiently plausible to be accepted at face value. If they are, they are not news, and the relevance of publishing them can be questioned. For an elaboration of this view of how knowledge claims should be assessed, see Hammersley (1998a). For a philosophically more sophisticated account of what is largely the same epistemological position, see Haack (2009).

2000a). As a result, on my argument here, it is unethical – in the sense that it involves deviation from the primary obligation of the researcher.

The success of academic research in producing conclusions that are consistently less likely to be false than those from other sources depends upon researchers being committed to the production of knowledge as their only immediate goal. As soon as other goals are allowed in, or validity is redefined to include ethical or political criteria, the danger of coming to erroneous conclusions is increased. And it is the primary duty of the researcher to seek to ensure that her or his conclusions are true. So I am arguing that there is a distinctive ethic, close in character to Clifford's 'ethics of belief', that applies to research as a specialised occupational activity.[24] Moreover, I believe that this is an ethical obligation that is currently under threat, not only from methodological arguments in favour of partisanship, but also as a result of rapidly growing pressure on researchers from commercial and governmental organisations to make their findings 'useful' and to maximise 'impact' (see Crossen 1994; Norris 1995; Bridges 1998).

The final criticism I will consider here concerns the fact that research is itself a practical activity; for the most part, it is carried out in the world, and must be adapted to that world. This fact is of significance because I have argued not only that other values as well as prudential considerations necessarily play a role in practical activities, but also that in such activities judgements about what is sufficient evidence for a knowledge claim to be accepted can reasonably vary across circumstances. This would seem to imply, contrary to my main argument, that prudential considerations, including the evaluation of knowledge claims partly in terms of consequences, must play a role in research.

Some care is required here in distinguishing between research findings, along with the argumentative structure on which they rely, and the various assumptions on which researchers depend in doing their work. My points about the priority of epistemic considerations in determining what is to be treated as true, and about the process by which the threshold of belief should be determined within research, apply to the treatment of *research findings* and the presuppositions on which they depend. However, the situation is different in evaluating the assumptions involved in *carrying out* academic enquiry. In doing a piece of research, one is faced with a host of decisions to which various kinds of belief are relevant: about whether access can be gained to a particular setting, whether one approach to negotiating access rather than another is likely to be more successful, how to represent the research to those being studied, what data collection methods to use, what sorts of interview question might facilitate or hinder getting high-quality data from informants, and so on. These are necessarily pragmatic matters, in the sense that the sorts of consideration I outlined as relevant in many practical decisions – consequentiality, remediability, etc. – will play a key role. Furthermore, in relation to many of the issues that they have to resolve for practical purposes, researchers are unlikely to have the evidence, or to be able to collect the evidence, that would be necessary to make a judgement in the way that is required for reaching research conclusions. However, there is no contradiction

---

[24]Note that this does not mean that other values are not relevant to research, only that they do not form part of its immediate or proximal goal.

here, since the pragmatic decisions involved in research must be made with a view to maximising the likelihood that the findings produced will be true, and not false; and that they will meet the high threshold of likely validity applied by the relevant research community.

CONCLUSION

In this chapter I have discussed a tendency on the part of researchers to treat some research findings whose validity has been shown to be at the very least uncertain as 'too good to be false'. For purposes of illustration, I discussed teacher expectancy theory, as originally developed by Rosenthal and Jacobson and widely accepted today in educational circles. In the main part of the chapter I considered what grounds there might be for this tendency to accept what is false or unproven, using a debate over the 'ethics of belief' as a starting point. Drawing on the work of Haack, I came to the conclusion that it is important to distinguish between the role of epistemic and other sorts of consideration, particularly those to do with the *consequences* of belief, in deciding what to treat as knowledge. However, I went beyond Haack's account to argue that there are differences not just across situations but also across roles in terms of the priority that ought to be given to truth as against other values in evaluating beliefs. I proposed that, for researchers, belief in substantive claims about their research fields must be evaluated exclusively in epistemic terms. By contrast, in many other activities other thresholds will properly be applied in judging whether to rely on knowledge assumptions, according to variation in the consequentiality of belief, the likely costs of different types of error, the remediability of costs, and so on.

I examined a number of possible challenges to this account. These related to the fallibility of all knowledge claims, the role of plausibility in assessing the validity of such claims, the idea that researchers should have at least equal commitment to some other values besides truth, and the point that since research is itself a practical activity, other values and prudential considerations must play a key role in evaluating possible operating assumptions. I argued that the last of these criticisms requires the introduction of an important qualification: that in evaluating beliefs for use in an instrumental way during the course of enquiry, researchers should adopt a flexible approach that takes account of a variety of ethical and prudential considerations, including the costs of different sorts of error. However, this *is* only a qualification: the overall implication of my argument is that the treatment of substantive knowledge claims by researchers must be governed by an orientation that is very close in character to Clifford's 'ethics of belief'.

So, what conclusion is to be drawn from my discussion of the tendency among researchers to treat some findings as 'too good to be false'? What it suggests is that this practice is ethically, as well as prudentially, wrong. The sole criterion by which knowledge claims should gain entry to and retain membership in the body of knowledge must be epistemic justification. To deviate from this orientation leads to corruption of the literature, and undermines the only basis on which researchers can justify their distinctive role and speak authoritatively.

The ethic of research forbids taking into account considerations to do with the consequences of a conclusion when we are assessing its validity. One implication of this is that researchers are required to present all findings as true that meet the threshold of validation, even if these findings seem to have unpalatable political implications. This is the other side of the requirement that we must refuse to treat findings as true that are not well-established even if we judge their promulgation as likely to have desirable practical or political consequences. In short, the ethic of research forbids treating findings either as 'too good to be false' or too bad to be true.

PART 2

THE DIALECTIC OF KNOWLEDGE PRODUCTION

6

MODELS OF RESEARCH: DISCOVERY, CONSTRUCTION, AND UNDERSTANDING

[...] we must change our imageries and metaphors from those of discovery and finding to those of constructing and making. (Smith and Deemer 2000: 878)

How odd it is that anyone should not see that all observation must be for or against some view, if it is to be of any service! (Darwin, letter to Henry Fawcett, 18 September 1861, in Burkhardt and Smith 1994: 269)

In this chapter, I begin by comparing two models of the research process. The first one, which I will call the discovery model, is widely assumed by lay audiences to capture that process, and is routinely employed by most researchers when they unselfconsciously talk or write about their work – it is a kind of default mode. The second approach treats research as a matter of construction. It is promoted by many qualitative researchers today, drawing on that range of ideas trading under the label of constructionism or constructivism. It emphasises that researchers (and others) play an active role in the enquiry process, that they thereby construct the accounts of the world generated by research, and that these accounts will reflect their authorship in various ways rather than some independent reality. This, then, is the construction model.

While apparently contradictory in principle, in practice the relationship today between the discovery and construction models is one of coexistence: they tend to operate side by side in the work of many researchers. Indeed, it may be that, despite some friction, the relationship between them is a symbiotic one. In other words, in the absence of anything better, we may need to draw on each of them for use on particular occasions. More specifically, as already noted, the discovery model still seems to underpin much practical talk about social research, despite the increasingly powerful influence of the construction model at the level of more abstract writing about methodology.[1] Yet neither of these two models is adequate, as the criticisms mounted against them make clear. Given this, later in the chapter I examine a third option which draws on work in hermeneutics, particularly that of Gadamer. I conclude that, in many respects, this hermeneutic or understanding model is more cogent; at least in a form that is based on what I have referred to elsewhere as subtle realism (Hammersley 1992a). Whether it can supplant the other two models is less clear. Perhaps, instead, it provides a context in which use of them is less problematic.

THE DISCOVERY MODEL

As its name implies, the discovery model portrays enquiry as aimed at uncovering reality. In its simplest version this involves going to sites where relevant events, processes, etc., are to be found, and then reporting back to audiences who have not themselves visited these places but have an interest in the information available there. Sometimes this may involve literal travel to observation sites. This is most obvious in the case of anthropologists studying societies that are geographically remote from where most readers of their research reports live. However, much the same idea has been applied to social worlds closer to home for Western social scientists, as for example in the work of the Chicago sociologists of the 1930s. Here, for example, is the famous instruction to his students from a key figure in the first Chicago School, Robert Park, indicating what is necessary if urban life in that city is to be properly understood:

> Go and sit in the lounges of the luxury hotels and on the doorsteps of the flophouses; sit on the Gold Coast settees and on the slum shakedowns; sit in the Orchestra Hall and in the Star and Garter Burlesk. In short, [...] go get the seats of your pants dirty in real research. (Robert Park, quoted in McKinney 1966: 71)

Park and other Chicago sociologists pointed out that even the inhabitants of large cities like Chicago were often unfamiliar with, or even unaware of, the character of the many other social worlds that existed side by side with their own; and that this was perhaps especially true of people in a position to make policy decisions. So the task of the researcher was to go to observe, and document the experience of people in, different areas of the city – perhaps especially those belonging to low-status communities – and to report back on what was found.

Research along the lines of this model need not always involve travel to unknown regions. Sometimes, it may require instead the collation of already available data that have never been put together before, or the discovery of a set of documents that no-one

---

[1] Many years ago, Mann (1981: 549) argued that all researchers, whatever their epistemological allegiances, 'practice a kind of "as if positivism"', and this seems to imply adherence to the discovery model on contructivist grounds!

interested in the matter knew to exist or had seen. Equally, what is involved could be interviewing people to collect data about or explore their perspectives or attitudes. The most important point is that, in line with the physical metaphor built into the term 'discovery', research is portrayed as involving movement, actual or virtual, from a position where some aspect of reality was obscured to one where it is exposed; so that, crudely speaking, what now appears is reality itself.

This view of the nature of research involves some important assumptions, all of which have been questioned. One is that there are phenomena which are independent of our knowledge of them. Another is that we can get into direct contact with these phenomena. A third is that truths about the world are things we see: that they are somehow embodied in reality. Finally, it is assumed that the truths that have been discovered can be communicated to others intact. To summarise, then, the task of researchers from the point of view of the discovery model is to uncover reality, and to report what they see honestly and clearly. In this way, they can reveal the truths discovered to others.

In its simplest form, the discovery model requires the researcher to have nothing more than normally working human perceptual, intellectual, and communicational abilities. As a result, the only grounds on which a research report can be challenged relate to:

a   the positioning of the researcher (did he or she actually get to a point where the nature of reality was revealed?); and

b   her or his honesty in reporting what has been seen.

Moreover, since getting into the right position to observe is treated as a relatively straightforward matter, dishonesty – intellectual fraud of one sort or another – is the only significant potential source of error.

Another feature of the discovery model is that it draws little distinction between the professional researcher and others. All that can be claimed as distinctive by the former is that more time and resources were available to pursue discoveries, and, possibly, possession of a more single-minded commitment to honesty in enquiring and reporting. Moreover, in the case of social research, the importance of the first of these features is often reduced, since some lay people will often be directly involved in the situation observed, and will have their own accounts of that situation. Furthermore, the second claim to distinction – honesty or disinterestedness – has come under increasing challenge with public recognition of the existence of ulterior motives on the part of researchers, and as a result of general scepticism about any claims to a neutral or dispassionate orientation. Indeed, any claim to *superior* honesty or disinterestedness is likely to be met with incredulity.

More sophisticated versions of the discovery model are possible, but these start to blur its differences from the other models. Thus, we might add into it specialised abilities and knowledge on the part of the researcher; such things as: intuition or genius; command of a distinctive theory and/or method; knowledge of the relevant scientific literature; and/or a capacity for reflection or scepticism. Of especial importance might be the ability to dis-identify from commonsense illusions and thereby to open the way for recognising underlying realities. However, it should be clear that these various bases for expertise are at least potentially incompatible with one another: intuition versus method; different methods against one another; all of these against theory; method or theory versus reflection; and so on. In this way, there is much more scope for disagreement and debate than with the simpler version of the model.

Moreover, while more sophisticated versions of the discovery model increase the scope for claims to professional expertise on the part of researchers, they also increase the space for challenge to the validity of the accounts produced. Dishonesty is no longer the only plausible source of error; various failings in expertise may also now be blamed. Even if the researcher was in the right position and was honest, did he or she have the necessary intuition, abilities (methodological, theoretical or substantive), etc., to see and report what was there? On top of this, whether a method was properly applied or a theoretical resource correctly interpreted can be made an issue. And the scope for this is increased when it is acknowledged that no method is an algorithmic procedure, or that all theory is open to conflicting interpretations.

Nevertheless, in these more sophisticated versions, the basic idea behind the discovery model remains. This is that, given the necessary capabilities, researchers can uncover reality and reveal its nature to others through describing it. The capabilities required are treated as no more than necessary preconditions: if these are met then reality reveals itself and can be revealed to others through descriptive reports. Other characteristics of researchers – such as their attitudes, social backgrounds, personalities, etc. – are treated simply as potential sources of error. And these only become relevant if and when the veracity of the account is challenged.

At the very least, the discovery model has considerable rhetorical force. In its simple form, the justification for the knowledge claims made under its auspices seems to lie in having found the site of the relevant data, uncovered them, and allowed them to speak for themselves. However, the cogency of this view of enquiry has long been questioned. In the next section I will look at some of the criticisms that have been made of it.

PROBLEMS WITH THE DISCOVERY MODEL

Over the course of the twentieth century, there was a great deal of criticism of the ideas associated with the discovery model, even as applied to natural science. This was based on two main epistemological arguments. The first is to the effect that we cannot gain direct access to reality. Our experience of the world is always mediated: by our perceptual capacities, and by the concepts built into languages and cultures. This mediation has been seen either as potentially introducing error into our experience or, more radically, as suggesting that experience can never simply conform to some reality beyond it, that there are necessarily multiple, experiential realities.

Along the same lines, the claims of empiricists to found knowledge on brute sense data that are simply given, were also rejected. One argument here was that anything that is simply given does not constitute a statement of knowledge and therefore cannot serve as the premiss for reaching a conclusion. Any premiss must be formulated as a descriptive knowledge claim, whether relating to sense impressions (phenomenalism) or to objects in the world that are held to have generated those sense impressions (physicalism or some other form of realism). And such descriptions cannot themselves be regarded as simply given. They are formulated in a language that uses category systems that necessarily rely upon assumptions. And these assumptions may be false, and are therefore open to possible doubt, or they may be viewed as arbitrary, as having no relationship to any reality beyond. Different observers may produce quite different accounts of the 'same' phenomenon, relying on varying languages or category systems; and there is no assumption-free way of choosing among these.

The second main criticism of the discovery model is that theories are always underdetermined by data. No evidence can ever logically compel assent to a theory, or can even falsify a theory with absolute certainty. Questions can always be raised which throw potential doubt on the validity of any inference from evidence to the truth of a theory. These may be to do with the evidence itself, which could contain error and be misleading, or they may relate to background assumptions on which the inference or theory relies. Putting the point the other way round, any set of data can always be used to support the validity of more than one theory. From this it may, but need not, be concluded that there is no rational basis for selecting among theories, that we are faced with a choice that is 'undecidable'.

A separate problem concerns the model of communication that the discovery model involves. It requires that the truth can be transmitted to audiences intact. This seems to treat communication as involving the encoding of a message at one end of the communication process and its decoding at the other in terms of the same, algorithmic coding manual. However, as Sperber and Wilson (1986) and others have pointed out, this is not a convincing account of the nature of human communication. Communication involves a much more uncertain process of inference, in which background knowledge and judgement necessarily play a key role.

These arguments have undermined overt defence of the simple discovery model, even though in practice it continues to be assumed in the methodological talk of both natural and social scientists. Indeed, the metaphor at the heart of it is so convenient, and so rhetorically powerful, that it is hard to abandon. A variety of alternatives have been proposed. One involves reversion to a strict empiricism in which knowledge claims do not refer beyond relationships among data to any underlying 'reality'. Thus, it is sometimes argued that we cannot claim that our theories portray phenomena that are independent of us; at best they are simply instruments for predicting future experience.[2] Other commentators have sought to retain a commitment to realism, but to detach this from other elements of the discovery model; and this is more or less the position I will adopt later. Finally, there are those who have emphasised the active role of the researcher in constructing, and by implication creating, the phenomena that are portrayed in research reports. This latter view, which has become very influential in some of the literature on social research methodology, will be my focus in the next section.

---

[2] Van Fraassen (1980) provides a sophisticated version of this approach.

THE CONSTRUCTION MODEL

At the centre of the construction model, as the term implies, is the idea that all knowledge is created, rather than truths being uncovered, or data speaking for themselves. In other words, it is argued that a great deal of work goes into the process of producing knowledge. It is not just a matter of going to the relevant site, or even of digging beneath appearances, to find reality. Rather, the researcher must draw on whatever resources he or she has available and *use* these, both to identify and to make sense of evidence. Up to now this might seem to be no more than a sophisticated version of the discovery model, but there is a key difference. Whereas with the latter the work of investigation involves establishing the conditions under which the truth can be revealed, for the constructionist that work is *constitutive of* the truth: in other words, the truth that is documented is not independent of the process of 'discovering' it. The implication drawn by many constructionists is that, while different accounts of the 'same' scene can be judged in terms of their value, this cannot take the form of assessing how well they correspond to the thing(s) to which they refer. Instead, a range of other criteria are recommended: notably, practical relevance, ethical appropriateness, political consequentiality, and/or aesthetic desirability.[3]

One important implication of some forms of constructionism is that research accounts are taken to reflect the social and personal characteristics of the investigator, a position that Taylor (1979: 1–2) has referred to as expressivism. In the discovery model true knowledge corresponds to the reality uncovered; indeed, it is isomorphic, if not identical, with it; and any effect of the researcher beyond establishing the preconditions required for valid knowledge is a source of bias. But with the construction model, what is produced is often taken necessarily to reflect who the researcher is, just as works of literature are often held to be an expression of the writer's character, personality, life-experience, and so on. In particular, it is frequently argued that what is produced reflects specific socio-cultural identities and interests of the researcher: gender, ethnicity, and social class are among the most frequently mentioned. Under the influence of constructionism, there has also been great emphasis on the similarities between research reports and forms of literature: that both employ rhetorical strategies of various kinds, through which representations of the world are created. As this indicates, constructionism carries very different assumptions about what is communicated in research reports: it is no longer a matter of conveying what was discovered intact to an audience. Rather, it perhaps involves creating a particular vicarious experience of the world for audiences, through employing literary resources attuned to them, or setting out to evoke certain responses in them.

In its most developed form, the construction model involves an anti-realism that denies the possibility, or at least the accessibility, of real phenomena existing independently of the research process. This anti-realism draws on an influential line of

---

[3]See Smith and Deemer (2000). It is perhaps worth noting that there is a tension within the notion of construction in terms of who is the agent. In some accounts this is individual human beings; in others, the latter are merely the vehicles by which some other agent – discourse, desire, or power, for example – constitutes the world. In yet another version, that of actor–network theory, agency is distributed across human beings, animals, and inanimate objects: see Law (1986).

philosophical argument that can be traced back both through more extreme forms of positivism, such as that of Ernst Mach, and through idealism, notably Kant's distinction between phenomena and noumena, to the debates among empiricists in the sixteenth and seventeenth centuries about the difference between primary and secondary qualities, and ultimately to the arguments of the ancient Greek sceptics. At the heart of the idealist version is the problem of understanding how there could be anything known that is not perceptually and/or conceptually formed by the process of coming to know it. And it is sometimes taken to follow from this that any claim to knowledge, in the sense of representations of how things are *in themselves* rather than as they appear to human beings, or even to particular human beings on particular occasions, is spurious. This argument is often combined with the idea that claims to knowledge must be understood as serving vested interests, or at least as primarily designed to have practical effects; in other words, they are 'performative' rather than referential.

This philosophical anti-realism was reinforced within the social sciences by changes in thinking about the nature and role of human agency over the second half of the twentieth century. Indeed, the trend towards constructionism can be found even in long-established traditions, such as symbolic interactionism. Here, a view of actors as actively making sense of the world and generating multiple perspectives (perhaps even 'multiple realities') developed. Within early interactionism this was in conflict with the commitment of most interactionists to something like the discovery model as a research methodology (see Hammersley 1992a: 44–5). Over time, this conflict tended to be resolved by abandonment of the discovery model, and its replacement by a more thoroughgoing constructionist perspective. This was encouraged initially by the influence of phenomenology, which was often treated as if it were epistemologically relativist, and later by postmodernism. These philosophies were taken to cast doubt on the very possibility of knowledge, interpreted as objective representations corresponding to the nature of the things themselves. Rather, the words 'knowledge' and 'truth' came to acquire explicit or implicit scare quotes around them, and were redefined as 'what is taken to be knowledge' and 'what is taken to be true'.[4] At the same time, this sort of constructionism is rarely adhered to consistently, and indeed there are questions about whether it ever could be, since (at the very least) the construction process itself must be treated as existing independently of descriptions of it, the latter treated as referential rather than purely 'performative'.

ASSESSING THE CONSTRUCTION MODEL

The construction model avoids all of the criticisms that were directed against the discovery model. Indeed, it puts the processes neglected by the latter, which were identified in those criticisms, at the heart of research. From this point of view,

---

[4]One area where these developments have been particularly influential is in the sociology of scientific knowledge. See, for example, Woolgar (1988). How constructionism became more radical over time can be discovered by comparing Woolgar's position with that of Berger and Luckmann (1967), who carefully distinguished their constructionist sociology of knowledge from epistemology.

discoveries become social constructions; in fact, they are achievements brought off by persuading others to 'recognise' them as true accounts.[5]

However, while constructionism escapes the charges directed at the discovery model, it is open to other serious criticisms. One of these is that it seems to undermine the very possibility of knowledge, as that word is normally used. If what is true is simply what is *taken* to be true by some group of people, in other words what they find persuasive, then what distinction can be made between knowledge and belief? Apparently this can be done only in terms of conformity or non-conformity to the consensus, or in terms of an application of the standards operating within a particular community. But this robs the word 'knowledge' of its distinctive meaning, one that we cannot do without even in our everyday dealings with the world. Given this, we might ask how it is that some forms of knowledge seem much more resistant to change than others, and appear to provide a reliable basis for action in the world. Can it simply be that no-one has yet found a way of persuading us that they are false? And, if someone did find a way, would this make the ideas false? Is it not, perhaps, that those ideas capture something real about the world with which we have to deal? The response of constructionists to such questions, often, is to suggest that stability of belief arises from the operation of power. However, any attempt to identify the forces involved is undermined by the fact that, to be consistent, this cannot be a claim to knowledge but only, in its own turn, an attempt to exercise power.

Constructionists vary somewhat according to the extent to which they embrace the sceptical, or at least relativistic, implications of the position. The most radical do so up to the point of accepting that the very argument for constructionism itself must be seen as no more than an attempt at persuasion (see, for example, Ashmore 1989). Others argue that the apparently sceptical implications of constructionism stem from a commitment on the part of critics to an unnecessary discipline called Epistemology, which demands that all knowledge be supported by philosophical justification.[6] They argue that while constructionism undercuts epistemological arguments, it leaves our everyday judgements about what is and is not true intact – a stance which may be used to undercut, and in fact cannot avoid undercutting, claims to superior knowledge on the part of scientists, and researchers more generally.

Neither of these positions seems effective. As regards the first, the cost of a consistent constructionism is acceptance that an internally coherent realism would be equally legitimate if it were found persuasive. And, for constructionists, whether or not something is found persuasive is an entirely contingent matter. The second argument involves a sharp distinction between philosophical epistemology and our everyday judgements about truth; one that is not viable. The questions that have preoccupied epistemologists came out of that everyday context, and continue to arise there occasionally. People sometimes ask themselves whether anything can be known about some particular domain, for example other people's experience. Equally, they sometimes wonder whether there can ever be knowledge that is beyond all doubt. These questions are not 'unnatural' inventions on the part of philosophers; nor are

---

[5]Brannigan (1981) spells out this argument in considerable detail.

[6]This is the position taken by Rorty (1982), for example.

thoughts about them irrelevant to our everyday judgements about the validity of knowledge claims, what is the best course of action to adopt, and so on.

This leads to recognition of a second problem with constructionism: that in ordinary life people distinguish between what is *taken* to be true, in other words what is believed, and what *is* true. While they may judge the likely truth of a knowledge claim in terms of its persuasiveness, they do not treat these two features of it as equivalent. One implication of this is that constructionism amounts to critique of a key aspect of what is taken to be common sense by many social actors. And the question then arises: what is the basis for this critique? It cannot be that constructionism provides a true account of the nature of knowledge. To be consistent, a constructionist could only claim that her or his account is more persuasive, in the empirical sense of persuading more people. Yet there seems little evidence to support this, and in any case a constructionist view would have to treat any such evidence as itself a rhetorical construct.

The source of the problem here is that constructionism conflates empirical questions about what people recognise as true, can be persuaded is true, etc., with normative questions about what people *ought to* believe, what they have *good reason* to believe, etc. This amounts to a category mistake (Ryle 1949: 17).[7]

A THIRD MODEL

It seems clear, then, that neither of these first two models is satisfactory as it stands: there are cogent arguments against both. At the same time, I do not want to suggest that they are completely in error, or that they are of no value. In my view, we usually get nearer to the truth by a process of approximation, in which we retain some elements of earlier accounts, or reformulate them, rather than simply abandoning them. Moreover, we need to recognise the heterogeneity of the activities that come under the heading of 'research'. It may be, for example, that the discovery model matches *some* kinds of enquiry reasonably well, in that with them the judgements, assumptions and construction work which it ignores can be assumed to operate unproblematically most of the time and in much the same way for everyone. However, *most* of the topics in which academic social researchers have an interest probably cannot be investigated successfully along the lines of the discovery model, so that here that model is misleading, and perhaps even serves often as an illegitimate rhetorical device, in the sense of covering up the role of the researcher in making sense of the phenomena concerned.

In these kinds of research it will be important to recognise the cognitive and social processes that the construction model highlights. However, these can be recognised without adopting the epistemological scepticism or relativism with which this model is commonly associated, however selectively. This is reflected in the fact that, contrary to what is sometimes suggested by many qualitative researchers who have strayed into the realm of philosophy, the dominant position there is not epistemological scepticism

[7]On the importance, and unavoidability, of normativity, see Korsgaard (1996).

or relativism. Most contemporary philosophical writers are realists of one sort or another; though there is a great deal of uncertainty, and indeed dispute, about what the term 'realism' means.[8]

So, what I want to do here is to sketch the outline of a model of the research process that draws elements from the other two, but which seeks to avoid most of the criticisms that have been directed at these. Whether it incurs other kinds of serious criticism I leave the reader to judge.

A good place to start is with the failings of the discovery model. Earlier, I identified some central assumptions of that model. The first was that there are phenomena which are independent of our knowledge of them. I regard this as true, but not in an entirely straightforward way; I will elaborate on this below. Another assumption of the discovery model is that we can get *direct* access to such phenomena. This is clearly false. The term 'access', like 'discovery' itself, implies the possibility of a decisive move which makes reality, or even truth, directly perceivable. An exemplar here would be seeking to demonstrate the falsity of the earth's appearance as flat to someone on its surface by producing pictures from an orbiting satellite which show that it is round. But, of course, what is 'recognised' in any scene depends upon the capabilities of the observer. Someone who is blind would not be able to see photographs of the earth. Similarly, someone who is incapable of imagining how one could rise so far above the earth's surface to take such photographs, or how photographs themselves are possible, would be unlikely to interpret them in the way that we do. The third assumption underpinning the discovery model is also problematic: that we can *see* truths about the world, that they are somehow embodied in reality. In my judgement, while recognition of some truths may be *stimulated* by what we see, we cannot *see* truths in a literal sense. After all, photographs can lie or mislead. Furthermore, knowledge of the world is often knowledge of processes that are not visible, not even in principle. Our understanding of the world does not capture it in the way that a photograph represents the scene that the camera was aimed at. And this is true in a deep sense, in that any knowledge we have amounts to an answer to some question, or set of questions. So, it is misleading to think of knowledge picturing or capturing reality; we must not forget that what is really involved is an answer to a set of questions.

What has to be accepted from the main criticisms of the discovery model, then, is that there is no knowledge whose validity is simply given. Any knowledge claim, however basic and however much it may seem to be obviously or demonstrably true, is fallible in that it might later need to be revised. This is the case even with deductive inferences from definitions, since potential for revision arises because the terms of no definition are absolutely clear in their meaning – there is always some scope for alternative interpretations. A second point that must be accepted is that there is no process of reasoning which guarantees the validity of the conclusion reached. Again, deduction may seem to represent an exception; but this is only true if we assume that the premises of the argument are sound, and there is no way of demonstrating the

---

[8]A useful discussion of different senses that can be given to 'realism' is to be found in Vision (1988). See also the entry on realism in Blackburn (2008).

absolute validity of any set of premisses.[9] The upshot of all this is that, as noted earlier, no evidence can verify, or for that matter falsify, a theory with absolute certainty.

Moreover, it is also true that research is a social process. So, the personal and social characteristics of the researcher will shape not just what is investigated but also what is 'discovered', as well as whether reports about the discovery are believed. But those characteristics are not simply a source of possible error, they can lead the researcher towards a true account just as easily as away from it. Indeed, scientific discoveries always depend upon a body of prior substantive and methodological knowledge that has been built up, and this will usually consist of both sound and false ideas. Furthermore, some people will be less likely, and others more likely, to recognise the truth about some matter than others, because of their interests or background assumptions.

What this means is that all of our judgements in the research process are fallible, but that they are *not all equally doubtful*. We can and do make judgements about the relative likely validity of different knowledge claims and of different sorts of evidence; and, while these may be wrong, there is no reason to assume that they are *always* wrong, or that they are no more likely to be correct than if we tossed a coin to decide among the possibilities, or relied upon some other source of information. The temptation to draw that conclusion on the part of sceptics and relativists stems from something they take over from the absolutist epistemology they reject. This is the idea that the validity of a claim must be known with absolute certainty if it is going to be given the title of 'knowledge'. But why should we define 'knowledge' in this way? After all, this is not how we use that term in everyday life; and, as Hume recognised, we could not operate in our lives on such a basis (Hume 1739).

So, what cannot be rejected in the discovery model, without leading to self-contradiction, is the distinction between belief and knowledge. The fact that someone believes something, or that a whole community of people believe it, does not make it true. As noted earlier, this is a distinction we all make in our everyday thinking and it is one that we could not do without. While we may judge the likely validity of a belief in terms of whether others believe it, especially those in whom we have confidence, this is not the same as treating 'A is true' as equivalent to 'A is widely believed'. And, as already indicated, treating them in that way would be to confuse an issue of evaluative warrant with a question of empirical fact.

Of course, this view renders enquiry a rather complex and uncertain business, in the sense that doubts can always be raised about the assumptions we rely on and about the judgements we make. And, indeed, it is an important obligation placed upon members of research communities that genuine doubts be explored. This is precisely what provides the basis for the claim, central to the authority of research findings, that research communities can produce knowledge claims that, typically, are more likely to be true than those coming from other sources. However, research does not, and could not, involve 'questioning all assumptions'. Rather, it involves treating as true what is 'beyond reasonable doubt' within the relevant research community, and revising judgements about what is and is not beyond reasonable doubt over the course of enquiry, in light of communal interpretation of evidence (Rescher 1978; Skagestad 1981; Haack 2009).

---

[9] I have spelt out this argument elsewhere: Hammersley (2002b).

One way of developing this line of thought is through drawing on work in hermeneutics. Originally in this discipline the concern was with interpreting texts, in the sense of resolving obscurities and uncertainties so as to capture the meanings communicated in them, and understanding why these meanings were inscribed in the texts in the ways that they were. Later, the focus was broadened to include other kinds of human communication, in fact the whole field of human actions.

The term 'understanding' does not seem to rely upon an implicit metaphor in the manner that 'discovery' and 'construction' do. Our everyday use of this word does not seem to depend much on the idea of standing under, among, or close to something in order to gain knowledge of it. Perhaps as a result, the term is employed in a variety of ways. Sometimes it is simply a synonym for 'having knowledge', so that we can substitute 'scientific understanding' for 'scientific knowledge' without changing the meaning significantly to most ears. However, at other times 'understanding' is *contrasted* with 'knowledge', so as to indicate a genuine grasp of, rather than simply an external relationship to, what is known. Here 'understanding' means to make something one's own, cognitively speaking: to know it from the inside.

This outside–inside contrast was central to early usage of the term in hermeneutics and in the methodological literature on history and the social sciences. In the nineteenth century 'understanding' came to be contrasted with 'explanation' by some writers on hermeneutics (see Von Wright 1971). It was argued that human beings, their actions, and their cultural products could be *understood* in a way that physical phenomena could not be; the latter could only be *explained* on the basis of correlations among outward characteristics. The justification for this idea, often attributed to Vico, was that we can understand what human beings do and say, even those who lived in the past or who belong to other societies than our own, because we share their fundamental nature; this gives us the potential to grasp the meaning of what they say and do 'from the inside'. By contrast, we do not share our essential nature in common with physical phenomena, and so we are only able to understand them externally.

This argument involved a very particular view of human nature in which the creation and communication of meaning is central. What is distinctive to humans, so the argument went, is that they actively make sense of the world and construct ways of life that have meaning for them; rather than their perceptions and interpretations of the world simply being more or less accurate reflections of its intrinsic nature or the automatic products of human biology. And, of course, different groups of human beings, and people in the same society in different historical periods, create different cultures – in other words, different patterns of meaning. This opens the way for the task of the historian and social scientist, which is to try to understand the distinctive character of the meaningful world in which the people being studied live. Such understanding is rarely acquired immediately or easily. It has to be worked for, and involves suspending some of the assumptions that the researcher has learned to take for granted in her or his own society. Nevertheless, it is assumed that understanding is always possible in principle; and this is facilitated by the capacity for constructing meanings, which the researcher shares in common with other humans.

Now, of course, the notion of meaning is a problematic one. Very crudely, we can identify three views of it in the history of philosophy. The first treats it as intrinsic to the world. This is the position adopted by Aristotle, but also by Hegel and Marx.[10] And, in fact, this is the kind of view of meaning that is required by the discovery model, to the extent that what are to be discovered are meanings. The second position argues that meanings are *imposed* by human beings on the world; they are not intrinsic to it, and are in that sense arbitrary. This idea can be found in post-Hegelian philosophy, notably in Nietzsche and also in Sartre. It corresponds to much usage of the construction model. Finally, there is an argument to be found in several twentieth-century philosophical traditions, notably some forms of pragmatism and phenomenology, that meaning is something that is made out of the world: it is not simply a reflection of the essential features of phenomena independently of our knowledge of them, but neither is it an arbitrary imposition. This idea is sometimes referred to as transactionalism, with meaning seen as a product of the transaction between an organism and its environment. Pragmatists have often adopted this view, though they vary considerably in how they interpret it, as on other matters. For example, Peirce retains the idea that there can be a body of knowledge, the one we reach at the end of enquiry, which captures the world as it is. By contrast, James and Dewey seem to adopt more radical forms of transactionalism that perhaps abandon any notion of correspondence. A somewhat different version of transactionalism can be found in the work of Heidegger and Gadamer, working their way out of phenomenology. For them, while meaning is 'realised' by humans, it is not simply a human projection on to the world but also a product of what was available to be 'realised'. For Heidegger, understanding 'being' seems to rely upon a notion of grace that has echoes of Christian theology: it is a matter of getting oneself into the proper spiritual state to be spoken through.[11] Here, a form of realism is retained, but the meaning produced does not simply capture the world as it is. Rather, it is just one of potentially many meanings that are 'realisable'.

Gadamer's version of the argument, which has become particularly influential, builds upon this. For him, understanding is always socio-historically located, in that we necessarily have to draw on what he provocatively refers to as prejudices: those assumptions that have come down to us as part of the socio-cultural tradition to which we belong. While we can suspend belief in, and even modify, each of those prejudices, we cannot suspend or modify all of them at once; in questioning any one we must rely upon others. The model of understanding for Gadamer is that of dialogue, so that historians are seen as engaging in a dialogue with the past. And, if understanding the past is to be achieved, what must happen is a fusion of the 'horizon' of the interpreter with that of the people whose beliefs and actions are to be interpreted. Moreover, it is important to underline that what is produced, while having the epistemic status of truth, is not the reality of a past age as it actually existed. Rather, at best, it simply captures those aspects of that reality that are available to the interpreters concerned and relevant to their questions.[12]

---

[10] In broad terms, the difference between them is that for Aristotle meanings were eternal, whereas for Hegel and Marx they were only realised over time, over the course of history.

[11] There is a curious parallel with the discovery model here, and I think it points to a significant weakness: the nature of understanding as *work* seems to have been downplayed.

[12] For an account of the development of hermeneutics, and the work of Gadamer, see Palmer (1969).

Central to nineteenth-century hermeneutics was the idea of the hermeneutic circle: that all understanding must presuppose some starting point, but that, once the process has begun, our understanding of particulars can be revised in terms of an understanding of the whole of which they form part; and interpretations of that whole can be modified in terms of changed understanding of particulars. This was not seen as a vicious circle, precisely because a starting point of shared humanity could be assumed. However, Gadamer's philosophical hermeneutics involves an important shift from nineteenth-century ideas.[13]

While older writers on hermeneutics had drawn a sharp distinction between enquiry in the natural and in the historical sciences, they had retained the idea that the latter could produce knowledge of past societies that has the same epistemic status as the knowledge produced by natural science. In this sense, while nineteenth-century writers on hermeneutics recognised historical variation in the meanings that human beings give to their world, in methodological terms they were still wedded to the first of the three views of meaning I identified, analogous to the discovery model. For them, the social and historical sciences, in following a distinctive scientific method, could produce eternally valid characterisations of the cultural meanings they investigated.

Gadamer challenged this assumption: he argued that all understanding, including that engaged in by scientists, is itself socio-historically located and therefore cannot produce knowledge that simply captures the reality of other societies, or of past historical periods. It is always itself a socio-historically located elicitation of meaning. However, as I have tried to make clear, this form of hermeneutics was not based on the second view of meaning but rather on the third. Thus, what is involved is not simply a projection but also, where enquiry succeeds, a realisation of meanings that exist, in potential form, independently of the enquirer and of the tradition to which he or she belongs. So, rather than supporting a constructionist view of the research process, Gadamer's position retains a version of realism; albeit one that is very different from that presupposed by the discovery model.[14]

So, as I am formulating it here, the third model – concerned with understanding – recognises that there can be no absolute givens in enquiry, and that any knowledge we produce is necessarily a product of construction work, both conscious and subconscious. Moreover, that work will reflect the cultural resources available to us, and our own position in the world. However, this model retains the idea that, at best, what is produced is a representation, albeit only of some part of reality from a particular perspective (that framed by our questions). At the same time, it is argued that any notion of a representation which implies capturing reality as it is, in its entirety, is misconceived. Reality is an inexhaustible fund of truths, because truths are always

---

[13]On the complex relationship between the positions of Dilthey and Gadamer, see Harrington (2001).

[14]Needless to say, my discussion here only captures some aspects of Gadamer's position. Moreover, it is at odds with how he is frequently interpreted, but see Wachterhauser (2002).

answers to questions; and the scope for questions, even about any small part of reality, is always potentially endless.[15]

What are the practical implications of this third model for researchers? I do not believe that it implies a radical reconstruction of how we should go about our work. As I indicated earlier, there may be forms of enquiry where the discovery model suffices because, although it is not an accurate representation of all that is involved, what it misses does not *usually* amount to a source of problems. And, for all research, we must retain the idea that the aim is to capture features of phenomena whose existence or non-existence is independent of our studying them. However, in much social research we are likely to need to pay attention to how researchers go about the work of constructing representations of the phenomena they are concerned with understanding, and not just in terms of whether the preconditions for discovering reality have been met. Even here, though, our concern needs to be restricted to what the construction process indicates about the limits of the knowledge produced, and about likely sources of error. In other words, by contrast with the constructionist model, there is no suggestion that the enquiry process must itself be explicated in full if what it produces is to be validated, or to be judged to be authentic.

CONCLUSION

In this chapter I have looked at two influential metaphors frequently used to represent the research process: those of discovery and construction. I argued that neither is satisfactory, and that there are important criticisms which undermine them. At the same time, I suggested that both these models do capture something important about what is involved in research, so that neither must be dismissed as entirely lacking in validity.

Given this, the third model that I outlined, focusing on the notion of understanding, and appealing to hermeneutics, drew elements from the other two, while acknowledging the criticisms that had been directed at them. I argued that while the meanings that inform people's beliefs and actions are not eternally fixed – they undergo change over time and vary across contexts – it is possible, at least in principle, to capture aspects of the meanings operating in any particular scene. While those meanings are in an important sense constructed, they are not sheer fabrications out of nothing. Similarly, while the sense that a historian or social scientist makes of social events and processes is itself a construction, to the extent that the account is sound, the meaning given is not arbitrary. So, while no account can capture a phenomenon as it is in its entirety, or in its essential nature, accounts *can* answer questions about phenomena in ways that accurately represent them. That, in my view, is the modest, and exclusive, task of enquiry.

---

[15]There is a further point, which I cannot address here, to do with the fact that there will always be many questions that cannot reasonably be asked about a particular phenomenon, because of a mismatch between their presuppositions and reality. 'Is the present King of France bald?' is a classic example invented, I believe, by Bertrand Russell.

7

MERELY ACADEMIC? A DIALECTIC FOR RESEARCH COMMUNITIES

The traditional and orthodox emphasis on the issues *How can I convince myself? How can I be certain?* invites us to forget the social nature of the ground rules of probative reasoning – their rooting in the issue of: *How can we go about convincing one another?* The dialectic of disputation and controversy provides a useful antidote to such cognitive egocentrism. It insists that we do not forget the buildup of knowledge as a communal enterprise subject to communal standards. (Rescher 1977: xii)

The life-blood of philosophy is argument and counter-argument. Plato and Aristotle thought of this occurring in what they called dialectic-discussion. Today, it might be argued that it is just the same, except that it operates upon a much wider scale, both historically and geographically. Argument and counterargument in books and journals is the modern version of dialectic. (Hamlyn 1988: 333)

The adjective 'academic' has long had negative as well as positive connotations. The negative ones probably grew in salience during the twentieth century – reflecting an increasingly instrumental or utilitarian view of knowledge, not only outside but also within the academy.[1] However, dismissal of the 'merely academic' can be traced back much further, for example to the writings of Francis Bacon in the early seventeenth century. Bacon is renowned for his assertion that 'knowledge is power', by which he meant that the application of scientific method could produce knowledge that would lead to inventions capable of improving the lot of humankind.[2] He insisted that

---

[1]The idea that knowledge can only be of instrumental value is false. Some things must have intrinsic value if infinite regress is to be avoided, and knowledge has a good claim to be among those things (see Hammersley 1995: 140–3).

[2]He seems to have seen no tension between this and the capacity of new technologies to serve the needs of monarchs and powerful social groups.

knowledge is for practical use, for 'the relief of man's estate' (see Quinton 1980: 30). However, he was not arguing that research should be aimed directly at producing inventions: he draws a distinction between 'experiments of light' (yielding valuable knowledge) and 'experiments of fruit' (producing immediate practical results), and insists on the priority of the former (see Rossi 1996: 44). In this respect, Bacon contrasts the new science that he proposes with the work of 'artisans'. But he is even more keen to contrast it with Scholasticism. He argues that this intellectual movement had been 'fruitful of controversies but barren of works' (quoted in Sargent 1996: 146). In other words, it had produced little knowledge of practical value, it was of merely academic interest. And one of the reasons for this, he argued, was that the Scholastics had been preoccupied with discussing the meaning of ancient texts rather than engaging in experimentation designed to generate new knowledge. In this way, Bacon was a key protagonist in what came to be labelled the battle between the ancients and the moderns (see Gaukroger 2001).

The picture of Scholastic discussion to be found in Bacon portrays it as endless and pointless discourse, addressing meaningless or unresolvable questions, and making fine distinctions for their own sake. And this image of intellectual life in the Middle Ages became widely accepted in the seventeenth, eighteenth, and nineteenth centuries.[3] Moreover, current notions of the 'academic' still draw on this image. Thus, in the *Oxford English Dictionary* academic discussion is referred to in one entry as 'not leading to a decision; unpractical; theoretical, formal or conventional'. Indeed, the prime aim of the participants might be seen as simply to keep the discussion going.[4]

It is worth comparing this aspect of Bacon's championing of modern science against medieval philosophy with the views of a philosopher who was his most notable critic in the twentieth century, Karl Popper. The main focus of Popper's criticism is Bacon's alleged inductivism: commitment to the idea that theoretical knowledge can be logically derived from the examination of data. Popper denies that this is possible, and indeed that there can ever be certainty that a theory is true. The only certainty that is available, Popper insists, is about the falsity of theories, once they have been tested and found wanting. And even here he distinguishes between the logical and methodological aspects of falsification; so that, in practice, we can never know with absolute certainty even that a hypothesis is false. For him, it does not matter where theoretical ideas come from, so long as they are open to falsification and are subjected to test. The fact that they may have arisen in the course of examining data offers no indication of their likely validity.

In some ways, Popper's criticism of Bacon is misdirected, since the latter does not claim that absolute certainty is possible, and he emphasises the importance of seeking

---

[3]In the eighteenth century, the rational metaphysics of Descartes and Leibniz came to be tarred with the same brush. Many *Philosophes* argued that the knowledge that science can produce is limited by human capabilities, so that rather than debating questions to which the answer cannot be known we must concentrate on gaining those kinds of knowledge that will be useful in improving the lot of humankind: see Baker (1975: 87–95).

[4]There are those, even in the modern world, who have sought to justify this. Canovan argues that this was Arendt's position; see Canovan (1988). And Malachowski (1990: xi) refers to Rorty's 'laudable aim of "keeping the conversation going"'.

critical cases that will offer the sharpest test of hypotheses. What is required for rigorous enquiry, Bacon insisted, is careful and systematic investigation of cases, employing what he calls eliminative induction, a method that relies on 'the greater force of the negative instance' (Quinton 1980: 58).[5] In these terms, the contrast between Popperian and Baconian philosophy of science is rather less sharp than is sometimes assumed (see Quinton 1980; Urbach 1987).

However, there are certainly respects in which Popper's and Bacon's views about science differ significantly. While Bacon saw science very much as a collective activity, he does not assign a central role to the scientific community in assessing knowledge claims; and especially not to scientific discussion concerned with clarifying the meaning of theoretical ideas, assessing the evidence for these, etc. Rather, he tends to see experimental investigations as producing knowledge directly.[6] The main reason why science must be a collective activity, from his perspective, is that it requires more work than any single individual is capable of: a division of labour is necessary. By contrast, while Popper is no admirer of the Scholastics, and is as convinced as Bacon of the importance of scientific experiment, he emphasises the role of discussion in science. He sees intersubjective testing of hypotheses as 'a very important aspect of the more general idea of inter-subjective *criticism*, or in other words of the idea of mutual rational control by critical discussion' (Popper 1959: 44; see also Popper 1966: 217–20). Indeed, in 'On toleration and intellectual responsibility', Popper claims that the method of science is 'quite simply: critical discussion in the service of truth' (1987: 29).[7] One way of formulating this is to say that at the heart of the research process is dialectic, what Rescher (1977: xiii) refers to as 'the communal and controversy-oriented aspects of rational argumentation and [scientific] inquiry'.[8]

Interestingly, Popper's emphasis on the role of critical discussion bears some similarities to the views of other authors whose positions are usually taken to be as far from his own as he saw himself being from Bacon. One of these is Jürgen Habermas, who confronted Popper in what came to be referred to as 'the positivist dispute in German sociology' (Adorno et al. 1976). Thus, Habermas also emphasises the collective and discursive character of rational investigation in pursuit of

[5]As Quinton points out, some twentieth-century criticism of Bacon, including that by Popper, has tended to overlook his emphasis on the negative instance. Note too that what Bacon was proposing can be interpreted as a more systematic form of what Aristotle regarded as the first stage of enquiry. Indeed, the methods of agreement and difference, identified by Bacon and developed by Mill, had been anticipated by philosophers working within an Aristotelian framework in medieval times: see Losee (1993: 32–4, and also Weinberg (1965). There is irony here: it seems that Bacon misinterpreted Aristotle, and was in turn misinterpreted by Popper.

[6]This is what I have referred to in Chapter 6 as the 'discovery' model of research. Even here there may be a danger of misrepresenting Bacon. As Quinton points out, he emphasised the significance of publicity and criticism in his discussion of the failings of 'the fantastic learning': astrology, natural magic and alchemy (Quinton, 1980: 30–2; see also Sargent 1996).

[7]It is in this spirit that Popper's philosophy has sometimes been labelled 'critical rationalism', see Albert (1985; 2002).

[8]Rescher bases his discussion on an analysis of medieval disputation as 'a stylized sequence of moves and countermoves' (Rescher 1977: 18). Of course, the notion of dialectic can be traced back to Plato and Aristotle; see Robinson (1953) and Evans (1977).

knowledge. The concept of the ideal speech situation, which is central to his early work, is in many ways an idealisation of academic discussion (see Habermas 1975: 107–8). Of course, Popper is concerned primarily with *scientific* discussion, whereas Habermas sees the rational orientation of the ideal speech situation as implicit in all human communication. Furthermore, Habermas believes that science is a false model for rationality; though this is because he regards it as instrumental or technical in character – in this respect his view of science is closer to that of Bacon than to Popper's. These points aside, the two authors are not very far apart in their views about the form that rational discussion should take. For both what is required is critical assessment that is free from both external constraint and internal compulsion. Furthermore, both philosophers see relationships among rational enquirers as necessarily egalitarian, rather than as hierarchical (an important contrast with Bacon). Nor does Popper regard rational discussion as the exclusive prerogative of researchers: he believes that democratic politics must take this form as well. So both these authors are committed to a notion of rational politics in which open discussion and publicity play a key role in determining policy, even though in other respects their political views are very different.

Perhaps even more surprisingly, parallels can also be drawn with the 'philosophical hermeneutics' of Hans-Georg Gadamer, who engaged in a well-known debate with Habermas, and whose position is in many respects an even greater distance from Popper's. Gadamer also emphasises the role of discussion in enquiry, and his conception of its nature is close in some respects to what the other two authors envisage. Thus, for Gadamer, 'every claim is legitimate only insofar as it opens itself to the possibility of counterclaim' (Sullivan 1989: 171). In other words, we must be prepared for our views to be refuted; we should be ready to have someone or something say 'no' to us. So what is required, according to Gadamer, is an openness in dialogue with other perspectives, a willingness to topicalise and reconsider the prejudices – the prior assumptions – on which our current understandings are based. Furthermore, like Popper and Habermas, for Gadamer dialogue is directed towards discovering the truth, though his conception of truth is different from both of theirs.[9]

A final comparison that can usefully be made on this issue is with Richard Rorty. He too sees discussion, or at least 'conversation', as central to enquiry. However, in more senses than one, Rorty is the joker in this pack. The other three authors regard rational discussion as directed towards and capable of achieving knowledge, in a sense of that term which goes beyond 'what we currently believe'. By contrast, for Rorty the purpose of the conversation engaged in by scientists, scholars, and others is edification rather than truth.[10] And this has implications for the nature of the conversation. The scholar, in Rorty's view, should be a cultural critic, commenting on anything that attracts her or his attention. Furthermore, where for the other writers, and especially for Popper, the language to be employed

---

[9]There has been some debate about the relationship between the positions of Popper and Gadamer: see Grondin (2003) and Albert (2002: 20–1).

[10]This is a contrast he takes over from Lovejoy (1917) to very different effect; see Rorty (1982: 169–71).

in discussion should be as clear and unequivocal as possible, for Rorty allusion and word play are to be celebrated. For him, science and philosophy become genres of literature. The emphasis is on invention, novelty, and style. In short, Rorty privileges a particular image of literary culture, seeing it as a form of discourse that lacks most of the features associated with science: 'rules, a constant vocabulary, respect for history, and argumentative rigour'. As a result, it 'fails to terminate in agreement, let alone progress'. In fact, it 'ignores everything an academic discipline stands for' (Fischer 1990: 237):

> Unable to engage in argument, 'operating without rules', adopting a 'relaxed attitude' towards terminology, and refusing to be 'bothered by realist questions such as "Is that what the text really *says*?"', literary intellectuals, as Rorty portrays them, cannot 'agree on what would count as resolving disputes, on the criteria to which all sides must appeal'. In this giddy form of life, 'the true and the good and the beautiful drop out', as norms, leaving critics free to engage in a kind of 'name-dropping, rapid shifting of context, and unwillingness to stay for an answer which [...] runs counter to everything that a professionalized academic discipline stands for'. Similarly, the past provides 'no containing framework, no points of reference' for literary intellectuals, who regard history as a kind of sandbox, full of 'material for playful experimentation'. (Fischer 1990: 235)[11]

Rorty is not arguing for an intellectual free-for-all; in that he insists on the virtue of civility, and beyond this on the 'willingness to talk, to listen to other people, to weigh the consequences of our actions upon other people' (Rorty 1982: 172). Indeed, Fischer qualifies his account, summarised above, by suggesting that Rorty 'praises literary critics not for dispensing with rules but for adopting a suitably playful or relaxed attitude towards the rules that they nonetheless follow' (Fischer 1990: 240). Nevertheless, the constraints are those of conversation rather than of rational enquiry: they are to do with maintaining solidarity and expanding the community in which the conversation takes place, rather than progressing towards truth (see Rorty 1991b).[12]

The views of these four authors, and especially of Rorty, highlight the need for clarity about the proper nature of academic discussion, if this is to be presented as at the heart of research. In the sections that follow I will try to provide this clarification.

---

[11]Fischer provides sources for the quotations from Rorty that he includes in this extract.

[12]Interestingly, at one point Rorty argues in favour of a Baconian view of science (Rorty 1991a: 172). I will not engage here with the philosophical issues which separate Rorty from the other three philosophers or those that differentiate the positions of the latter. For critical assessments of Rorty's work that I find compelling, see Haack (2009: ch. 9) and Haskell (1996). Rorty is by no means the only commentator to challenge the ideal of dialogue outlined here: see Derrida's responses to Gadamer's attempts to engage in dialogue with him, in Michelfelder and Palmer (1989). Also of interest here are Rescher's (1993) arguments for pluralism.

VIRTUES AND VICES IN ACADEMIC DISCOURSE

My aim in this section and the next one is to specify some key aspects of the attitude or orientation that is properly constitutive of academic discussion, viewed as a means of producing sound knowledge. This will involve trying to explicate the character of rational communication in an academic context.[13]

Popper provides a starting point here. He argues that scientific or rational discussion relies on three ideas: 'I may be wrong and you may be right'; 'let us talk things over rationally'; and 'we may get nearer the truth, even if we do not reach agreement'.[14] He emphasises that the first of these ideas does not imply relativism, only fallibilism. As regards the second, he unpacks 'rational talk' as 'talking things over with the aim of finding out what is true and what is false [...] while forgetting, as far as this is humanly possible, the question of who is wrong and who is right' (Popper, 1987: 26–7). The final idea underlines the fact that we can never know with absolute certainty when we have discovered the truth. At the same time, it emphasises that we can get nearer the truth through one or more party to the discussion discovering errors in their beliefs. Popper also insists that: 'Real progress in science is impossible without toleration, without feeling sure that we can publicly state our thoughts wherever they may lead us' (1987: 29).[15]

Popper argues that scientists must make every effort to avoid 'speaking at cross purposes', and that this involves trying 'to express their theories in such a form that they can be tested, i.e. refuted (or else corroborated) by [...] experience' (Popper 1966: 218). He denies the possibility that Robinson Crusoe could engage in science proper, on the grounds that there must be others to check the results, in order to:

> correct those prejudices which are the unavoidable consequences of [the individual scientist's] peculiar mental history [...] to help him to get rid of that strange blindness concerning the inherent possibilities of our own results which is a consequence of the fact that most of them are reached through comparatively irrelevant approaches. [...] [I]t is only in attempts to explain his work to *somebody who has not done it* that he can acquire the discipline of clear and reasoned communication which too is part of scientific method. (Popper 1966: 219)

---

[13]For present purposes, I am leaving aside the question of whether this model could or should be applied beyond that context, in the way that Popper and Habermas, at least, propose.

[14]There is a close similarity here with the six principles that Palmer (2003) identifies in Gadamer's work, the first three of which are 'the other person could be right', 'look for common ground' and 'avoid ad hominem argument'.

[15]In many respects, we can see these commitments as discursive embodiments of the scientific norms identified by Merton: see Merton (1973a) and the discussion in Ziman (2000: ch. 3). It should be noted that the third commitment indicated by Popper assumes the notion of verisimilitude, which is by no means straightforward: see Miller (1994: chs 10 and 11).

Popper sums up his argument as follows:

> what we call 'scientific objectivity' is not a product of the individual scientist's impartiality, but a product of the social or public character of scientific method; and the individual scientist's impartiality is, so far as it exists, not the source but rather the result of this socially or institutionally organized objectivity of science. (1966: 220)

Interestingly, we find a rather similar account of the requirements of participation in academic communities put forward by a severe critic of Popper's political philosophy, Willmoore Kendall. He adds some features that Popper might have rejected but which are nevertheless important. According to him, those who belong to an academic discipline:

> demonstrably proceed on some such principles as these: (a) The pursuit of truth is indeed forwarded by the exchange of opinions and ideas among many; helpful suggestions do indeed emerge sometimes from surprising quarters; but one does not leap from these facts to the conclusion that helpful suggestions may come from just anybody. (b) The man or woman who wishes to exercise the right to be heard has a logically and temporally prior obligation to *prepare* himself for participation in the exchange, and to prepare himself in the manner defined by the community. Moreover, (c), from the moment he begins to participate in the exchange, he must make manifest, by his behaviour, his sense of the duty to act as if the other participants had something to teach him – the duty, in a word, to see to it that the exchange goes forward in an atmosphere of courtesy and mutual self-respect. Next (d), the entrant must so behave as to show that he understands that scholarly investigation did not begin with his appearance on the scene, that there is a strong presumption that prior investigators have not labored entirely in vain, and that the community is the custodian of – let us not sidestep the *mot juste* – an *orthodoxy*, no part of which is it going to set lightly to one side. (e) That orthodoxy must be understood as concerning first and foremost the frame of reference within which the exchange of ideas and opinions is to go forward. That frame of reference is, to be sure, subject to change, but this is a matter of meeting the arguments that led originally to its adoption, and meeting them in recognition that the ultimate decision, as to whether or not to change it, lies with the community. (f) The entrant, insofar as he wishes to challenge the orthodoxy, must expect barriers to be placed in his way, and must not be astonished if he is punished, at least in the short term, by what are fashionably called 'deprivations'; he must, indeed, recognise that the barriers and the deprivations are a necessary part of the organised procedure by which truth is pursued. (g) Access to the channels of communication that represent the community's central ritual (the learned journals, that is to say) is something that the entrant wins by performing the obligation to produce a craftsmanlike piece of work. (h) The ultimate fate of the entrant who disagrees with the orthodoxy but cannot persuade the community to accept his point of view is, quite simply, isolation within or banishment from the community (Kendall 1960: 979).

These accounts, from Popper and Kendall, not only outline what the purpose and proper nature of academic discussion should be, but also point to a series of virtues and vices that are defined by this framework. Thus, certain forms of argument are ruled out as inappropriate, in particular what Haack (1998: 8) refers to as 'pseudo-inquiry'. She identifies two types. The first is 'sham reasoning', where people make a case for the truth of some proposition 'which no evidence or argument would induce them to give up' (p. 8). In other words, the enquirer has a *prior and unbudge-able commitment* to the proposition for which he tries to make a case' (p. 9). The other kind of pseudo-enquiry is 'fake reasoning', where an inquirer is indifferent '*to the truth-value* of the proposition for which he seeks to make a case' (p.9). Rather, the primary concern is with what is taken to be the desirable effect of its being accepted as true (or treated as false).[16]

Other types of pseudo-discussion could be added, focusing not so much on background purpose but rather on target or means. For instance, ad hominem argument is ruled out, in the sense of criticism that *instead of engaging with the points made* moves straight to a diagnosis of why they were made, the sort of person who would make them, and so on; these being treated by the critic as demonstrating their falsity. This is, of course, by no means a new tactic. It was explicitly ruled out of scholastic debate, though it no doubt occurred in more informal discussions. And it is certainly to be found in the Renaissance, where discussion of religious issues often descended into polemic. Here, for example, is an extract from Thomas More's response to Luther, on behalf of Henry VIII of England, written under a pseudonym in 1523:

> Since he [Luther] has written that he already has a prior right to bespatter and besmirch the royal crown with shit, will we not have the posterior right to proclaim the beshitted tongue of this practitioner of posterioristics most fit to lick with his anterior the very posterior of a pissing she-mule until he shall have learned more correctly to infer posterior conclusions from prior premises? (More 1969: 123, quoted in Kenny 1983: 51)

While by no means new, various later developments in Western thought have encouraged the use of ad hominem arguments that judge the validity of views according to their sources, notably Marxism, Nietzschean genealogy, Freudian analysis, and the forms of sociology of knowledge deriving from these. Indeed, some versions have assumed that the cognitive validity of any statement is entirely determined by psycho-social dynamics, discursive and/or socio-historical processes. However, while it is important to recognise that we are all shaped by such processes, there are good reasons to reject this kind of determinism: true and false conclusions can be generated by the same processes; and the explanation of beliefs in terms of causal processes is itself a knowledge claim; and is undermined if this form of argument is applied across the board as, consistently, it must be.

---

[16]From my point of view, what is wrong with these kinds of argument is not intrinsic to them; I am not suggesting that they are never appropriate. They are illegitimate, as Haack's label indicates, when they pretend to be deployed in a process of enquiry, because they are at odds with the guiding orientation of that activity.

Another argumentative device that is ruled out of academic discussion, on the model I am putting forward here, is what Woolgar and Pawluch (1985) refer to as 'ontological gerrymandering'. What they mean by this is expediently and inconsistently moving the line backwards and forwards between what can be treated as reality and what must be regarded as doubtful *in order to suit the argument that the writer is putting forward*. Here the strategies used by epistemological sceptics to deny the possibility of any kind of knowledge are deployed selectively to undermine opponents' arguments, but are suspended when it comes to the critics' own claims to knowledge, even though they logically apply there too.

This relates to a more general obligation: to present consistent lines of argument, rather than vacillating among divergent positions according to whichever is the easier to defend.[17] It is worth noting that what is demanded here is not life-long consistency – there is no ban on changing one's mind – but rather that such changes be made explicit or at least acknowledged. This contrasts with the situation in politics, and many other practical roles, where people become identified with a particular position and their credibility is often judged by how well they defend it.

In the next section I want to try to provide a more systematic account of the constitutive principles of academic discussion, building on these points.

THE CONSTITUTIVE PRINCIPLES OF ACADEMIC DISCUSSION

What I mean by academic discussion here is the whole communicative process within a research community, this being devoted primarily to putting forward and assessing knowledge claims relevant to the field of study. In these terms, contributions to journals, and even the writing of whole books, are simply moves in a larger communicational game: they are neither starting points nor end points. They are themselves responses to previous moves, and there will usually be subsequent responses to them. And they must be viewed in this context.[18]

My starting point is that the constitutive principles of academic discussion can only be identified relative to its exclusive immediate goal: discovering the truth about some matter of fact.[19] This is what marks academic discussion off from ordinary, or 'desultory', conversation; from other kinds of conversation-with-a-purpose, such as

---

[17]Many years ago Gellner (1968: 21–2) accused some representatives of the 'linguistic philosophy' he was criticising of this kind of inconsistency.

[18]This points to a need to broaden the meaning of 'peer review'. There is a tendency to assume that it applies only to the pre-publication stage, but this is simply the first part of the peer review process, amounting to a precautionary device to filter out what is furthest from meeting the disciplinary requirements for knowledge. Thus, what is published will also be assessed by peers, and indeed any researcher must be prepared to answer questions and respond to challenges from fellow researchers. Moreover, as I argued earlier, research-based knowledge claims should not be treated as well-established knowledge until they are treated as valid by most of the relevant research community.

[19]This would include discovery of facts about conceptual implications, which I take to be a key element of the work of philosophers.

meetings designed to reach a decision; from political debates, where the aim of the participants, very often, is to win the argument; and from legal trials, where lawyers work to give those they are representing the best chance of getting a judgement in their favour, within the procedural rules of the court.

From this goal of discovering the truth about some factual matter, several subordinate commitments follow.

A FOCUS ON THE COGENCY OF ARGUMENTS, NOT ON THEIR IMPLICATIONS

There should be an exclusive concern with the *soundness* of arguments and evidence, *rather than with their practical implications or the consequences of expressing them*. It is important to note that this includes their implications for the identities of the speakers. This is part of what Popper meant by insisting that we must be able to state our thoughts 'wherever they may lead'. It is also related to his emphasis on the need to downplay concern with 'who is right and who is wrong'. While reputation within the relevant research community will no doubt have some effect on how people listen to and interpret what is said, as Kendall indicates, the rules of academic discussion counterbalance this by requiring that all members of that community are listened to, at least initially.

Usually, outside of academic discussions, attention to the validity of the knowledge claims people make, or of the assumptions on which they rely, is combined with an interest in what are, or are taken to be, the practical implications of what they say; or with what are likely to be the practical consequences of their saying it. Indeed, very often, statements of fact will be treated as recommendations of, or demands for, action. For instance, the statement that 'hospitals have cancelled many routine operations because beds are needed for flu victims' will sometimes be taken as an indictment (of the relevant managements or authorities). Of course, statements of fact do not always carry *unambiguous* implications of this kind. For example, when an increase in the number of students passing an examination is reported, this may be taken to indicate the growing intelligence and effort of the candidates, and the success of the education system, *or* it can be treated as implying that standards are slipping. Even in such ambiguous cases, however, factual statements are being read primarily for their practical implications. Furthermore, as communications, they will often be interpreted as *intendedly* carrying these implications. In fact, in non-academic discourse we sometimes draw on the practical implications of what people might have been saying to try to determine exactly what they were *actually* saying, when this is not made clear.

The reason for disengaging claims to factual knowledge from their practical implications or consequences, in academic discussion, is that it allows sustained attention to be given to the *truth* of those claims, and this increases the possibility that anything that is taken for granted in error will be exposed. It is also designed to reduce the danger that assessments of validity will be biased by other concerns. What is involved here is a separating out of different forms of evaluation that frequently occur together in other contexts, and often influence one another. This process of detachment is required for knowledge to be pursued in the most effective way possible.

Much the same applies to the issue of motivation. As already noted, very often in everyday life, when people say something we search not just for intentions but also for motives; in other words, we try to see what they say as part of some larger action project. However, in the case of academic discussion the larger action project should be, *and ought to be assumed to be*, discovery of the truth about the matter at issue. This is not to say that it is necessary to believe that fellow academics are motivated solely by a concern with the truth, even less that they actually are apolitical or uninterested in life generally, that they are not concerned about how they are seen by others or about their career interests, and so on. Indeed, it is important to recognise that they will have such potential motives. The point is simply that the participant in an academic discussion is expected to try to behave *as if* discovery of the truth were the only immediate goal, and to assume that fellow participants are similarly motivated – *unless and until there is overwhelming evidence that other considerations have distorted their work, in the sense of leading it astray from what would be rational in pursuit of the truth.*

So, a distinctive feature of academic discourse is that in examining knowledge claims much of the wider implicational context is suspended. This is crucial to the capacity of research to produce knowledge that is more likely to be true, on average, than information from other sources. And it is worth reiterating that this implies distinctive responsibilities on the part of both those putting forward knowledge claims and those assessing them. The former must limit themselves to factual claims, and present sufficient evidence in support of these; while audiences must focus exclusively on the truth of what is being claimed, putting aside any interest in practical implications or consequences. Furthermore, each side must assume, in the absence of overwhelming evidence to the contrary, that the other is primarily committed to discovering the truth, rather than to any other goal.

The suspension of routinely accepted connections between a knowledge claim and both its practical implications/consequences and the motives for making it, amounts to a slowing down of the process of assessment, compared with those kinds that go on in many non-research contexts. The importance of the necessary slowness of research, by contrast with many other activities, needs to be emphasised today since there are strong pressures against recognising it (see Pels 2003). Needless to say, there are losses as well as gains associated with this slowness, but these are an unavoidable cost of the academic mode of production (see Hammersley 2002a).

TOLERATION AND OPEN-MINDEDNESS

A second subsidiary commitment follows on from the suspension of normal connections between knowledge claims and their implications, or what are taken to be the likely consequences of stating them: this is the need for tolerance. It is important to be clear what 'tolerance' or 'toleration' means here: a willingness to live with the expression of views with which one disagrees, or of which one disapproves. But toleration is only a minimum requirement: it is also desirable that there is a willingness to explore views that are different from or even discrepant with one's own; to try to understand what they mean and the grounds on which they are being put forward. Closely associated with this is a preparedness to live with uncertainty about the truth of relevant matters, rather than immediately seeking closure and certainty.

Also crucial is tolerance of criticism. In ordinary conversation, and in some other kinds of talk, disagreement and criticism may be avoided or disguised, for the sake of civility or not causing trouble.[20] However, in the case of academic discussion, criticism must be tolerated while civility is maintained. The fact that the criticism is of arguments rather than people facilitates this, though of course it cannot eliminate the feelings generated by public criticism. Criticising someone's research always potentially impugns their competence or motives, even when a clear disclaimer is provided.

The complement to this is that the appropriate response to criticism is a search for common ground from which it may be possible to develop arguments that overcome the disagreement. However, as Popper emphasises, the goal is not to produce agreement but to discover error (see also Rescher 1993). By contrast with other types of social interaction, where agreement may be reached by negotiation and compromise, these moves are ruled out as illegitimate in an academic context.[21] Rather, the attempt to reach agreement through rational discussion is used as the most effective means of detecting and eliminating cognitive error. As Popper notes, it is possible to move towards truth in such discussion even where no agreement is produced.

It is perhaps worth emphasising that this toleration of other views is not endless. Views will be judged in terms of their plausibility and credibility, and that of the evidence offered in support of them, at each point in the exchange. Where views are judged to be highly implausible and/or not credible, the search for common ground may be abandoned quite soon, on the basis that none seems likely to be found. However, the threshold for such abandonment is much higher in academic discussion than it is in lay discussions, because there is a need to err on the side of avoiding accepting as true what is false (see Chapter 5). Thus, counter-arguments must be given at least some attention: they must not be dismissed out of hand. The difference between academic discussion and other forms, then, is a matter of degree, one stemming from a specialised concern with just one of the goals that may guide everyday conversations, that of discovering the truth about some factual matter. Nevertheless this difference is important.

Finally, as I have indicated, tolerance should also include the capacity to live with uncertainty, what the poet Keats referred to as 'negative capability': there must be an acceptance that the outcome of the discussion could be inconclusive, that the issue may not currently be resolvable. In other words, it must be recognised that a legitimate conclusion may be that we do not know the answer to some question, that the evidence available is not yet sufficient, one way or the other. Whereas in many situations

---

[20]Pomerantz (1984: 83–90) has argued that, generally speaking, disagreement is a dispreferred response in conversation.

[21]By 'an academic context' I mean discussions of the likely truth of research findings. In their practical dealings with one another, academics will often need to rely upon compromise and negotiation.

those occupying particular roles are expected to know or have an opinion about all relevant matters, in academic discussion it is acceptable to declare that there is not currently enough information to make a sound judgement. Here, this should not be taken to imply incompetence, or an unacceptable unwillingness to come to a judgement. Indeed, a claim to knowledge where many others in the research community judge that there is insufficient evidence is likely to be taken as a much more telling sign of incompetence.

Again, what we have here is a matter of degree, not a dichotomy between academic and other forms of discussion. What is implied is not toleration of total doubt. There will be many matters that an academic working in a particular field will be expected to know and to accept as valid. Expressions of uncertainty about these will not be automatically dismissed, but very convincing evidence for why currently accepted justifications are less compelling than is usually believed will be required, if these expressions of uncertainty are to be accorded validity and not to count against an academic's reputation.

CLARITY OF PRESENTATION AND THE PROVISION OF SUFFICIENT EVIDENCE AND INFORMATION

A third subordinate commitment constitutive of academic discourse requires that arguments and counter-arguments be presented in a way that is as clear as possible for the audience, and that provides the data and information required for them to come to a conclusion about the truth of what is claimed.

This can be elaborated by drawing on Grice's account of conversational maxims. He starts from the idea that conversation is governed by what he calls the 'cooperative principle'. His conception of conversation here assumes that its purpose is 'the maximally effective exchange of information' (Grice 1989: 28), while recognising that this does not capture the purposes involved in all conversations. However, I suggest that the cooperative principle does approximate reasonably closely to what ought to be involved in scientific communication. Grice summarises this principle as follows: 'make your conversational contribution such as is required, at the stage at which it occurs, by the accepted purpose or direction of the talk exchange in which you are engaged' (1989: 26). And he identifies four maxims that specify the requirements of cooperation in more detail, concerned with: quantity, quality, relation, and manner.[22] I will use these as a framework for discussing the requirements placed on contributions to academic discussion, though there is some overlap amongst them.

(a) *The maxim of quantity.* The requirement here is that speakers make their contributions as informative as is required, *but no more so*. In the academic context, this can be taken to include the following:

---

[22]Grice recognises that these maxims are often breached precisely in order to communicate a message. This may also occur in the context of research communications, but my primary focus here is on the way in which they serve as guiding norms.

- Make an oral or written input to the discussion when you have something to say that contributes significantly to the process of knowledge development; do not enter the discussion simply for the purpose of defending some prior position, building your reputation, heightening the public profile or publication record of your institution or unit, etc.
- Include in what you say or write as much evidence, and as much information about how this evidence was produced, as is necessary – *but no more than this*.

This maxim prescribes a mean between the poles of too little and too much, as regards both when to contribute and what to contribute. Of course, what is required is necessarily a matter of judgement.

As regards *what* contribution would be worthwhile *when*, there are few guidelines, since much will depend upon local circumstances of both time and place. Nevertheless, it is possible to indicate some of the considerations that ought to be taken into account. Contributions must be attuned to the present state of development of the discipline concerned, responding to the claims and criticisms that are currently live in that field. This can involve pointing to what might be a productive direction in which new investigations could be pursued as well as filling gaps in, or challenging, what is currently accepted as sound knowledge. Equally important, knowledge claims should exceed an appropriate threshold of likely validity. Both fanciful speculation and radical scepticism about the very possibility of knowledge are likely to be ruled out. Moreover, whatever contribution is offered should clearly indicate what is taken to be its likely level of validity, this ranging from an interesting possibility that might need to be considered to a well-established fact.

In relation to the content of research reports, it is possible to identify some essential components: a statement of the question to be addressed, and perhaps of its importance; an account of the methods used; a presentation of the main findings; and a summary of the conclusions, which may go beyond those findings (see Hammersley 1998a). Of course, even if accepted, such a list does not resolve all the issues. First of all, there is the question of *how much* evidence and/or information is required under each heading. Here, judgements must be made about what ought to be necessary, but there must also be some anticipation of what colleagues are likely to *believe* is required. What is needed is determined, first of all, by the relationship between what is claimed and what is currently taken to be well-established knowledge in the field. For example, if a knowledge claim being made is strongly implied by that existing knowledge, then relatively little evidence and information may be judged necessary.[23] If, by contrast, the claim runs counter to some element of what is judged well-established knowledge, much more evidence and information will be required. And, of course, there will be differences in view within any research community about what is and is not judged sufficiently plausible to be accepted at face value; and the threshold probably ought to be at least the lowest level of what is commonly accepted among a substantial portion of members of that community.

---

[23]However, claims that are strongly implied by existing knowledge will usually be open to question in terms of the maxim of relation or relevance, on which see below.

Similarly, how much evidence is required depends upon credibility: is the knowledge claim which is being presented, or being challenged, of a kind that researchers could know simply by looking at some situation they were observing, with relatively little chance of error? Is it the kind of matter about which an account from an informant (of some kind) can be taken to be reliable? If so, then little further evidence will need to be presented. If, as is almost always the case with the central claims of a research report, the knowledge claim is not itself strongly credible in this sense, then further evidence will be required, until we reach a level of evidence that *is* sufficiently plausible and/or credible to be accepted. Here, again, there may be significant variation within the relevant research community about what is and is not judged sufficiently credible to be accepted at face value, as well as about the range of evidence that is required. The aim must be to provide what should be sufficient to persuade most of a potentially sceptical research community.

A more fundamental problem must be mentioned. This is that all judgements rest upon tacit knowledge, which by its nature cannot be fully explicated. Thus, while credible evidence will often involve appeal to observation by the researcher, the skill involved in producing this may not be widely distributed in the general population, so that readers may not be well-placed to evaluate the evidence (see Ziman 2000: 91–2). To take an example from medicine, while X-ray photographs provide highly credible medical evidence for those who are competent to read them, they do not provide this for those of us without that competence. Much the same *may* be true with some sorts of evidence in social research, for a variety of reasons. For instance, if we assume that there are culturally significant variations across and within societies, and that understanding actions depends upon having the relevant local cultural knowledge, which a researcher has to learn, then it may be that few people in the research community will have the relevant competence. Here, the competences involved are a component of the very cultural activities that are being studied by the researchers concerned (see Hammersley and Atkinson 2007). Moreover, this cultural competence probably cannot be formulated in language in a manner that allows it to be *transferred* intact from one person to another; even though language can be used to facilitate its being learned. The point is, then, that while there must be an attempt to provide readers with what they need in order to understand and assess the data and the inferences from them, this is not entirely straightforward even in the physical sciences, and it may be more difficult to achieve in the case of the social sciences because of reliance upon cultural competence of various kinds. Certainly, it can never avoid some reliance upon trust.

Let me turn now to the other, perhaps more surprising, side of the maxim of quantity: that too much information should not be provided. One reason for this requirement is that unnecessary information makes research reports longer than they need to be, and therefore introduces inefficiency. This is not an insignificant consideration in a world in which the literature in most research fields is growing rapidly. An equally important point is that excessive evidence and information obscures the line of argument, and thereby results in reports being less clear: it makes it harder to distinguish the wood from the trees. A third, closely related, issue is that it is central to Grice's argument that the maxims, including the maxim of quantity, are employed by *audiences* as well as by speakers/writers. As part of the process of understanding, audiences must assume, at least initially, that anything which has been included in a statement or set of statements is there because it is of significance, so that anything present which is actually unnecessary creates problems of interpretation that may be difficult and time-consuming to resolve.

This argument against the inclusion of unnecessary information carries several implications. One is that it underlines the importance of making clear in the body of a research report what is central and what is less so. One way of doing this is through meta-statements, for example lists indicating the central findings and conclusions. Another is the use of footnotes and appendices to include material that is less directly relevant, but still perhaps necessary for certain purposes and for some audiences. It is worth noting that these features are sometimes picked out by critics of social scientific writing who complain about its tedious, pedantic character – but they are essential to the process of clear communication for research purposes. The requirements are not the same as they are, say, for journalism.

This aspect of the maxim of quantity has important implications for arguments in favour of reflexivity. As we saw in Chapter 1, this principle is sometimes interpreted to mean that research reports should include detailed information about the researcher as a person, especially her or his social identity and biography, and perhaps also epistemological, ontological, political and ethical assumptions. In short, the argument is that the researcher and research process ought to be included within the focus of the research report (see, for example, Stanley and Wise 1983; 2002). However, this will breach the maxim of quantity, and in my view it arises from a confusion about the purpose of research and about how it is to be assessed.[24] In part, it stems from the belief that research can and should be made 'transparent', its whole process of production laid bare. However, this is neither possible nor necessary.

As I made clear earlier, the publication of research findings is only one stage in the communicative process that is at the heart of academic research: after publication, further evidence and information may need to be provided in response to questions or criticism. In other words, the initial judgements of the researcher about what evidence and information were required may prove to be false. And any such misjudgements should be rectified subsequently. There is an obligation on researchers to respond to criticism by, as far as possible, providing the additional evidence and information that is necessary; though, of course, this cannot go on for ever.

(b) The maxim of quality. The maxim of quality amounts to the injunction: do not say or write what you believe to be false, or anything for which you lack adequate evidence. The relevance of this maxim to research is obvious; though it requires qualification so as to allow people to present hypothetical arguments or as-if models. The necessary reformulation of the maxim might read: do not say or write what you believe to be false, or anything for which you lack adequate evidence, without indicating any deficiency in these respects. In other words, offering deficient forms requires explicit justification; moreover, these will not warrant

---

[24]It also creates problems for universalism, one of the norms that Merton (1973a) identified as constitutive of science. See Ziman (2000: 38).

publication on their own, but must be accompanied by other claims that are not deficient in this respect.

While commitment to this maxim is crucial for academic discussion, once again *judgement* is required in applying it: notably in determining what is true and what constitutes adequate evidence. Moreover, such judgement must be formed in the context of the research community: on each occasion it must involve anticipation of the judgements of other members of that community, rather than relying *solely* upon the judgement of the individual researcher.

There is an asymmetrical relationship here. Judgements about the truth or falsity of a knowledge claim must be individual, in the sense that no researcher should put forward as true what he or she personally believes to be false or inadequately supported. However, neither should researchers put forward as true, without qualification, or evidence, knowledge claims which they believe to be true but which they know that a substantial proportion of their colleagues would doubt. In such a situation, lack of consensus must be acknowledged, and evidence in support of the knowledge claim provided, or a source where it can be found supplied. Furthermore, the evidence presented must be such as could reasonably be expected to convince a substantial proportion of the relevant research community, irrespective of their background beliefs. There is no requirement here of an unerring ability to predict the responses of others, simply that a reasonable attempt must be made to do this in any publication. Equally important, as noted in the previous section, there must be a willingness to provide clarification and further evidence in the face of collegial doubt. This is not always present.

Also involved in the maxim of quality is the obligation to make clear exactly what knowledge claims are being made. For instance, they need to be distinguished from the presuppositions of the analysis and from any broader implications that might be drawn from the findings. This requirement may seem obvious, but it is one that is not always met in research reports (see Foster et al. 1996; Hammersley 1998a). Presuppositions can take a variety of forms: there are value assumptions used to establish the relevance of the research focus, and also factual assumptions – descriptive, explanatory, and/or theoretical – about the field to which the focus relates. These presuppositions may be regarded as a matter of commonsense or as well established by previous research; or they may be treated as working assumptions. But their status needs to be made explicit. Much the same is true of implications that could be drawn from the findings, whether these are about the truth or scope of a particular explanatory model or the likely consequences of some policy or practice.

A further requirement of the maxim of quality is that the *character* of the findings be made clear. What I mean by this is that readers need to know whether they are definitions (and, if so, what *kind* of definition, see Robinson 1954), descriptions, explanations, or theories. Furthermore, if the conclusions of the research involve generalisation from the findings about the particular cases studied, as is common, it should be made clear to what population generalisation is being made, and by what means.[25]

Finally, while this maxim requires that nothing be put forward as true which lacks adequate evidence, without this deficiency being indicated, it is also often important

---

[25]For a discussion of these various points, see Hammersley (1998a).

for researchers to indicate the *level* of confidence they have in the validity of their findings, and the reasons for this.[26] There is no need to assume that all findings must be presented with the same level of likely validity. For publication of findings to be justified, it is necessary that they exceed the appropriate threshold of probable validity (see Hammersley 1995: ch. 4); but they can vary in how far above that threshold they reach. And where they stand in relation to that threshold should be made explicit to the audience. This is not a matter of attributing specific probabilities, but rather of indicating the level of certainty in informal terms. Thus, findings must not be presented with great confidence when they are actually still open to reasonable doubt. Equally important, however, those that are believed to be certain should not be put forward in a tentative fashion. Once again, an Aristotelian mean is involved. Presenting claims in an overly modest way can be merely a device for avoiding criticism; and, whatever the motive, the result may be to obstruct their effective assessment.[27]

(c) The maxim of relevance. This, the third of Grice's maxims, what he calls 'the maxim of relation', requires that what is said be relevant to what has previously been said. In the context of conversation, it is relatively easy to understand what this involves: what someone says at each point, whether continuing what they have been saying or responding to what someone else has said, must have an obvious link to what went before, or it must be explicitly introduced as a new topic.[28] In conversation, this link is often left implicit, on the expectation that the hearer will recognise it without difficulty, or sometimes with the intention of forcing the audience to work it out. Indeed, making the link too explicit may be seen as insulting the intelligence of co-participants. However, in the case of academic discussion there is more of an obligation to make the relevance of any contribution explicit, and to rule out any unintended implications.

The issue of relevance arises in various ways within the context of academic contributions, and especially as regards lengthy research reports. First, the relevance of the study to the field needs to be indicated, and perhaps also its wider relevance to important value principles, policy issues, and so on. Secondly, it must be made clear how the material presented is relevant to answering the particular research question that is being addressed. Thirdly, in presenting evidence in support of various claims, just how and why this is relevant to the claim may need to be indicated: in other words, the assumptions on which inference from the evidence to the validity of the claim is based need to be made explicit. Finally, the implications of the findings within the appropriate body of knowledge ought to be spelt out. Most fundamentally, contributors to academic discussion must indicate that, in each context, they have

---

[26]This reflects Locke's formulation of the ethics of belief: see Price (1969: Lecture 6 and *passim*).

[27]In my view, the literature of social science has suffered increasing corruption through the widespread use of modal formulations where what is actually intended is a strong claim to knowledge. To mention just one form of this, authors write 'I would argue that' when they are indeed arguing the point being presented, or often simply assuming that it is true. There is a similar problem with usage of formulations such as 'It appears to be the case that', where the claim goes beyond appearances. While apparently innocent, usage of such formulations obscures the communication of differential confidence in likely validity.

[28]There are, of course, many complexities involved, and Grice declares that he finds these 'exceedingly difficult' (1975: 46). On this issue see Sperber and Wilson (1986).

included all of the information and data that would be relevant, not only those which support the particular claims they are making. One aspect of this is that in interpreting any account, an audience will make assumptions about the background against which the events, actions, etc., that are being described or explained took place, by relying on ideas about 'what is usual in this sort of situation'. Hence, any deviation from what might be thought to be usual needs to be indicated by the researcher.

What we can draw from this maxim, above all, is that research communications must not only relate to what is taken to be the body of knowledge in a field, and provide some news in relation to this, but also make the connection and contribution clear to readers: studies may extend the body of knowledge, fill a gap within it, or throw doubt on some element of it. Similarly, the relevance of each part of what is presented to the other parts must be spelled out.

(d) The maxim of manner. Grice summarises this maxim as: be perspicuous. And he identifies several components, including: avoid obscurity of expression; avoid ambiguity; and be orderly.

As regards obscurity and ambiguity, it is sometimes argued that the writings of social scientists are jargon-ridden and wilfully obscure. There is no doubt some truth in this. However, if the primary audience for academic research is fellow researchers, then what is required is writing that is clear *to them*; and what is clear to them may not be clear to others. Furthermore, as I noted earlier, according to Grice's maxim of quantity, it is important to give only what is sufficient for an audience. To exceed this is actually to reduce the efficiency of communication and perhaps also the clarity of the message. Thus, specialised terms may well need to be employed, as well as names of other writers referred to, even though these are not known outside the field. More than this, what is written will be designed for the kind of reading that academics are expected to do, which is different from that required in many other contexts: the emphasis is on presenting the information required clearly, not on having an entertaining or elegant style. These latter considerations are suppressed, though not entirely eliminated, in line with their degree of importance for the purpose at hand.

So, it is essential that what is said and written needs to be as clear and unambiguous as possible for a research audience.[29] This is a matter not just of guarding against obscurity and ambiguity inadvertently occurring, but also of not using these in order to make one's case appear stronger or more significant than it is. While it is important to defend a mode of presentation that is distinctive to the academic context, and that may not be intelligible to lay people, it ought to be noted that quite a lot of academic writing in the social sciences today breaches this maxim. And sometimes it seems to do this not through negligence, but wilfully. It is designed deliberately to provoke readers, or to tease them. Moreover, with the division of research communities into 'paradigmatic' camps, distinctive modes of language have developed whose function, as much as anything else, is to signal allegiance. These run foul of the requirement that communications should be addressed to all who work in a particular research field, not just to those who share the same philosophical, theoretical, or political commitments.

---

[29]There have been arguments against this, see Lather (1996) and MacLure (2003: ch. 6). See also Law (2004). For a discussion of this issue, see Hammersley (2008a: 140–3).

The part of this maxim relating to orderliness also has some important implications for how research reports should be written, which are perhaps of particular significance for qualitative researchers. In some areas of quantitative research, there is a standard format for presenting findings. However, anthropology texts and much qualitative sociology do not conform to any standard format. This is not a problem in itself, since orderliness does not require standardisation. But it *is* necessary that the essential elements of a research report, outlined earlier, be presented in an order that enables readers to find them easily. And there are dangers, for example, in putting the findings or conclusions at the beginning, in the way that would be done in a newspaper report: this runs the risk of blurring the distinction between these and the assumptions on which the account relies. Nevertheless, the fundamental requirement is that there is a coherent argumentative structure, in which each point leads on to the next, in a way that presents candidate answers to a clearly specified set of questions. Exactly how this is done can be left open.

The various commitments that I have identified in this section mark out a quite distinctive form of communicative interaction, one that is designed to serve the specialised purpose of contributing to a body of knowledge. What must be underlined here is that the establishment and maintenance of an academic context of this kind depends upon those involved operating routinely on the basis of these commitments. In many respects the researcher must act, both in doing the research and in writing the report, as a representative member of the research community; and part of this involves anticipating what questions others would ask and seeking to provide the answers to those questions in the course of the report. In this sense the research report is dialogical in character, even when it is not dialogical in form. And audiences too must act on behalf of the research community, acting on a principle of charity which assumes that what is presented is intended to be clear and convincing. A dialogical orientation is required here too.

Popper is correct to point to the institutional character of this form of communicative interaction; with individual researchers being socialised into the rules, and commitment to them being maintained by sanctions against those who deviate. However, the institution would not survive without individual commitment. In my view, the institutional and individual aspects are reciprocal – each depends upon the other (Haskell 1998: 60). Thus, just as the idea that all falsifiable hypotheses should be treated as equally worth testing undermines the prospect of scientific progress (Rescher 1978), so too would any widespread failure in the commitment of individual researchers to treat discovering the truth as their prime concern.

CONCLUSION

I have argued that collective, dialectical assessment of knowledge claims is essential to the process of academic knowledge production. In this chapter I have sought to spell out the rules or norms that ought to govern discussions within academic research communities. I began by noting that there is considerable agreement about what is required among philosophers with very different orientations. Furthermore, these rules are frequently acknowledged by academics in the course of their discussions, most obviously when complaining about the behaviour of colleagues.

It is important to underline that, from the point of view of the model of academic enquiry I have defended in this book, discussion of the kind specified here plays a central role in the knowledge production process. For one thing, nothing should be treated as established knowledge in a field, or communicated to lay audiences, until it has been subjected to, and survived, collective assessment of this kind. Equally important, anticipation of the reaction of what we might call, paraphrasing George Herbert Mead, the 'generalised academic other' plays a crucial role at all stages of the research process. Researchers must not rely solely on their own judgements about what seems likely to be true, what is reliable evidence, what would be the best way of pursuing their enquiries, and so on; they must also anticipate likely judgements on the part of their colleagues about these matters, adapting their behaviour to take account of these. In an important sense, throughout their work there should be an internal dialogue between themselves and the imagined and actual responses of others to what they are doing. In this way, the relevant research community shapes every aspect of the work of each of its members.

It is worth noting that the form the discussion takes corresponds to some key features of the stereotype of academic discussion which, I suggested, is based to some extent on seventeenth-century criticism of Scholasticism. Thus, it will often be concerned with matters whose relevance to practical concerns is remote, and obscure to lay people. Secondly, discussion will often take a long time to reach a conclusion that is widely accepted, or it will result in the acknowledgement of continuing uncertainty. Moreover, previously established conclusions are sometimes subsequently opened up to doubt again. Thirdly, the orientation of academics engaged in discussion will be concerned entirely with the likely cognitive validity of the arguments put forward, even where these have significant potential practical implications. As a result, viewed from the pragmatic perspectives of other activities, what is said may seem to be irrelevant, wrong-headed, or even outrageous.

What I am suggesting, then, is that there are important respects in which academic discourse properly differs from other kinds. It is not the appropriate form in other circumstances; and, more important still for my purposes here, the kinds of discourse that occur in other situations are not appropriate in an academic context concerned with investigating the validity of knowledge claims. It is a distinctive type of discourse that requires an unusual orientation on the part of the participants. However, it is not *totally* different from what occurs elsewhere. Rather, it involves variation of features that are to be found in all forms of discussion. Moreover, I am not suggesting that this kind of discourse only occurs in academic contexts. It may sometimes occur in other situations. But a distinctive requirement of the academy is that it is, or should be, institutionalised there.

Following on from this, we might ask whether it operates effectively within social scientific communities today. Relying on my own experience, I suggest that to a significant degree it does not. Much more common than a dialectic of the kind outlined above is the 'exchange of opinions', or sometimes just the trading of abuse. This problem is, of course, by no means restricted to social science, but in some parts of that field it is a severe problem (see Hammersley 1995: ch. 4; 2000c). Deviation from the norms may be prompted, of course, by knowledge claims that are regarded as offensive, that are by no means 'merely academic'. In the next chapter I will consider a case in point.

8

ACADEMIC LICENCE AND ITS LIMITS: THE CASE OF HOLOCAUST DENIAL

By academic freedom I understand the right to search for truth and to publish and teach what one holds to be true. This right implies also a duty: one must not conceal any part of what one has recognized to be true. (Albert Einstein, see Calaprice 2000:71)

[…] academic freedom is not an abstract philosophical value with a pedigree in the writings of Mill and other Enlightenment rationalists, but a form of guild protectionism. (Fish 2001a: 522)

In the Introduction, I suggested that some academic licence or freedom is an essential condition for the kind of knowledge production process distinctive to universities. This chapter focuses on the question of whether there are any proper limits to this licence, for example as regards what topics can be discussed and what arguments pursued – and what the nature of, and grounds for, these limits should be. Holocaust denial will be used as a test case to explore these issues.[1]

The concept of academic freedom is by no means a straightforward one. It is sometimes treated as identical with the principle of freedom of expression, whose origins lie, to a large extent, in the liberal political philosophy that emerged in Western Europe during the seventeenth century. This was concerned with placing limits on the authority of the state. Initially, the rationale for liberalism was primarily negative: toleration of a range of beliefs and practices, especially religious ones, was deemed a requirement for civil peace; though this toleration was by no means all

---

[1]The bulk of academic literature on the Holocaust is, of course, historical but there is some social scientific work as well, notably Bettelheim (1960) (see Marcus 1999), Bauman (1989), and Alexander (2009). There is no significant difference between the two sorts of work for my purposes here.

encompassing (see Fish 1994). Later, more positive justifications for freedom of expression arose.

One of these was that freedom of expression, and especially freedom of the press, is an important bulwark against absolutism and corruption in government, these being central preoccupations of eighteenth- and early nineteenth-century radicals. Another influential idea that emerged around the same time was that others' autonomy in coming to their own beliefs must be respected, this being seen as integral to the dignity of a person (see Dworkin 1998). For both these reasons, it came to be argued that other people have a *right* to express their views even if we disagree with them, a principle famously expounded by Voltaire in the eighteenth century. From this perspective, the only proper constraint on expression, as on other actions, is where its exercise interferes with *others'* autonomy. A third justification for freedom of speech is the idea that only if the expression of diverse views is allowed will error or truth be discovered through debate. This became particularly influential in notions of discursive or deliberative democracy (Dryzek 1990; Gutmann and Thompson 1996; Elster 1998).[2]

While these rationales for freedom of expression in the public sphere have influenced modern understandings of academic freedom, it is a mistake to treat the two notions as equivalent.[3] As Russell (1993) points out, the origins of the concept of academic freedom lie in medieval ideas about the proper autonomy of the church from the state, and of universities as relatively independent from the church. He writes: 'from the very beginning of the history of universities in the West, the claim to free intellectual enquiry and to control over their own teaching and degrees has been identified with the claim to the privileges of a self-governing corporation to run its own affairs' (p. 15).

In the Middle Ages, church and state had come to be seen as each having its own domain, in the sense of a range of matters over which it had authority, and in which the other should not interfere. An important component of this on the side of the church was treatment of the priesthood as a vocation concerned with spiritual matters that transcend the mundane issues to do with organising and sustaining human life on earth. There was, of course, a great deal of tension and conflict over the boundaries between the two domains, but the principle of distinct spheres of authority, religious and secular, continued to be recognised, or at least given lip-service, even after the Reformation, when the priesthood's right to interpret the word of God was challenged. Furthermore, the notion of a vocation was extended beyond the priesthood to other occupations, including that of the university academic, these also

---

[2]Many of these arguments are to be found in John Stuart Mill's influential essay 'On Liberty' (Mill 1859; see O'Rourke 2001), but also to one degree or another in earlier sources, such as von Humboldt (1792) and in the work of Kant. For recent discussions of freedom of expression, see Simon (1994), Alexander (2005) and Warburton (2009). Fish (1994) provides a rather different, illuminating and controversial perspective: 'there's no such thing as free speech, and it's a good thing too'.

[3]For discussions of the concept of academic freedom, see Lovejoy (1937), Dewey (1976), Arblaster (1974), Pincoffs (1975), Russell (1993) and Menand (1998). See, especially, the illuminating discussions provided by Haskell (1998) and Dworkin (1998) of the nature of academic freedom and its difference from the principle of free speech.

being viewed as committed to a higher ideal, in this case the production of knowledge and the provision of education.[4] An essential part of this notion of vocation was the idea that the professions should be above financial or political concerns; and, indeed, that they needed to be insulated from these. Another parallel, in the case of universities, is that the medieval church was international in character, with its supreme authority lying in the Vatican. In a similar way, academic researchers claim to be part of international communities that are self-governing, although these are republican rather than monarchical in character.

The origins of the various universities that now exist, even those in Western Europe and North America, are, of course, quite diverse, and this has affected their relationships with other institutions, religious and secular, producing a range of different patterns. Furthermore, even in those countries where the medieval model had been influential, it is possible to detect a major shift, towards the end of the twentieth century, away from recognition of universities as occupying a separate sphere, in which they exercise unique authority, towards regarding them as instruments of the state, the latter now being treated as primarily an economic agency concerned with facilitating industry and trade. Alongside this, they are often viewed increasingly as primarily commercial enterprises, whether privately or publicly owned.[5] This is, of course, part of a broader trend, with similar encroachments being made by the state, and by external commercial enterprises, into the work of other professions.

It is against this background that it is important to recognise the differences between the general principle of freedom of expression and the notion of academic freedom. The latter amounts to a form of occupational licence that has a distinctive function: to facilitate the production of academic knowledge.[6] As such, it has an instrumental purpose – it is not of value in itself in the way that freedom of expression is often taken to be. Moreover, its instrumental character implies that it should only be exercised where, and to the extent that, it facilitates the production of knowledge. So, the licence allowed must be determined according to what is and is not likely to serve this function.

Another part of the context for my discussion here is that, today, there are social scientists who denounce any 'policing' of the boundaries of research. They insist that there should be no constraints on academic licence, dismissing those who argue for boundaries as, to quote one recent example, 'self-appointed, in-house arbiters of excellence' engaging in 'intellectual McCarthyism' (Peim 2009: 236 and 240). In opposing 'tighter border controls', this author suggests that 'space should be left open to what may seem foreign, intrusive and improper in a cosmopolitan spirit of hospitality' (Peim 2009: 247).

---

[4]The role of monasteries and convents in pursuing these activities in medieval society no doubt facilitated this.

[5]This needs to be seen in the context of what Halsey (2003) refers to as 'the adaptation of corporate structures of feudal origin to the economy of modern countries' (p. vii), though there is an undertone of historicism in this phrase that should prompt caution.

[6]Hughes (1958; 1971) argued that those occupations that have come to be labelled professions have been assigned a licence to carry out some specific type of activity, and have successfully claimed a mandate to decide how this can best be done. I am including both of these processes under the heading of 'occupational licence' here.

What is proposed here seems to be in the spirit of Levinasian ethics, and is thus of broader scope even than traditional liberal rationales for freedom of expression, and so it prompts the question of whether there are any limits to academic freedom. It should be clear that Holocaust denial represents a test case for the principles of academic freedom, in this form and others, since most people find it not only false but morally objectionable. Indeed, many argue that it must not be tolerated. For academic researchers the question arises, however, of how they are to reconcile such policing with the idea that it is their responsibility fearlessly to question taken-for-granted assumptions, always to be open to new ideas, and so on. On this basis, should not the arguments of Holocaust deniers be given serious consideration within the relevant academic communities? It is worth noting that Holocaust deniers often claim that the academic community has irrationally set its face against the very possibility that their arguments are true, and for political reasons.

So, the question I want to address in this chapter concerns the proper limits to open-mindedness or toleration in research contexts, and also the issue of what kinds of work should be allowed to claim the title of research in the public sphere. I will begin by outlining the character of Holocaust denial and then look at the arguments that have been employed for and against toleration of it. After that, I will consider the general validity of these arguments and their implications for academic freedom.

WHAT IS HOLOCAUST DENIAL?

The meaning of 'Holocaust denial' varies somewhat across occasions of use. In part, this reflects the fact that applying this term amounts to an attribution of deviance: it labels what is judged unacceptable. Thus, the label is rarely self-applied. Furthermore, in general usage it covers a range of specific factual and evaluative claims, largely negative in character, that by no means necessarily go together.[7] These include the following:

Denial of the factual claim that:

- Some German concentration camps were designed systematically to kill Jews and others, notably by gassing. (Claims that there were gas chambers are sometimes dismissed, or it is argued that the chambers were intended for de-lousing clothing.)
- The number of Jews killed in the camps was several million.
- A very large proportion of deaths in the camps were the product of direct killing.
- Hitler ordered or knew about what was going on in the camps.
- What was done in the camps was, in large part, a product of anti-Semitism.

---

[7]Key examples of Holocaust deniers are Robert Faurisson and David Irving, but there are also more marginal cases, such as revisionist historians who have sought to draw comparisons between the Holocaust and other attempts at genocide and/or to explain it in ways that go beyond the specifics of German history, for instance Andreas Hillgruber and Ernst Nolte. On Faurisson, see Vidal-Naquet (1981; 1992). On Irving, see Guttenplan (2001) and Evans (2002). On Hillgruber and Nolte, see Kampe (1987), Baldwin (1990) and Maier (1998). For comparisons of the Holocaust with other examples of attempted genocide, see Rosenbaum (1996).

Denial of the evaluative claim that:

- Treatment of prisoners in the camps was worse than the conditions for Germans generally at the time. (It is sometimes argued that, especially as the war went on, the standard of living of the German population went down sharply, along with that of those interned in camps.)
- The concentration camps were worse than internment policies carried out by other countries.
- What happened in the camps was worse than the Allies' bombing of German cities.

Typically, then, Holocaust denial involves: a rejection of some of the generally accepted facts about what went on in German concentration and death camps in the 1940s and why; and an explicit or implicit downgrading of any moral evaluation of this, both by pointing out what are taken to be morally equivalent or even worse offences, and by providing justifications or at least pointing to extenuating circumstances that allegedly mitigate what was done.

There is a further feature that is sometimes treated as part of Holocaust denial, especially in relation to the so-called Historians' Debate in Germany (Maier 1998): what is often referred to as 'normalisation'. This involves rejecting the common idea that the Holocaust was a uniquely evil event in history, and that because of this it cannot be understood or explained in the usual terms employed by historians, psychologists, and social scientists; indeed that to attempt to do this is itself unacceptable, because it fails to acknowledge the abnormal character of what happened. Holocaust deniers generally insist that the idea that the Holocaust is distinctive in these ways is simply a political myth that has been promoted to serve the Zionist cause.[8]

RESPONSES TO HOLOCAUST DENIAL

There is variation not just in what is counted as Holocaust denial but also in views about how Holocaust deniers ought to be treated, both within the research community and in the public sphere more generally, ranging from suppression to toleration. Moreover, the grounds appealed to in such debates can differ sharply.

I will look first at the arguments of those who insist that Holocaust denial must *not* be tolerated. A number of reasons have been put forward for this position. First, there are political and ethical arguments about the consequences of allowing Holocaust denial to be voiced. For example, there is the claim that by downplaying the crimes of the National Socialists it facilitates the growth of neo-Nazi movements within Germany

---

[8]There are also commentators who by no means deny the facts of the Holocaust but nevertheless argue that the 'Holocaust industry' has exploited it for commercial and political purposes, see Evron (1983) and Finkelstein (2000). Along the same lines, Bauman argues that: 'The Jewish state tried to employ the tragic memories as the certificate of its political legitimacy, a safe-conduct pass for its past and future policies, and above all as the advance payment for the injustices it might itself commit' (1989: ix).

and elsewhere, movements which are evil and dangerous. Indeed, it is often pointed out that some forms of Holocaust denial are little more than an ideological cover for such movements.[9] In short, the claim is that Holocaust denial is designed to make, or at least will have the effect of making, the world safe for anti-Semitism, and that it denies Jewish people a right to live in the post-Holocaust world (Shermer and Grobman 2002: 16).

The Holocaust denier is also sometimes viewed as a 'paper Eichmann' (Vidal-Naquet 1992), as doing again to Jews, albeit on paper, what Eichmann and the Nazis had done to them, precisely through denying that first offence. In other words, Holocaust denial is seen as a continuation of the attempted genocide of the Jews, an attack on their communal sense of identity, and on their claim to a position in the world. Also relevant here is the distress and suffering caused by Holocaust denial to survivors, and to the families of those who died in the camps.

A rather different argument against toleration of Holocaust deniers, specifically within academic contexts, is that they do not abide by the basic rules to which historians should be committed in handling evidence and arguments, and which are essential to all rational thought. An influential example of this position is that of Lipstadt (1993), though she does not propose complete suppression of Holocaust denial. Her argument is that Holocaust deniers are engaged in a 'purely ideological exercise' in contrast with what is required by 'genuine historiography' (p. 2). She insists that it is important 'to make the critical distinction between a conclusion, however outrageous it may be, that has been reached through reasonable inquiry and the use of standards of evidence, on the one hand, and ideological extremism that rejects anything that contradicts its preset conclusions, on the other' (p. 25). In these terms, Holocaust deniers should not be tolerated, within academic contexts, because they seek to disguise their ideological motives by pretending to be genuine historians engaged in uncovering historical falsehoods.

Lipstadt broadens this argument into a general defence of reason. She describes Holocaust denial as:

> a threat to all who believe that knowledge and memory are among the keystones of our civilisation. Just as the Holocaust was not a tragedy of the Jews but a tragedy of civilization in which the victims were Jews, so too denial of the Holocaust is not a threat just to Jewish history but a threat to all who believe in the ultimate power of reason. It repudiates reasoned discussion the way the Holocaust repudiated civilized values. [...] Like any form of prejudice, it is an irrational animus that cannot be countered with the normal forces of investigation, argument, and debate. [...] Holocaust denial is the apotheosis of irrationalism. (pp. 19–20)

In the course of her discussion, Lipstadt suggests that post-structuralism, postmodernism, and other forms of relativism have paved the way for the successful spread of Holocaust denial. She claims that they have done this by questioning the legitimacy of all claims to truth, rational grounds for belief, etc. She writes:

---

[9]An important element of the case made by the defence in David Irving's civil action against Lipstadt and Penguin books was his associations with such groups: see Guttenplan (2001).

[T]he 'climate' [these sorts of ideas] create is of no less importance than the specific truth they attack. [...] It is a climate that fosters deconstructionist history at its worst. No fact, no event, and no aspect of history has any fixed meaning or content. Any truth can be retold. Any fact can be recast. There is no ultimate historical reality. Holocaust denial is part of this phenomenon. (Lipstadt 1993: 19; quoted in Eaglestone 2001: 7)

According to this, the success of Holocaust denial in recent years is partly a result of the new intellectual climate in which 'much of history seems to be up for grabs and attacks on the Western rationalist tradition have become commonplace' (p. 17). Here Lipstadt cites the work of Nelson Goodman, Richard Rorty, and Stanley Fish. She notes that while their work has its virtues, it also:

fostered an atmosphere in which it became harder to say that an idea was beyond the pale of rational thought [...] it created an atmosphere of permissiveness toward questioning the meaning of historical events and made it hard for its proponents to assert that there was anything 'off limits' for this sceptical approach. The legacy of this kind of thinking was evident when students had to confront the issue. Far too many of them found it impossible to recognize Holocaust denial as a movement with no scholarly, intellectual, or rational validity. A sentiment had been generated in society – not just on campus – that made it difficult to say: 'This has nothing to do with ideas. This is bigotry.' (p. 18)

Lipstadt is not alone in the belief that 'postmodernist' ideas paved the way for Holocaust denial, or that they make challenging it more difficult.[10] However, there are also those who denounce Holocaust denial specifically on the basis of postmodernist ideas. Thus, Eaglestone argues that Lipstadt's criticism of postmodernism reflects a misunderstanding of its nature. Indeed, he insists that, in fact, it represents an even stronger bulwark against Holocaust denial than does Lipstadt's rationalism (Eaglestone 2001; 2004).[11]

Eaglestone argues that Holocaust denial has grown in influence precisely because it has been able to disguise itself as 'objective historical work', and therefore as rationally authoritative. By contrast, he claims that postmodernism's questioning of the very possibility of objectivity provides a much better basis for denouncing Holocaust denial. This is because it demands that the value framework within which any historical work is carried out be made explicit. Yet Holocaust denial fails to do this; and

[10]See Evans (1997: ch. 8). Shermer and Grobman (2002: 27) argue that changes in ideas about historical scholarship have encouraged Holocaust denial: that the relativism that flourished in the US historical community between the wars, and which was revived in the second half of the twentieth century as a result of trends from literary studies, provides 'a seedbed for pseudo-history and Holocaust denial'. At the same time, they see these changes as broadly progressive, despite involving some 'paradoxes', and they regard the Holocaust deniers as distorting these theoretical and methodological ideas as much as they do the facts about the Holocaust.

[11]For a more sophisticated version of this argument, see Fish (2001a). For a sympathetic but critical discussion of postmodernism in the context of historiography, see Thompson (2004). See also Jenkins (1997).

it also fails to observe those procedures for handling argument and evidence that are currently institutionalised within the community of historians. In other words, Holocaust deniers operate in what is, in terms of those procedures, an unreasonable manner. So, 'Holocaust denial isn't bad history: it isn't any sort of history at all, and simply can't be discussed as if it is' (Eaglestone 2001: 57).[12]

The difference between Lipstadt and Eaglestone here is that, whereas the former treats the procedures employed by historians as largely fixed and as of transcendent value, reflecting the character of Reason, for Eaglestone their validity cannot lie beyond their (current) institutionalisation in the community of historians. Nevertheless, for him this provides a sound enough basis for dismissing the claim of Holocaust deniers to be historians.[13] Moreover, he argues that the latter must be judged not just in this way, but also according to a more existential notion of truth that reflects our values as human beings (Eaglestone 2004). In much the same spirit Wyschogrod (1998: xi) writes:

> What is it that must precede the conveying of history? Must there not be the declaration of a double passion, an eros for the past and an ardor for the others in whose name there is a felt urgency to speak? To convey that-which-was in the light of this passion is to become a historian. Because the past is irrecoverable and the others in whose stead the historian speaks are dead, unknowable, she cannot hope that her passion will be reciprocated. To be a historian then is to accept the destiny of the spurned lover – to write, photograph, film, televise, archive, and simulate the past not merely as its memory bank but as binding oneself by a promise to the dead to tell the truth about the past.

Eaglestone draws on the work of a variety of French 'postmodernist' writers in presenting his case. However, the most important reference in *Postmodernism and Holocaust Denial* is to Lyotard's book *The Differend* (1988).[14] In this, Lyotard begins from Faurisson's argument (as presented by Vidal-Naquet 1992) that only those who died in the gas chambers could be credible witnesses to the existence and purpose of those gas chambers, and that since there can be no such witnesses it must be concluded that there were no gas chambers designed to exterminate the Jews, or at least that we cannot know whether there were any. Rather than treating this as a fallacious piece of reasoning, or even as relying on a false methodological standard, Lyotard uses it to address the issue of what he calls 'differends': situations in which a claim about

---

[12]For an argument along similar lines, see Fish (2001a: 503–5 and *passim*).

[13]There are questions, however, about how far Eaglestone's position in this respect reflects that of those writers he identifies as postmodernist. Evans' (1997: 102) commentary on postmodernist arguments in historiography results in the following judgement: 'Whatever useful opportunities this line of thinking offers history as a discipline, there is no doubting the hostile intent towards traditional norms of historical judgment on the part of many of those who have developed it.'

[14]See also Lyotard 1986, and Jenkins' (2003) assessment of the implications of Lyotard's work for historiography. Sedgewick and Tanesini (1995) provide a brief, clear and accurate account of Lyotard's theory of phrases on which the notion of the differend relies. They also subject his position to cogent criticism. See also Bennington (1988).

injustice cannot be expressed because it is impossible to 'phrase' it within the dominant discourse or language game.

Lyotard is opposed, in principle, to any attempt, on the part of historians or others, to seek to resolve a dispute of the kind generated by Holocaust denial through appealing to reason – in the sense of fixed, universally applicable principles. He argues that employing such principles can only be an imposition, by one side on the other. Instead, we must simply recognise that there is an injustice, that the victims are silenced, are prevented by the discursive regime in operation from voicing their experience. Indeed, for Lyotard the unrepresentable persists within *any* representation. He insists that there must be critical sensitivity to the violence inscribed in the heterogeneous genres through which knowledge is determined.

Lyotard is particularly concerned, then, with the way in which Holocaust denial suppresses the voices of those killed in the camps, and of survivors. But he does not see historical scholarship as a remedy for this: the Holocaust is a wrong that cannot be expressed within that genre. It should be noted, though, that applying this approach to the dispute between Holocaust deniers and their critics among historians and other academic scholars implies that there is an incommensurability between the two positions: that they employ different genres or phrase universes, and that the terms of one position cannot be translated into the other. Both sides employ distinctive linguistic regimes, ones which differentially upgrade and downgrade various kinds of evidence, give voice to and silence various types of speaker, and so on. And this seems to have the effect of rendering historical scholarship and Holocaust denial equivalent in epistemic status. As a result, his argument could be used to suggest that Holocaust deniers are being unjustifiably silenced by the discourse of the historians who denounce them, especially those who (like Lipstadt) seek to place them outside the boundaries of reason.

Contrary to Eaglestone's presentation, then, Lyotard's position could be used to recommend toleration of Holocaust denial. Equally there are also those who argue explicitly for toleration on the basis of the value of reason. The best known example is Noam Chomsky. He has not simply advocated tolerance of Holocaust denial but also signed a petition demanding that freedom of speech be maintained for one Holocaust denier: Faurisson. Furthermore, a piece he wrote on the civil libertarian aspects of the Faurisson affair appeared as a preface to a book by this author when it was published by a French far-Left group.[15]

Chomsky argues that the quality of Faurisson's work is irrelevant to the issue of his freedom of speech (Chomsky 1981a: 231). He points out that Faurisson's conclusions are diametrically opposed to his own views, but he continues as follows: 'it is elementary that freedom of expression (including academic freedom) is not to be restricted to views of which one approves, and that it is precisely in the case of views that are almost universally despised and condemned that this right must be most vigorously defended' (p. 231). Furthermore, he argues that the reaction to his own support for Faurisson displays a failure to distinguish between 'defense of the right

---

[15]Though, when he discovered that it was to be used for this purpose, he tried to stop it. For a rather negative evaluation of Chomsky in this context, see Rubinstein (1981). See also Finkelkraut (1998: 134 Note 15).

of free expression and defense of the views expressed' (p. 232). And he notes that he has been consistent on this principle:

> At the height of the Vietnam War, I publicly took the stand that people I regard as authentic war criminals should not be denied the right to teach on political or ideological grounds and I have always taken the same stand with regard to scientists who 'prove' that blacks are genetically inferior, in a country where their history is hardly pleasant, and where such views will be used by racists and neo-Nazis. (pp. 232–3)

Chomsky concludes:

> one may ask if the proper response to publication of material that may be used to enhance racist violence and oppression is to deny civil rights. Or is it, rather, to seek the causes of these vicious developments and work to eliminate them? To a person who upholds the basic ideas professed in the Western democracies, or who is seriously concerned with the real evils that confront us, the answer seems clear. (pp. 233–4)

He argues that it is:

> something of a scandal that it is even necessary to debate these issues two centuries after Voltaire defended the right of free expression for views he detested. It is a poor service to the memory of the victims of the Holocaust to adopt a central doctrine of their murderers. (p. 234)

Above all, Chomsky sees the defence of free speech as necessary to avoid the situation where 'the state will determine what is "true", depriving those who "lie" by its lights the right to do so' (1981b: 12).

It is clear from this outline of responses to Holocaust denial that they generate conflicting arguments and raise some fundamental questions about the proper nature and scope of toleration, both within the academic community and beyond.

HOLOCAUST DENIAL AND ACADEMIC FREEDOM

Many of the commentators quoted in the previous section do not draw any sharp distinction between the attitude appropriate towards Holocaust denial in academic contexts and that required in the public sphere. However, my focus here is specifically on academic freedom. I will be concerned with whether Holocaust denial should be tolerated in academic research communities, and if not why not (see McKinnon 2006, Chapter 10).

A first point to make is that, in terms of the account of academic enquiry I have presented in this book, the argument that the views of Holocaust deniers should be dismissed or suppressed because of their political implications or anticipated consequences is ruled out at the start. The fact that discussing their views may fuel neo-Nazi movements, or that they are offensive or disrespectful to Holocaust survivors or their families, is not relevant in this context. Such dangers have to be tolerated, unless they are extremely severe.[16] Instead, the academic focus must be entirely on whether or not the claims made by Holocaust deniers are likely to be true.

Earlier, when outlining those claims, I distinguished between factual and evaluative ones, and separated both of these from the argument that the Holocaust is a normal, not an abnormal, event. These issues will need to be approached differently.

FACTUAL CLAIMS

There is no doubt that the core elements of Holocaust denial are believed to be false by almost all historians and social scientists, and for good reasons. As Shermer and Grobman (2002), and others, argue: the convergence of evidence to the conclusion that there was a systematic attempt to eliminate large numbers of Jews and others through gassing, and by other means, and that this was sanctioned if not organised from the very top of the Nazi state, is overwhelming. It is true that the numbers killed seem likely to be lower than some of the highest estimates, but they still run into millions. Moreover, while the reasons why the policy was instituted, and how it was implemented, are complex, the broad character of what was done, how and why, consists of facts that are not doubted by most researchers within the relevant academic communities.

But to say that these factual claims about the Holocaust are not currently doubted by most historians and social scientists, and that they have good reasons for believing what they do, is *not* to say that any questioning of this conventional wisdom should be ignored or suppressed. Does not the academic commitment to openness require that any doubts about the validity of this knowledge be taken seriously? After all, we know that most of what is currently treated as knowledge will turn out to be false in the future, in at least some respects. Moreover, as I argued in Chapter 5, academic enquiry should err on the side of avoiding false positives. For these reasons, academic researchers must not seek to protect what is currently regarded as established knowledge from all criticism.

While this is true, I will argue that there is no obligation on the part of academic researchers to treat as serious, or accept as legitimate, all doubts, all questioning of established knowledge.[17] After all, while much of what we believe may be false in some respects, we also know that most of what is currently regarded as false will still be viewed that way in the future. And to take seriously *all* criticisms of what is currently treated as true would undercut any possibility of progress in developing knowledge.

---

[16]In other words, there may be circumstances where, for some greater good, academic freedom should be suspended in some respect. However, on the basis of the sort of liberal political philosophy that underpins both the principle of free speech and that of academic freedom, these occasions must be *very* exceptional, and should not involve a permanent ban on any topic.

[17]This is one aspect of Kendall's (1960) critique of Popper's commitment to openness.

If academic researchers were to be continually questioning *all* their assumptions about what is currently known – and especially if they were to seek to avoid relying upon *any* taken-for-granted assumptions – then they could never hope to develop a body of knowledge. This is because there is *always* scope for raising doubts, given that the validity of no empirical claim can be *demonstrated* in the way that the formal validity of deductive inferences can be, or in the manner that some mathematical theorems can be proved. So, judgements always have to be made about how *significant* potential doubts are; and, if they are no more serious than those relating to many other assumptions on which we routinely rely in the relevant field and elsewhere, then researchers will rightly dismiss them. In line with this, those who continue to raise questions about such matters will legitimately be ignored, at the very least, unless they can provide new and compelling reasons for taking their doubts seriously. What this means is that, once conclusions have been accepted as established knowledge within a discipline, a strong case must be made for opening them up to doubt again; and this case must be such as to persuade a majority of researchers in the field, not just those who, for one reason or another, might have motives for doubting them.

On these grounds alone, it might be argued that there is sufficient justification for academic researchers to ignore or reject the main factual claims of Holocaust deniers, since they do not provide strong evidence for suspending belief in what are taken to be well-known facts. Of course, responding to doubts about what is currently treated as established knowledge is not an all-or-nothing matter: there is a spectrum of possible reactions, relating to the various sorts of decision that members of academic research communities make, for example in organising and speaking at conferences, in editing and refereeing journals and books, recruitment to departments, and so on. At one end of the spectrum, expressions of doubt could be taken very seriously, being treated as representing a position that deserves attention. Moving along the spectrum, doubters could be given opportunities to express their views but without according these much significance. Or, shifting towards greater intolerance, they may, for instance, be denied space on conference platforms or in journals, on the grounds that they have nothing worthwhile to offer. Finally, there could be active suppression of their views, preventing the arguments being made, because these are interfering with the process of knowledge production.

Lipstadt adopts a sophisticated position on this issue, which may derive from the distinction between freedom of expression in the public sphere and academic freedom. She argues that:

> The deniers have the absolute right to stand on any street corner and spread their calumnies. They have the right to publish their articles and books and hold their gatherings. But free speech does not guarantee them the right to be treated as the 'other' side of a legitimate debate. (1993: 17)

So, while she does not believe that Holocaust denial should be banned, she refuses to share a platform with its exponents, on the grounds that to do so is to 'give them a legitimacy and stature that they in no way deserve. It would elevate their antisemitic ideology [...] to the level of responsible historiography' (p. 1).

Generally speaking, Holocaust denial has been ignored or suppressed in academic contexts, but it has been subjected to detailed challenge by academics in the public sphere (see, for example, Lipstadt 1993; Shermer and Grobman 2002; Evans 2002). The latter can be seen, at least in part, as a response to another offence that Holocaust deniers commit: besides doubting what is established knowledge without good reason, they put their own claims forward in the public realm as the products of scholarly enquiry when most other members of the relevant academic communities believe those claims to be false. In doing this, it can be argued, they misuse the authority of academic research, in an attempt to get their views publicity.

There is, however, a third, even more important, charge made against Holocaust deniers: that they engage in sham reasoning (Haack 1998). In other words, their aim is not to discover the truth but rather to defend a view to which they are already committed, for political or other reasons. At best, they act like lawyers who are seeking to win a case by presenting whatever evidence they can in support of it. At worst, they are propagandists who are willing to invent evidence and to deny truths in order to persuade audiences to accept their message (Lipstadt 1993; Evans 2002).

Where the first offence – challenging existing knowledge without good reason – opened up Holocaust deniers to the charge of being poor historians or social scientists, this third accusation implies that they are *fake* scholars, pretending to pursue academic research when they are actually engaged in a quite different task. What lies behind this charge is identification of a pattern of systematic error in judgement and inference on the part of Holocaust deniers that is directed towards a particular conclusion. For instance, they are accused of rejecting witness accounts on the general grounds that such evidence is weak, but then using this sort of testimony themselves where it seems to be favourable to their own position. They also often fail to distinguish between there being no proof of a claim and its being false, again where doing so supports the conclusion they wish to reach. Worse still, they quote selectively from the evidence, and over- or mis-interpret it, to serve their purposes. Shermer and Grobman (2002: 34) accuse Holocaust deniers of conveniently disregarding 'any convergence of evidence; instead they pick out what suits their theory and ignore the rest. They divorce their chosen details from the overall context.' At base, the argument is that they selectively apply methodological judgements about evidence (see Lipstadt 1993; Evans 2002).

We need to remember, of course, that the label of sham reasoning is not self-applying. Indeed, there is sometimes room for reasonable disagreement about whether or not the charge is justified. Part of the problem here is that conclusions are always underdetermined by evidence, that we cannot logically induce them from the data; so researchers must make judgements that are always potentially contestable, about what are and are not reasonable inferences. Moreover, sham reasoners often disguise their practice in various ways: adding qualifications which are later silently dropped, recognising counter views at one point but ignoring them at others, and so on. Lipstadt notes that:

In order to maintain their facade as a group whose only objective is the pursuit of truth, the deniers have filled their publications with articles that ostensibly have nothing to do with World War II but are designed to demonstrate that theirs is a global effort to attack and revise historical falsehoods. Articles on the Civil War, World War I, and Pearl Harbor are included in their journals as a means of illustrating how establishment historians, with ulterior political motives, have repeatedly put forward distorted views of history. The deniers aim to undermine readers' faith in 'orthodox' historians' commitment to transmitting the truth. They argue that this tactic of distortion by 'court historians' for political means reached its zenith in the Holocaust 'myth'. (p. 21)

In Chapter 7, I argued that it is a requirement of academic discussion that we do not immediately assume that those who disagree with us are not committed to a proper academic orientation. And, of course, we are always likely to suspect sham reasoning when people continue to resist what we regard as convincing arguments and put forward claims that we regard as patently false, so it is important to remember that we could be mistaken about what others are doing. This is an essential caution, but it does not mean that we cannot, and should not, sometimes come to the conclusion, over time, that sham reasoning is taking place. And while judgement is always involved, this does not mean that any conclusion about this matter is as good as any other. Moreover, as with decisions about the likely validity of arguments and evidence, the charge of sham reasoning must be a collective assessment made within a research community. In other words, what is crucial is the view that most members of that community reach about whether or not sham reasoning has taken place. It is not that this determines the truth of the charge, but rather that – so long as the academic research community is in good order – this is the best means of coming to some conclusion about its likely validity. And the general view about Holocaust denial among historians and social scientists is that it relies upon sham reasoning.[18]

There are a couple of additional points that need to be made here. One is that the sorts of errors that are signs of sham reasoning are by no means restricted to Holocaust deniers: they are probably to be found in the work of many historians and social scientists. Who is engaging in sham reasoning, and who should be excluded from the academic community on these grounds, is therefore always a contested matter. Indeed, Holocaust deniers frequently accuse historians who criticise their work as themselves engaging in sham reasoning. Furthermore, it seems likely that, in practice, decisions about this matter are often influenced by practical values – in this case, an understandable disgust at what is being argued – even though they should not be.

The second point is that the argument about sham reasoning involves drawing a sharp line between academic enquiry, on the one hand, and 'the purely ideological exercise' in which Holocaust deniers are engaged (Lipstadt 1993: 2), on the other. Yet, as Lipstadt and others point out, some of the methodological ideas that are currently influential in many areas of the social sciences and the humanities threaten this distinction. There are historians and many social scientists who overtly question the possibility of even approximating true knowledge of the social world. They argue that there are necessarily different perspectives, even different realities, which must be

---

[18]For a discussion of other examples within the study of history where sham reasoning has been identified, see Evans (1997: ch. 4).

regarded as true in their own terms. Furthermore, many insist that research is inevitably partisan, in the sense that it cannot avoid being committed to, or serving, some set of practical values or interests.[19] If we accept these arguments, then Holocaust denial cannot be rejected on the grounds that it is not properly committed to pursuit of the truth, nor on the basis that it involves an unwarranted questioning of what is taken to be well-established knowledge. It could only be rejected through evaluating the goals that Holocaust deniers are pursuing and/or the anticipated consequences of their work.

However, I have argued that such evaluations are outside the legitimate scope of academic enquiry and should not be grounds for intolerance in that context. Moreover, there is probably much less agreement about value issues among people generally than there is about factual issues within many academic communities, so that the grounds for suppressing Holocaust denial in these terms may be very weak. Evidence for this is the fact that, as we saw in reviewing responses to Holocaust denial earlier in this chapter, there is considerable disagreement among its opponents about whether or not it should be suppressed in the public sphere. And there are conflicting public attitudes towards the German law that proscribes it. In addition, on the basis of the sceptical and relativist arguments that are now so influential among social scientists, and some historians, it is hard to see what kind of ethical judgement could gain general acceptance. As Gillian Rose has commented: 'no one seems to have considered what philosophical resources remain for an ethics when so much of the live tradition is disqualified and deadened' (1996: 1).

As we saw, Eaglestone (2000; 2004) seeks to counter these arguments by two means. First, like Lipstadt and others he rejects Holocaust denial on the grounds that its proponents do not follow the ground rules of traditional historical scholarship, though what is distinctive about his position is that he treats this scholarship as a language game or genre that is self-constituting, rather than being justified in terms of its capacity to discover the truth about past events. Secondly, he appeals to a deeper notion of truth, different from the one that is built into historical scholarship: what he refers to, drawing on Heidegger and Levinas in particular, as existential truth (2004: 142).

Neither of these arguments is convincing. In the case of the first, without some specification of a goal to which the language game or genre of historical scholarship is directed, it is hard to see how it can have any point. There is also no source of justification for why the rules are as they are, why they cannot be changed or be subject to arbitrary challenge. Indeed, as Sedgewick and Tanesini (1995) show, even Lyotard, on whose work Eaglestone is relying here, does not manage to escape dependence upon a moderate form of essentialism, according to which our distinctions can capture differences that exist in the world independently of our making them – in this case differences between types of activity. These authors argue that, in itself, Lyotard's theory of phrase regimes and genres provides no basis for distinguishing between 'playing a game "badly" and playing another game' (Sedgewick and Tanesini 1995: 272). In effect, in making this first argument Eaglestone is simply

---

[19]See, for example, the sorts of position taken in White (1966), Root (1993), Munslow (1998), Jenkins (2003); Eaglestone (2004), Munslow and Rosenstone (2004) and Denzin and Lincoln (2005).

trading on the reader's likely assumption that historical work is directed towards providing answers to questions about the past that correspond to the facts, even though he declines to accept this assumption himself.[20]

The second argument – about 'existential truth' – is problematic because it opens up a field in which there is endless scope for rival claims about what is true, on the grounds that particular claims are 'true for us', 'resonate with our experience', etc., not least because there will be differences over who 'we' are. Indeed, it is hard to see why Holocaust deniers could not themselves use this concept of truth. The danger is illustrated by an example cited by Finkelstein (2000: 61). In 1995, Binjamin Wilkomirski (legal name Bruno Dössekker, born Bruno Grosjean) published what purported to be an autobiographical account of his life as a child in two concentration camps, but which was later shown to be a fraud. Finkelstein quotes Israel Gutman, a former inmate of Auschwitz, and a Holocaust lecturer at Hebrew University, to the effect that it is 'not that important' whether this account is genuine, that 'Wilkomirski has written a story which he has experienced deeply; that's for sure. [...] He is not a fake. He is someone who lives this story very deeply in his soul. The pain is authentic.' Finkelstein comments, with incredulity, 'So it doesn't matter whether he spent the war in a concentration camp or a Swiss chalet; Wilkomirski is not a fake if his "pain is authentic"?' The key point is that determining what is and is not 'authentic' pain, and what are 'authentic' expressions of it, are not factual but rather evaluative matters. Calling such evaluations true – rather than applying adjectives such as 'just' or 'convincing' – obscures the fact that what are involved are judgements in terms of practical rather than epistemic values, and ignores the need to retain a distinction between the two (Habermas 2003).

EVALUATIVE CLAIMS

On most judgements, what happened in German concentration and death camps would be ranked among examples of the most inhumane treatment of fellow human beings in history. However, making such judgements, and assessing how these crimes compare with others, is a practical not an epistemic or theoretical matter: and, on the view adopted in this book, it cannot be dealt with effectively or legitimately entirely on the basis of academic enquiry; even though the latter can provide factual information and conceptual clarification that would assist such judgements. This is not to imply that practical value judgements are necessarily irrational or unimportant – they are neither.[21] However, different conclusions will often be reached depending upon

---

[20]There is a similar problem with Fish's (2001a: 512) argument: despite his efforts to avoid appealing to general principles of reasoning, in effect he nevertheless accuses Holocaust deniers of engaging in pseudo-enquiry.

[21]That they are necessarily irrational is sometimes taken to be central to Max Weber's doctrine of value-neutrality. However, his views on this issue were complex. He believed that there are fundamental value commitments that are necessarily irrational, but that we can nevertheless assess the rationality of particular value judgements, for example according to whether they follow coherently from the commitment claimed (see Bruun 1972; Ciaffa 1998). Here, Weber is adopting

the value framework employed; and, while there can be rational argument about which evaluative frameworks are more and less appropriate for which purpose, there is almost always room for considerable disagreement about this, both reasonable and unreasonable. Moreover, there is no reason to believe that rational discussion about these matters would result in convergence to a single answer, even in the very long run (see Chapter 3).[22]

Above all, my point here is that academic enquiry has no distinctive authority in these matters. Given this, the evaluative claims of Holocaust deniers should be ignored by academic researchers. Indeed, putting forward evaluative claims is, in my view, itself at odds with any claim they make for the academic status of their work. At the same time, it must be noted that a great many genuine historians and social scientists also present evaluative conclusions as part of their work (see Evans 1997: ch. 2), and this raises problems for any dismissal of Holocaust denial on these grounds.

THE ISSUE OF NORMALISATION

The final component of Holocaust denial, one that is also central to the work of revisionist historians, rejects the often-made claim that the Holocaust is unique in history, in the sense that its intrinsically evil character transcends normality, implying that it should be treated in a fundamentally different way from other events. A number of features are often identified as making the Holocaust unique: that it occurred in the heart of Europe, in a country renowned for its cultural achievements; that it was a systematic attempt to exterminate a whole people; the sheer scale of the enterprise; and its industrialised character.

In the literature, very different attitudes are taken towards what uniqueness means. For some it means that the Holocaust represents a distinctive *combination* of features, and perhaps also one that thereby carries important implications for historical and sociological understanding. This is the position adopted by Bauman (1989: ch. 4), for example, who argues that it challenges mainstream sociological understanding of modern society. Along the same lines, others present the Holocaust as a watershed or turning point in history. There are those, however, who view its character in a more radical way, for example as a 'break with civilisation' (Diner 1990: 143). More generally, Aschheim paraphrases Friedländer as arguing that: 'the singularity of the event lay in its fundamentally transgressive and taboo-breaking nature, in the fact that those who embarked upon and implemented this project went beyond all thinkable limits',

---

a kind of foundationalism; and, in my view, as in other cases this needs to be replaced by the notion of a network of beliefs, in which some are more central and others more peripheral, but with this status varying with context, and over time. Moreover, 'rational' is a matter of plausible reasoning, not of logical or empirical demonstration.

[22]One of the reasons for this is that there are several dimensions to the framework underlying any evaluation: the object being evaluated (for example, are we evaluating actions, the agents involved, intentions, or outcomes?); the standard in terms of which some object is being judged (is this justice, responsibility, well-being, honour, or what?); and the benchmark employed (the highest standard, relative to some comparative case, a minimal threshold?).

that the perpetrators engaged in 'radically transgressive, morality-defying behavior' (Aschheim 1996: 15–16). Others argue that the Holocaust can only be understood in theological terms, for example as a 'tremendum' which signals the mystery of the overwhelming power of radical evil, whose irruption produces a caesura in history (Cohen 1981). This comes close to treating the uniqueness of the Holocaust as implying inexplicability (see, for example, Wiesel 1985) – as beyond what is understandable by any form of enquiry and beyond any form of representation. In these terms, Cohen (1981: 1) refers to it as 'unthinkable but not unfelt'. As Rose (1996: 43) notes, for some the Holocaust amounts to a 'breakdown in divine and/or human history [that] de-legitimises names and narratives as such, and hence all aesthetic or apprehensive representation'.[23]

For those holding the more radical of these views, analysing the Holocaust in the normal terms employed by historians and social scientists is inappropriate, to put it mildly. For example, Cohen suggests that: 'There is something in the nature of thought – its patient deliberateness and care for logical order – that is alien to the enormity of the death camps. The death camps are a reality which, by their very nature, obliterate thought and the humane program of thinking' (1981: 1). And sometimes this argument is presented in terms of an ethical imperative to bear witness to the experience of those killed in the camps and of those who survived, that experience being regarded as in an important sense inexpressible, at least via the usual modes of scholarly research (see Lyotard 1988; Eaglestone 2004; Jenkins 2004).

This argument leads to rejection of the 'normalising', 'historicising' or 'relativising' effect of applying an academic approach to the Holocaust. For example, Friedländer argues that 'systematic historical research, which uncovers the facts in their most precise and most meticulous interconnection, also protects us from the past, thanks to the inevitable paralysis of language. This is the exorcism and the involuntary evasion to which we are all subject' (1993: 89). He claims that the way in which language is often used in historical texts about the Holocaust:

> neutralizes the whole discussion and suddenly places each one of us, before we have had time to take hold of ourselves, in a situation not unrelated to the detached position of an administrator of extermination: interest is fixed on an administrative process, an activity of building and transportation, words used for record-keeping. And that's all. (p. 91)

The argument here is that in writing about the Holocaust we inevitably take a stand towards it, even when we use the apparently neutral modes of representation characteristic of historical writing; *indeed that these modes of writing imply an inauthentic attitude, analogous to that of the perpetrators*. This reflects the fact that it is 'a boundary experience of the historical as such' (Rüsen 1997: 119).

This kind of argument is sometimes taken to imply a challenge to academic historiography more generally, not just that dealing with the Holocaust; to the extent that this is conceived as exclusively or primarily concerned with description and

---

[23]There is a link here with the category of the sublime, see the discussion in Braiterman (2000).

explanation, abjuring or downplaying evaluation.[24] For example, Rüsen (1997: 116) writes:

> The Holocaust calls into radical question the very character of what is historical. It cannot be incorporated within the representational confines of a usual research object for historical inquiry. Rather, in recoil, it exerts a meta-historical impact on the very way in which the methods and categories are constituted.

For some, what this implies is a rejection of history and social science, conceived as empirical investigations into factual matters, in favour of an approach that is explicitly evaluative, whether labelled as a form of social enquiry or as a kind of philosophy. An example can be found in Leo Strauss's challenge to Weber's principle of value neutrality. He writes:

> The prohibition against value judgments in social science would lead to the consequence that we are permitted to give a strictly factual description of the overt acts that can be observed in concentration camps and perhaps an equally factual analysis of the motivation of the actors concerned: we would not be permitted to speak of cruelty. Every reader of such a description who is not completely stupid would, of course, see that the actions described are cruel. The factual description would, in truth, be a bitter satire. What claimed to be a straightforward report would be an unusually circumlocutory report. The writer would deliberately suppress his better knowledge, or, to use Weber's favorite term, he would commit an act of intellectual dishonesty. (Strauss 1953: 52)

For Strauss, this signals the impossibility, or perhaps the fraudulence, of social science in its predominant forms.

Much more recently, this argument about the broader significance of the Holocaust for the disciplines of history and social science has been taken up by those writing under the banner of postmodernism (see Evans 1997: ch. 1). For example, appealing to Levinas, Eaglestone (2004: 157) writes: 'History which aims at truth as correspondence destroys others as lives, and reincarnates them as things, as historical events.' Moreover, while this writer seems to leave open some space for conventional kinds of historical work, other commentators mount a more fundamental challenge. Drawing on the work of Lyotard (see Drolet 1994: 263–4), Jenkins claims:

> what is to be registered is not what can be empirically demonstrated/proven, but that the Holocaust/Auschwitz *are the names of a silence*. And that this silence/silencing cannot be adequately dealt with by phrases of a cognitive kind. That is, that if one is to respect the annihilation of the Jews (and those 'others' silenced with them) then one must respect that silence. No amount of empirical detail, no amount of new 'evidence' or old evidence newly raked-over, no witness or testimony can ever represent the lost screams of the victims.

---

[24]Friedländer (1992: 4–5; 1993: 92) does not seem to generalise the argument in this way.

One can only register the final silence by letting it speak 'for itself'; it is not possible to ever fill in the detail – ever to challenge effectively at the empirical level a revisionist like Faurisson – over the death camps. And it is, therefore, the memory of that silence – a silence that we cannot ever fully 'know' – that ensures that, although this 'event' is something that we cannot ever fully remember, we cannot ever fully forget it either. It is, through its problematical, unresolvable silence, an *immemorial* event. [...]

Thus, to respect the impossibility of ever 'coming to terms with' or 'understanding' the silencing of the Holocaust's victims – to keep its possible meanings interminably open – we need a remembrance testifying to that silencing precisely by *not* 'representing' it. It is the *historian's* ethical responsibility to ensure that the Holocaust/Auschwitz forever haunts us. Consequently, for Lyotard, how this 'event' is treated gives weight to his suggestion that actually *all* events are 'immemorial'. That 'the past', both in general and in particular, can never be fully known; that no amount of empirical work can ever entail its definitive significance; that there is no entailment between cognitive and speculative/prescriptive phrase regimes or genres and that this is an excellent thing. Consequently, for Lyotard, the Holocaust/Auschwitz is *a sign of history*, a sign of the limits of the empirical/cognitive genre; the limits of any history suffering from the delusion that it is an epistemology. (2004: 3–4)

Of course, these arguments about normalisation, and the wider challenges to historiography and social science, have not gone unchallenged. The problem is one with which many historians have struggled (see Friedländer 1992; Baldwin 1990). Bauer, for example, while insisting that historians cannot and should not seek to avoid taking a value stance towards the Holocaust, insists that it must not be treated as inexplicable, not least because understanding it is essential if we are to prevent it happening again (Bauer 2001: ch. 2). From a rather different perspective, Rose has dismissed what she refers to as 'Holocaust piety' in favour of 'Holocaust ethnography' (Rose 1996: 41–3 and *passim*). She views the sacralisation of the Holocaust (Novick 1999) as reflecting a major, and undesirable, philosophical shift, of which postmodernism is an instance:

Athens, the city of rational politics, has been abandoned: she is said to have proven that enlightenment is domination. Her former inhabitants have set off on a pilgrimage to the New Jerusalem, the imaginary community, where they seek to dedicate themselves to difference, to otherness, to love – to a new ethics, which overcomes the fusion of knowledge and power in the old Athens. (p. 21)

She regards this move as futile and misguided. She claims that: 'New Jerusalem, the new ethics, has been developed from a dangerously distorted and idealised presentation of Judaism as a sublime other of modernity' (p. 26). Later, she writes:

In this way the search for a decent response to those brutally destroyed is conflated with the quite different response called for in the face of the 'inhuman' capacity for such destruction. To argue for silence, prayer, the banishment equally of poetry and knowledge, in short, the witness of 'ineffability', that is, non-representability, is to mystify something we dare not understand, because we fear that it may be all too understandable, all too continuous with what we are – human, all too human. (p. 43)

The broader 'postmodernist' challenge to historiography has also been subject to criticism on the grounds that it is an exaggerated form of the kind of scepticism that has long been a normal part of historical work. It is excessive in that it undercuts the possibility of knowledge of any kind, including that which postmodernists them selves unavoidably claim (see Evans 1997: ch. 3).

The conception of academic enquiry I have been defending in this book implies that historians and social scientists cannot make, and should not claim to present, authoritative judgements about the moral status of the Holocaust. For this reason, they cannot treat the Holocaust as unique, as somehow standing outside of history and of ordinary reality. Furthermore, to allow that there is any event of this kind – this one or others, such as the birth of Christ – would be to break with a fundamental tenet of academic enquiry: that it can, in principle, address factual questions about any event, action, or institution. To treat some phenomena as beyond its reach would 'block the road of inquiry', perhaps the worst of all scientific vices according to the American philosopher Charles Sanders Peirce (see Skagestad 1981). The danger of this is illustrated by the way in which some writers, notably Jenkins, generalise the argument about the ineffability of the Holocaust to all events. Here there is a rapid move back from viewing the Holocaust as unique towards treating it as signalling the inexplicability of all events.

Part of what is at issue here is the very function of historical and social scientific writing: whether it is concerned with describing and explaining actions and events, or whether it is intended to provide a proper ethical, political, or practical response to those actions or events: for instance, one that serves the memory of some collectivity, is true to the experience of victims, is designed to counter neo-fascism, etc. I have argued in this book that it is fundamental to academic enquiry that it is restricted to the first of these tasks. This involves accepting that all actions and events have unique characteristics but that, at the same time, aspects of them can always be grasped, and indeed can only be grasped, through the use of general categories; and that explanations for them must be framed in ways that do not assume that what we judge to be good and what we judge to be bad are caused by quite different processes.

There are at least three objections that can be raised against the attempt to pursue this academic ideal. First, there is the argument that, in practice, historians and social scientists cannot actually prevent their value attitudes towards the phenomena being studied from biasing their descriptions and explanations. For instance, Friedländer (Broszat and Friedländer 1988: 41) has argued that 'a kind of purely scientific distancing from the past, that is, a passage from the realm of knowledge strongly influenced by personal memory to that of some kind of "detached history", remains, in my opinion, a psychological and epistemological illusion'. However, while it is true that this move is difficult, and may be impossible for those who have direct links with the events concerned, it is possible to *approximate* to this stance. And the effort to do this is essential in pursuing the proper goal of academic enquiry. It is important to note that what is required here is not that one's evaluative attitudes towards the phenomena being studied are abandoned, or even that they are prevented from having any effect on academic work. Indeed, attempts to do this are undesirable since these attitudes can facilitate understanding, not just obstruct it. The point is to try to prevent their causing error by seeking to suspend them (in the manner of phenomenological philosophy) for the purposes of academic work. While there are practical difficulties in this, and we can never know for certain that error has not entered our judgements, to treat objectivity as impossible would be to deny ourselves any prospect of developing academic, and perhaps any other kinds of, knowledge.

A second challenge to the academic ideal concerns whether it is possible for historians and social scientists to describe and explain events like the Holocaust – or, in fact, any actions, events and institutions – without necessarily *through the language used* implying some evaluative attitude towards them. As we saw, one of the criticisms of attempts to apply a normal historical approach to the Holocaust is that the language used may seem to excuse or even justify what happened, *simply because it does not condemn it*. Equally important, many words that serve descriptive and explanatory purposes also carry evaluative connotations (see Foster et al. 2000). And it is certainly true that in our ordinary usage of language we often convey evaluations via descriptive and explanatory accounts without making the value conclusions explicit. Similarly, in reading or hearing accounts provided by others, we frequently take evaluations to be implied, as either intended or inadvertently revealed.

However, the meaning of utterances or written statements is not fixed by semantics or general usage; instead, this occurs pragmatically, through the institutional circumstances in which language is being used on any particular occasion. Given that it is a requirement of academic work that evaluative conclusions are avoided, terms should only be used with descriptive or explanatory intent, and, correspondingly, we should not read evaluations into the descriptive and explanatory accounts provided in academic research reports. In other words, an effort must be made to make clear that the descriptive and explanatory terms being used are not intended to carry evaluative implications, and those reading research reports must interpret what is said purely as description and explanation, themselves suspending any potential evaluative inferences. In short, doing academic work requires special kinds of writing and reading that are, or should be, institutionalised within research communities; and these will determine the meanings of the language used.

It is of course true that, as Strauss suggests, a merely factual account of what happened in the camps could be taken as a satire, or be regarded as excusing what went on. However, there is no reason why such an account *must* be read in this way. And a key point of Weber's doctrine of value neutrality is that those who participate in scientific research communities should be primarily concerned with the validity of descriptions, explanations, and theories; not with the ethical or political implications of what is described, explained or theorised. This is necessary, according to Weber, because it facilitates the production of factual knowledge, and because consensus cannot be assumed, or easily reached, about value issues. This is true even of such an extreme event as the Holocaust.

A rather different question that might be asked concerns whether the normal vocabularies of motive employed by historians and social scientists can comprehend the nature of an event like the Holocaust, or indeed perhaps fully grasp *any* social action or event. One argument here is that the character of events, actions, and institutions as good or bad, right or wrong, is built into their very nature, so that any accurate description of them *must* be evaluative. From this perspective, to describe them in morally neutral terms is actually to misrepresent them. This is a view that was characteristic of the teleological approach of Aristotelian science and of medieval Christianity. Rejection of it was integral to the emergence of natural science in the seventeenth century; and, on the basis of the subsequent history of this field, certainly seems to have been justified, in epistemic terms at least. The justification for rejecting this view may be less obvious in the case of the social sciences. After all, evaluation is a central human (and, indeed, animal) activity, so that, in describing people's behaviour, social scientists and historians must give attention to the evaluations that they make. Nevertheless, in my view a clear distinction can and should be maintained between doing this and *endorsing* or *challenging* those evaluations; despite the fact that in extra-academic contexts this distinction frequently goes unrecognised, for both good and bad practical reasons.

There are other challenges to academic objectivity that do not rely upon the claim that value and purpose are intrinsic to the world. Instead, it may be questioned whether the kinds of writing and reading involved in academic history and social science are ethical; implying that they are in an important sense amoral or even inhuman. This is a contentious issue: from one point of view it involves weighing the likely benefits of the knowledge produced by academic work against the offensiveness of its language in dealing with events like the Holocaust. However, tolerating this offensiveness is at the heart of what I have referred to as academic licence. My point here is simply that such licence is essential if academic enquiry is to flourish, and perhaps even for it to survive.

This problem arises in a particularly sharp form in history and the social sciences because in order to understand people's behaviour we have to adopt an 'appreciative' stance (Matza 1969), in other words to try to see the world from their point of view, to treat their thoughts and behaviour as intelligible and as rational within some framework; even while at the same time locating their perspectives and actions, and the institutions in which these are implicated, within an explanatory framework. What is required here is not that people's views and actions be treated as justifiable, but rather that we come to understand how and why they see these views and actions as justifiable or excusable. Equally, explaining people's beliefs and actions in different terms from those they use themselves does not necessarily imply that the latter are false, though it may challenge some of the factual assumptions they make.

Different sorts of complaint, in this respect, are generated as regards the treatment of the victims and the perpetrators of the Holocaust. In relation to the former, what is likely to be found objectionable is the insistence that, rather than taking what the victims say at face value, we must check the validity of their accounts, as far as this is feasible; the possibility of error, and even of lying, must be addressed. Furthermore, their actions may be explained in quite different terms from how they represent these themselves. An example is Bettelheim's (1960) suggestion that the behaviour of some concentration camp inmates arose from a psychodynamic process whereby they came to identify with and imitate the dress and behaviour of their guards. This interpretation is likely to be at odds with the accounts given by these people themselves, and would probably be found offensive by them and by others (see Marcus 1999).

As regards 'appreciative' treatment of the perpetrators in academic research, the objection here is likely to be the reverse. The complaint will be that serious attention is given to what they say, including their justifications and excuses, when it should not be; for example, because they are simply evil. Furthermore, some of their accounts of what they intended, and why, may be treated as true, even though their reports will certainly not be accepted at face value. The objection is likely to be that they are being treated as if they were virtuous, or at the very least honest, when they are not.

What this discussion of the issue of normalisation makes clear is that, *in this very specific sense*, all historians and social scientists *ought to be* Holocaust deniers. It is a basic assumption of historical and social scientific work that all events are caused by material and socio-cultural factors, rather than being the product of good or evil. While the extreme character of the Holocaust must be recognised, it should not be treated as, by its very nature, inexplicable, as demanding silent witness, or as only open to theological interpretation; in other words, as requiring the abandonment of normal historical and social scientific forms of enquiry. There is a fundamental clash of perspectives here. And we should not underestimate the hurt that an academic approach can cause, in treating actions and people who are viewed as beyond the pale in exactly the same way as those who are seen as heroic victims. At the same time, it is equally important to emphasise that academic enquiry is not the only way in which the Holocaust, or any other set of events, can legitimately be approached. Nor, in itself, does academic work provide an adequate ethical, political, or practical response. The contribution it makes is limited to supplying and clarifying facts about such events. This is valuable, but it is not sufficient in practical terms to determine attitude or action; it is complementary to the evaluations that are essential if we are to respond appropriately to the Holocaust, and to any other events.

The discussion here brings out another fundamental point. This is that, while academic enquiry is committed to neutrality in relation to practical values, as regards its conclusions, restricting its focus to description and explanation, as a form of practice it is not compatible with all political, religious, and ethical stances. In particular, as we have seen, it is at odds with those that infuse the world with teleological forces for good or evil, truth or falsity. For example, when Levinas (1989: 488) writes '[t]he diabolical is endowed with intelligence and enters where it will', this signals a perspective that is fundamentally at odds with the sort of academic enquiry I am defending in this book. The same is true of views that require that, in all we do, we must bear witness to some specific set of non-epistemic values, so that the suspension of those values in the course of academic enquiry, or in any other sort of work, is proscribed as a form of inauthenticity, unfaithfulness, etc. Specifically, academic enquiry is at odds with those political, ethical, and religious views which insist that any investigation must be carried out within the framework they provide, either on the grounds that this embodies fundamental truths about human life and the world that cannot be questioned or ignored, or because not to do so would be morally offensive.

There is a direct parallel here with the position of liberal political philosophy. This insists that the state should not enforce any particular idea of the good life, allowing citizens to pursue their own goals and ideals. However, it is recognised by most commentators today that this is not a purely formal requirement. In other words, liberal states *do* always embody some substantive ideals about human living, however 'thin' these are; and they do thereby rule out ways of life that are at odds with those ideals – most obviously, but not only, those that are not prepared even to tolerate a society in which others are allowed to pursue different ways of life (see Gutmann 1980; Galston 1991). And just as liberalism may be seen as essential in societies whose citizens have diverse religious, political, and ethical affiliations, so too it might be argued that the academic ethos reflects a requirement of modern, urban societies. A central feature of these societies is a high level of occupational specialisation, and this demands a considerable degree of autonomy, in terms of value commitments, among the various roles that people play. As they move from one role to another, different responsibilities and obligations come into play and take precedence, even over deeply held views that are entrenched in other parts of their lives (see Wirth 1938; Emmet 1966: ch. 7). This is not an all-or-nothing matter, a licence for sheer hypocrisy, but it is an ethical requirement attached to particular roles. The primary responsibilities of a doctor are not the same as those of a patient's relative, a lawyer, a politician, or a citizen. Each role prioritises some matters and puts others in the background. Exactly the same is true of academic research: this requires that epistemic values be the exclusive criteria in judging knowledge claims, and that discovering the truth about some matter is the only immediate goal. As a result, other matters are backgrounded, without denying their importance for other purposes.

CONCLUSION

In this chapter I have examined the nature of and limits to academic licence, using Holocaust denial as a test case. I argued that the concept of academic freedom is closely tied to what I referred to in the Introduction as the academic ethos: in other words, its character and justification are determined by the distinctive function of academic research. A range of very different responses to Holocaust denial were identified, some of which sought its proscription while others insisted on its right to be heard. Moreover, while some appealed to notions of science and reason, others rejected these. I argued that the political and ethical implications or consequences of Holocaust denial should not be grounds for suppressing it within the academic context; that it must be judged entirely on epistemic grounds. For instance, it is possible, though not very likely, that academic study of the Holocaust will significantly affect the growth of far-Right political groups. However, such potential consequences must, generally speaking, be treated as part of the cost of academic licence.

Distinguishing between factual and evaluative claims made by Holocaust deniers, and also noting the more fundamental issue of normalisation, I examined what the appropriate response of academic researchers ought to be. I argued that in relation to the factual claims, for the most part these should be ignored or suppressed, and challenged in the public sphere, because they are incompatible with what is established knowledge in the relevant academic fields, and because no strong evidence has been provided for reconsidering their validity. Furthermore, Holocaust deniers often engage in sham reasoning in presenting their case. This means that rather than simply being dismissed as poor scholars, they should be treated as fake scholars, misusing scholarship for unscholarly purposes. However, I suggested that Holocaust deniers are by no means alone in using sham reasoning, that it can perhaps be identified in the work of many social scientists and historians. Furthermore, if we allow sceptical arguments, of the kind promoted by some of those operating under the banner of postmodernism, then drawing a boundary between what should and should not be included within academic enquiry, on either of these grounds, becomes much more difficult, if not impossible, in a reasoned way.

In the case of the evaluative claims made by Holocaust deniers, I argued that these fall outside the area about which academic enquiry can claim authority: they are matters of practical judgement. Furthermore, the fact that Holocaust deniers put forward such claims itself places them beyond the proper scope of academic enquiry; though, here again, many historians and social scientists effectively do the same.

Finally, examining the issue of normalisation, I argued that we must reject any claim that the Holocaust is uniquely evil, that it stands outside of history and ordinary reality, and therefore is not open to academic investigation. All actions, events and institutions must, as a matter of principle, be treated as amenable to this. Academic study of the Holocaust may well be found distressing and insulting by survivors of the camps and their families, since it cannot take their testimony at face value but must assess it in much the same way as other kinds of data; and must also take note of the accounts of the perpetrators. It is essential, though, to recognise the limits to what academic enquiry claims to provide: it can produce knowledge that is of great practical value, but it cannot, in itself, serve as a proper response to the Holocaust or offer solutions to practical problems.

I ended by highlighting an important point about the nature of academic neutrality: that it is not compatible with all religious, ethical, or political standpoints. In particular it is at odds with those that insist on the world being viewed as shaped by intrinsic forces for good and evil, or ethical views which demand that the same value principles govern all activity, so that academic research must be framed within these, and must express explicit evaluations of what is being studied. There is a parallel here with liberal political philosophy, with its rejection of the idea that the state should promote any particular conception of the good life. It, too, cannot tolerate *all* viewpoints or practices. This mode of governance involves costs as well as benefits; and, in just the same way, academic freedom comes with a price. But this is true of all forms of occupational specialisation.

EPILOGUE

In this book I have examined various aspects of the concept of academic social science. On my interpretation, this involves exclusive immediate dedication to the production of descriptive and explanatory knowledge, and a heightened methodological awareness compared with lay forms of enquiry. I argued that this is at odds with calls for social scientists to be organic, public, or even specific intellectuals. It also involves a commitment to objectivity and other key virtues, and an insistence on a distinctive approach to the role of criticism and to assessing the validity of knowledge claims. At the same time, I emphasised the communal character of this kind of social science. I argued that academic knowledge production is not simply a matter either of discovery or of construction, but necessarily involves a process of understanding that is dialectical in character. This generates the need for further virtues, centred on how knowledge claims, and evidence in support of them, are presented, the treatment of others' claims to knowledge, and the appropriate response to criticism. What is required here is the preservation of an intellectual enclave within which the primary focus is on the likely validity of factual knowledge claims, not on their political and practical implications or consequences. I also argued that the reverse side of dedication is the exercise of academic licence. Social scientists must have the freedom to investigate topics that they judge to be important, even if these are regarded as trivial or repulsive by others; to determine how best to investigate these questions; and to develop lines of argument that may seem arcane or offensive to lay people. In the final chapter I explored the limits to this freedom, while at the same time noting that similar charges of deviation from academic norms to those made against Holocaust deniers could be directed at many other social scientists and historians, even if to a lesser degree.

It is important to recognise that the model of academic enquiry I have presented here is not an artificial ideal brought in from outside. Its requirements are still often acknowledged by many social scientists, in how they actually behave or in their complaints about colleagues' behaviour, and this includes those who openly challenge the model. Moreover, complete conformity could not reasonably be expected; nor would this ensure that academic enquiry produces worthwhile knowledge. Indeed, some of the psychological and social forces that lead to deviation are essential to that outcome. While social science must be a cooperative enterprise in the ways that I have outlined, it is also a competitive one: much of its dynamism stems from this.

Haskell (1998: 47) writes:

> The price of participation in the community of the competent is perpetual
> exposure to criticism. If there is anything at all that justifies the special authority
> and trustworthiness of community-sponsored opinions, as I believe there is, it
> lies in the fact that these truth claims have weathered competition more severe
> than would be thought acceptable in ordinary human communities.

Similarly, while the norms I have discussed imply a moderation of passionate
commitment to the truth of particular ideas, a passion for knowledge is nevertheless
crucial to the academic enterprise.

All this said, an evaluation of the practices of many social science communities
today in terms of this academic model would highlight major divergences. Some of
these are quite fundamental in character – for example, denial among a substantial
number of qualitative researchers in several fields that their primary goal is the production of knowledge and/or that the truth of knowledge claims is the most important, or is a legitimate, issue. Another kind of deviation is the division of research into
paradigms or approaches whose assumptions are protected from discussion: they are
either asserted and rejected by the contending parties, or they are simply tolerated as
part of a détente (Hammersley 1984; 1992b; 1998c). Furthermore, in my judgement,
many of the published findings of social science do not meet the threshold of likely
validity necessary to warrant publication. Indeed there is often a considerable distance
between the level of support offered by the evidence presented and any legitimate
claim that these findings are valid. For example, quantitative work frequently relies
on measurement procedures whose validity is extremely doubtful, and on modes of
statistical analysis that do not control all the variables likely to be relevant. In the case
of qualitative work, not only is careful description of the phenomena studied not
always provided, but speculative claims are made about causal processes, sometimes
while simultaneously denying that causal analysis is involved. While it is possible to
use comparative analysis to identify the role of various factors in producing some
outcome in a particular set of situations, it is rare to find studies that do this effectively. Above all, there is a general failure to acknowledge the weakness of the
evidence offered and the implications of this, or to recognise what would be required
in order to produce stronger evidence.[1]

Of course, the failings I am pointing to here derive, in part, from the sheer difficulty of doing social scientific work. But in the Introduction I identified various
trends, both external and internal, that are undermining any capacity academic social
science has for achieving its mission. These include changes in the ways in which
research is funded, and in how universities are organised (see Tuchman 2009). From
a different direction, the rise of qualitative research has been associated in recent

---

[1]For assessments of quantitative and qualitative work along these lines, see Foster et al. (1996) and
Hammersley (2008a; 2010a). In a key respect, the kind of analysis championed by Ragin (2008)
stands as a reproach to most qualitative work. Whatever problems there may be with qualitative
comparative analysis, it does at least address the issue of causal analysis directly; its only genuine
predecessor being analytic induction. See Hammersley and Cooper (2010).

decades with conceptions of the purpose and character of social science that challenge what I suggested are its hinge assumptions: notably about the nature of knowledge, the desirability of this knowledge for its own sake, and the possibility of producing the kinds of knowledge at which academic social science aims.

The effect of these trends has been to generate research communities in many fields of social science that, to one degree or another, are dysfunctional in terms of the academic ideal. One aspect of this is the tendency for findings to be treated either as discoveries whose validity stands independently of dialectical assessment by the research community, or as constructions that simply reflect the personal characteristics of the researcher or the rhetorical strategies employed, rather than representing phenomena that exist independently. Furthermore, as a result of time pressures generated by the intensification of work in universities, plus huge increases in the amount of literature in most fields produced by pressures to publish, discussion of the results of particular studies now tend to be minimal, with only occasional exceptions. Moreover, where a study is cited this will often be either an appeal to it as a supporting reference or use of it as a negative example, in other words as symbolising an approach or conclusion which the author rejects.

As a result of all this, there is little cumulative development of knowledge in most social scientific fields (see Rule 1997), though I would not deny that many ideas have been fruitfully explored, factual evidence provided, and methodological problems recognised and clarified. But there is an even more fundamental problem. The implication of my argument seems to be that where a research community is no longer operating close to the dialectical model I outlined in Chapter 7, especially where the metaphor of battle prevails, there is little point in any individual researcher conforming to the norms built into that model: knowledge production of this kind can only work as a cooperative venture. The other side of research communities being self-constituting is that they can also be self-deconstructing. And any attempt to reform them, so as to remedy the problem, cannot be done through dialectical processes alone; it will almost certainly require negotiation and the exercise of power. But how could it be justifiable to institute or defend endogenous dialectical processes in this way?

As I made clear in the Introduction, I am not optimistic that academic social science of the kind I have argued for here can survive in the face of current countertrends. Key elements of it, such as the idea that knowledge is valuable in itself and the commitment to value neutrality, are now dismissed out of hand by many social scientists, usually via caricature. While this kind of social science is *worth* defending, it may not be defensible in practical terms at the present time or in the foreseeable future.

REFERENCES

Abrams, P. (1972) *Origins of British Sociology 1834–1914*, Chicago, University of Chicago Press.

Adorno, T. W., Albert, H., Dahrendorf, R., Habermas, J., Pilot, H. and Popper, K. R. (1976) *The Positivist Dispute in Germany*, London, Heinemann. (First published in German in 1969.)

Afary, J. and Anderson, K. (2005) *Foucault and the Iranian Revolution*, Chicago, University of Chicago Press.

Albert, H. (1985) *Treatise on Critical Reason*, Princeton, NJ, Princeton University Press.

Albert, H. (2002) 'Critical rationalism and universal hermeneutics', in Malpas, J., Arnswald, U. and Kertscher, J. (eds) *Gadamer's Century: Essays in honor of Hans-Georg Gadamer*, Cambridge, MA, MIT Press.

Alexander, J. (2009) *Remembering the Holocaust*, Oxford, Oxford University Press.

Alexander, L. (2005) *Is there a right to freedom of expression?*, Cambridge, Cambridge University Press.

Althusser, L. (1990) *Philosophy and the Spontaneous Philosophy of the Scientists*, London, Verso.

Anderson, D. (2004) 'Peirce's common sense marriage of religion and science', in Misak, C. (ed.) *The Cambridge Companion to Peirce*, Cambridge, Cambridge University Press.

Ankersmit, F. (1994) *History and Tropology: the rise and fall of metaphor*, Berkeley CA, University of California Press.

Anscombe, E. (1965) 'The intentionality of sensation', in Butler, R. (ed.) *Analytical Philosophy, Second Series*, Oxford, Blackwell.

Arblaster, A. (1974) *Academic Freedom*, Harmondsworth, Penguin.

Aristotle (1984) *Politics*, in Barnes, J. (ed.) *The Complete Works of Aristotle*, Volume 2, Princeton, NJ, Princeton University Press.

Aron, R. (1983) *The Committed Observer*, Chicago, Regnery Gateway.

Aronson, R. (1977) 'The individualist social theory of Jean-Paul Sartre', New Left Review (ed.) *Western Marxism: A critical reader*, London, New Left Books.

Aronson, R. (1980) *Jean-Paul Sartre: Philosophy in the world*, London, Verso.

Aronson, R. (1987) 'Sartre on Stalin: a discussion of "Critique de la Raison Dialectique, II"', *Studies in Soviet Thought*, 33, 2, pp. 131–43.

Aschheim, S. (1996) *Culture and Catastrophe: German and Jewish Confrontations with National Socialism and Other Crises*, New York, New York University Press.

REFERENCES

Ashmore, M. (1989) *The Reflexive Thesis*, Chicago, University of Chicago Press.

Axtell, G. (ed.) (2000) *Knowledge, Belief, and Character: Readings in virtue epistemology*, Lanham, MA, Rowman and Littlefield.

Ayalti, H. (1949) *Yiddish Proverbs*, New York, Schocken Books.

Baker, K. M. (1975) *Condorcet: from natural philosophy to social mathematics*, Chicago, University of Chicago Press.

Baldwin, P. (ed.) (1990) *Reworking the Past: Hitler, the Holocaust and the Historians*, Boston, MA, Beacon Press.

Ball, S. J. (1995) 'Intellectuals or technicians? The urgent role of theory in educational studies', *British Journal of Educational Studies*, 43, 3, pp. 255–71.

Bar On, B.-A. (1993) 'Marginality and epistemic privilege', in Alcoff, L. and Potter, E. (eds) *Feminist Epistemologies*, New York, Routledge.

Bataille, G. (1991) *The Accursed Share, Volume 1: Consumption*, New York, Zone Books. (First published in French in 1949.)

Bateson, N. (1984) *Data Construction in Surveys*, London, Allen and Unwin.

Bauer, Y. (2001) *Rethinking the Holocaust*, New Haven, CT, Yale University Press.

Bauman, Z. (1987) *Legislators and Interpreters: On modernity, post-modernity and intellectuals*, Cambridge, Polity.

Bauman, Z. (1989) *Modernity and the Holocaust*, Cambridge, Polity.

Becker, H. S. (1967) 'Whose side are we on?', *Social Problems*, 14, pp. 239–47.

Becker, H. S. (1970) *Sociological Work*, Chicago, Aldine.

Becker, H. S. (1994) 'Professional sociology: the case of C. Wright Mills', in Rist, R. (ed.) *The Democratic Imagination*, New Brunswick, NJ, Transaction Books.

Becker, H. S. (1998) *Tricks of the Trade*, Chicago, University of Chicago Press.

Bell, C. and Newby, H. (1977) *Doing Sociological Research*, London, Allen and Unwin.

Bell, J. (2005) *Doing Your Research Project*, Fourth edition, Maidenhead, Open University Press.

Benda, J. (1928) *The Treason of the Intellectuals*, New York, Norton, 1969. (First published in French in 1928.)

Bennington, G. (1988) *Lyotard: Writing the event*, Manchester, Manchester University Press.

Berger, P. and Luckmann, T. (1967) *The Social Construction of Reality*, Harmondsworth, Penguin.

Berlin, I. (1990) *The Crooked Timber of Humanity*, London, Murray.

Bernstein, R. (1983) *Beyond Objectivism and Relativism*, Oxford, Blackwell.

Bettelheim, B. (1960) *The Informed Heart: Autonomy in a Mass Age*, Glencoe, IL, Free Press.

Bird, A. (2000) *Thomas Kuhn*, Princeton, NJ, Princeton University Press.

Bird, G. (1986) *William James*, London, Routledge & Kegan Paul.

Blackburn, S. (2008) *The Oxford Dictionary of Philosophy*, Second revised edition, Oxford, Oxford University Press.

Blakeley, T. (1968) 'Sartre's "Critique de la raison dialectique" and the opacity of Marxism–Leninism', *Studies in Soviet Thought*, 8, 2/3, pp. 122–35.

Bottomore, T. (1975) *Marxist Sociology*, London, Macmillan.

Bourg, J. (2007) *From Revolution to Ethics: May 1968 and Contemporary French Thought*, Montreal, McGill–Queens University Press.

Bowen, E. (Bohannan, L.) (1954) *Return to Laughter*, New York, Harper.

Brady, M. and Pritchard, D. (eds) (2003) *Moral and Epistemic Virtues*, Malden, MA, Blackwell.

Braiterman, Z. (2000) 'Against Holocaust-sublime', *History and Memory*, 12, 2, pp. 7–28.

Brannigan, A. (1981) *The Social Basis of Scientific Discoveries*, Cambridge, Cambridge University Press.

Bredin, J.-D. (1986) *The Affair*, New York, Braziller.

Brewer, J. (2003) *C. Wright Mills and the Ending of Violence*, Basingstoke, Palgrave Macmillan.

Bridges, D. (1998) 'Research for sale: moral market or moral maze', *British Educational Research Journal*, 24, 5, pp. 593–608. (Reprinted in Bridges 2003.)

Bridges, D. (1999) 'Educational research: pursuit of truth or flight into fancy?', *British Educational Research Journal*, 25, 5, pp. 597–616. (Reprinted in Bridges 2003.)

Bridges, D. (2003) *Fiction written under oath? Essays in philosophy and educational research*, Dordrecht, Kluwer.

Bridgman, P. (1955) *Reflections of a Physicist*, New York, Philosophical Library.

Brooks, S. and Gagnon, A. (1988) *Social Scientists and Politics in Canada: Between clerisy and vanguard*, Kingston, McGill–Queen's University Press.

Brophy, J. (ed.) (1998) *Expectations in the Classroom*, Advances in Research on Teaching, Volume 7, Greenwich CT, JAI Press.

Broszat, M. and Friedländer, S. (1988) 'A controversy about the historicization of National socialism', *Yad Vashem Studies*, 19, pp. 1–47. (Reprinted in Baldwin 1990.)

Bruun, H. H. (1972) *Science, Values and Politics in Max Weber's Methodology*, Copenhagen, Munksgaard.

Bruun, H. H. (2007) *Science, Values and Politics in Max Weber's Methodology*, Second edition, Aldershot, Ashgate.

Bruyn, S. (1966) *The Human Perspective in Sociology: The Methodology of Participant Observation*, Englewood Cliffs, NJ, Prentice Hall.

Brym, R. (1980) *Intellectuals and Politics*, London, Allen and Unwin.

Bulmer, M. (1984) *The Chicago School of Sociology*, Chicago, University of Chicago Press.

Burawoy, M. (2005) 'For public sociology', *American Sociological Review*, 70, 1, pp. 4–28.

Burkhardt, F. and Smith, S. (eds) (1994) *The Correspondence of Charles Darwin*, Volume 9, 1861, Cambridge, Cambridge University Press.

Burtt, E. A. (1924) *The Metaphysical Foundations of Modern Physical Science*, London, Routledge & Kegan Paul.

Calaprice, A. (ed.) (2000) *The Expanded Quotable Einstein*, Second edition, Princeton, NJ, Princeton University Press.

Canovan, M. (1988) 'Friendship, truth and politics: Hannah Arendt on toleration', in Mendus, S. (ed.) *Justifying Toleration: Conceptual and historical perspectives*, Cambridge, Cambridge University Press.

Carter, K. and Delamont. S. (eds) (1996) *Qualitative research – The emotional dimension*, Aldershot, Avebury.

Caute, D. (1964) *Communism and the French Intellectuals 1914–1960*, London, André Deutsch.

Cesara, M. (1982) *Reflections of a Woman Anthropologist: No hiding place*, London, Academic Press.

Chamberlain, K. (1999) 'Methodolatry and qualitative health research', *Journal of Health Psychology*, 5, 3, pp. 285–96.

Chomsky, N. (1981a) 'His right to say it', *The Nation*, 232, 2, February 28, pp. 231–4.

Chomsky, N. (1981b) 'Freedom of expression? Absolutely', *The Village Voice*, July 1–7, pp. 12–15.

Christofferson, M. (2004) *French Intellectuals Against the Left: The antitotalitarian moment in the 1970s*, New York, Berghahn.

Ciaffa, J. (1998) *Max Weber and the Problems of Value-Free Social Science*, Lewisburg, PA, Bucknell University Press.

Clarke, J. and Newman, J. (1997) *The Managerial State*, London, Sage.

Clifford, W. K. (1947) *The Ethics of Belief and Other Essays*, London, Watts. (A more recent edition was published by Prometheus Books in 1999. 'The ethics of belief' was first published in 1877, in *Contemporary Review*, 29, pp. 283–309.)

Cobban, A. (1990) *A History of Modern France*, Volume 3 1871–1963, Second edition, London, Penguin.

Cohen, A. (1981) *The Tremendum: A theological interpretation of the Holocaust*, New York, Crossroad.

Cohen, G. A. (1982) 'Karl Marx and the withering away of social science', *Philosophy and Public Affairs*, 1, pp. 182–203.

Coleridge, S. T. (1830) *On the Constitution of Church and State*, London, Dent, 1972.

Collier, A. (2003) *In Defence of Objectivity: On realism, existentialism and politics*, London, Routledge.

Collini, S. (1991) *Public Moralists: Political thought and intellectual life in Britain, 1850–1930*, Oxford, Oxford University Press.

Colquohn, R. (1986) *Raymond Aron*, Two volumes, Newbury Park, CA, Sage.

Coser, L. (1965) *Men of Ideas: A sociologist's view*, New York, Free Press.

Cozzens, S., Healey, P., Rip, A. and Ziman, J. (eds) (1990) *The Research System in Transition*, Dordrecht, Kluwer.

Crossen, C. (1994) *Tainted Truth: The manipulation of fact in America*, New York, Simon and Schuster.

Daston, L. (1994) 'Baconian facts, academic civility, and the prehistory of objectivity', in Megill, A. (ed.) *Rethinking Objectivity*, Durham, NC, Duke University Press.

Daston, L. and Galison, P. (2007) *Objectivity*, New York, Zone Books.

Dear, P. (1992) 'From truth to disinterestedness in the seventeenth century', *Social Studies of Science*, 22, 4, pp. 619–31.

De Beauvoir, S. (1974) *Memoirs of a Dutiful Daughter*, New York, Harper and Row. (First published in French in 1958.)

Debray, R. (1981) *Teachers, Writers, Celebrities*, London, New Left Books.

DeGroot, G. (2008) *The 60s Unplugged: A kaleidoscopic history of a disorderly decade*, London, Macmillan.

Demeritt, D. (2000) 'The new social contract for science: accountability, relevance and value in US and UK science and research policy', *Antipode* 32, 3, pp. 308–29.

Denscombe, M. (2007) *The Good Research Guide*, Third edition, Maidenhead, Open University Press.

Denscombe, M. (2009) *Ground Rules for Social Research*, Second edition, Maidenhead, Open University Press.

Denzin, N. K. (1970) *The Research Act*, Chicago, Aldine.

Denzin, N. K. (2010) *The Qualitative Manifesto: A call to arms*, Walnut Creek, CA, Left Coast Press.

Denzin, N. K. and Lincoln, Y. S. (eds) (2005) *Handbook of Qualitative Research*, Third edition, Thousand Oaks, CA, Sage.

DePaul, M. and Zagzebski, L. (eds) (2003) *Intellectual Virtue: Perspectives from ethics and epistemology*, Oxford, Oxford University Press.

De Toqueville, A. (1856) *The Old Regime and the French Revolution*, English translation, New York, Doubleday, 1955.

Dewey, J. (1976) 'Academic freedom', in Dewey, J., *John Dewey: The Middle Works*, Carbondale, IL, Southern Illinois University Press.

Dews, P. (1986) 'The *nouvelle philosophie* and Foucault', in M. Gane (ed.) *Towards a Critique of Foucault*, London, Routledge & Kegan Paul.

Dews, P. (1987) *Logics of Disintegration: Post-structuralist thought and the claims of critical theory*, London, Verso.

Diner, D. (1990) 'Between aporia and apology: on the limits of historicizing National Socialism', in Baldwin, P. (ed.) *Reworking the Past: Hitler, the Holocaust and the Historians*, Boston, MA, Beacon Press.

Dinwiddy, J. (1989) *Bentham*, Oxford, Oxford University Press.

Douglas, H. (2009) *Science, Policy, and the Value-free Ideal*, Pittsburgh, PA, University of Pittsburgh Press.

Douglas, J. D. (1976) *Investigative Social Research*, Beverley Hills, CA, Sage.

Drolet, M. (1994) 'The wild and the sublime: Lyotard's post-modern politics', *Political Studies*, XLII, pp. 259–73.

Dryzek, J. S. (1990) *Discursive Democracy: Politics, policy, and political science*, Cambridge, Cambridge University Press.

Durkheim, E. (1969) 'Individualism and the intellectuals', translated as part of Lukes, S. 'Durkheim's "Individualism and the intellectuals"', *Political Studies*, 17, 1, pp. 14–30. (Originally published in French in 1898.)

Dworkin, R. (1998) 'We need a new interpretation of academic freedom', in Menand, L. (ed.) *The Future of Academic Freedom*, Chicago, University of Chicago Press.

Eaglestone, R. (2001) *Postmodernism and Holocaust Denial*, Cambridge, Icon Books.

Eaglestone, R. (2004) *The Holocaust and the Postmodern*, Oxford, Oxford University Press.

Eisenhart, M. (1998) 'On the subject of interpretive reviews', *Review of Educational Research*, 68, 4, pp. 391–9.

Eisner, E. (1992) 'Objectivity in educational research', *Curriculum Inquiry*, 22, 1, pp. 9–15. (Reprinted in Hammersley, M. (ed.) (1993) *Educational Research: Current issues*, London, Paul Chapman.)

Elashoff, J. D. and Snow, R. E. (eds) (1971) *Pygmalion Reconsidered*, Worthington OH, Charles A. Jones.

Ellis, C. and Bochner, A. P. (2000) 'Autoethnography, personal narrative, reflexivity: researcher as subject', in N. K. Denzin and Y. S. Lincoln (eds) *Handbook of Qualitative Research*, Second edition, Thousand Oaks, CA, Sage.

REFERENCES

Elster, J. (ed.) (1998) *Deliberative Democracy*, Cambridge, Cambridge University Press.

Emmet, D. (1966) *Rules, Roles and Relations*, London, Macmillan.

Erlandson, D. A., Harris, E. L., Skipper, B. L. and Allen, S. D. (1993) *Doing Naturalistic Inquiry: A guide to methods*, Newbury Park, CA, Sage.

Evans, J. D. G. (1977) *Aristotle's Concept of Dialectic*, Cambridge, Cambridge University Press.

Evans, R. J. (1997) *In Defence of History*, London, Granta.

Evans, R. J. (2002) *Lying about Hitler: History, Holocaust, and the David Irving Trial*, New York, Basic Books.

Evron, B. (1983) 'Holocaust: the uses of disaster', *Radical America*, 17, 4, pp. 7–21.

Eyerman, R., Svensson, L. and Söderqvist, T. (1987) Introduction, in Eyerman, R., Svensson, L. and Söderqvist, T. (eds) *Intellectuals, Universities and the State in Western Modern Societies*, Berkeley, CA, University of California Press.

Farrell, F. B. (1996) *Subjectivity, Realism and Postmodernism*, Cambridge, Cambridge University Press.

Fay, B. (1975) *Social Theory and Political Practice*, London, Allen and Unwin.

Ferlie, E., Ashburner, L., Fitzgerald, L. and Pettigrew, A. (1996) *The New Public Management in Action*, Oxford, Oxford University Press.

Festinger, L. and Katz, D. (eds) (1953) *Research Methods in the Behavioral Sciences*, New York, Dryden Press.

Feyerabend, P. (1975) *Against Method: Outline of an Anarchistic Theory of Knowledge*, London, New Left Books.

Finkelkraut, A. (1998) *The Future of the Negation: Reflections on the question of genocide*, Lincoln, NB, University of Nebraska Press. (First published in French in 1982.)

Finkelstein, N. (2000) *The Holocaust Industry*, London, Verso.

Fischer, M. (1990) 'Redefining philosophy as literature: Richard Rorty's "defence" of literary culture', in Malachowski, A. R. (ed.) *Reading Rorty: Critical responses to philosophy and the mirror of nature (and beyond)*, Oxford, Blackwell.

Fish, S. (1994) 'There's no such thing as free speech and it's a good thing, too', in *There's No Such Thing as Free Speech and it's a Good Thing, Too*, New York, Oxford University Press.

Fish, S. (2001a) 'Holocaust denial and academic freedom', *Valparaiso University Law Review*, 35, pp. 499–524.

Fish, S. (2001b) *The Trouble with Principle*, Cambridge, MA, Harvard University Press.

Forster, M. (1989) *Hegel and Skepticism*, Cambridge, MA, Harvard University Press.

Foster, P. (1992) 'Teacher attitudes and Afro/Caribbean educational attainment', *Oxford Review of Education*, 18, 3, pp. 269–81.

Foster, P., Gomm, R. and Hammersley, M. (1996) *Constructing Educational Inequality*, London, Falmer.

Foster, P., Gomm, R. and Hammersley, M. (2000) 'Case studies as spurious evaluations: the example of research on educational inequalities', *British Journal of Educational Studies*, 48, 3, pp. 215–30.

Foucault, M. (1980) 'Truth and power', in Foucault, M., *Power/Knowledge: Selected interviews and other writings 1972–77*, Hassocks, Harvester.

Foucault, M. and Deleuze, G. (1977) 'Intellectuals and power', in Bouchard, D. F. (ed.) *Language, Counter-Memory, Practice: Selected essays and interviews by Michel Foucault*, Ithaca, NY, Cornell University Press. (First published in French in 1972.)

Van Fraassen, B. (1980) *The Scientific Image*, Oxford, Oxford University Press.

Friedländer, S. (1992) Introduction, in Friedländer, S. (ed.) *Probing the Limits of Representation: Nazism and the 'Final Solution'*, Cambridge, MA, Harvard University Press.

Friedländer, S. (1993) *Reflections on Nazism: An essay on Kitsch and death*, Bloomington, IN, Indiana University Press.

Friedman, M. (2001) *Dynamics of Reason*, Stanford, CA, Center for the Study of Language and Information.

Friedrichs, R. (1970) *A Sociology of Sociology*, New York, Free Press.

Fuller, S. (1999) 'Making the university fit for critical intellectuals: recovering from the ravages of the postmodern condition', *British Educational Research Journal*, 25, 1, pp. 583–95.

Fuller, S. (2005) *The Intellectual*, London, Faber and Faber.

Furedi, F. (2006) *Where Have All the Intellectuals Gone?*, Second edition, London, Continuum.

Gadamer, H.-G. (1975) *Truth and Method*, Second edition. (English translation, London, Continuum, 2002.)

Gage, N. (1971) 'Foreword' to Elashoff, J. D. and Snow, R. E. (eds) *Pygmalion Reconsidered*, Worthington, OH, Charles A. Jones.

Gage, N. (1989) 'The paradigm wars and their aftermath: a "historical" sketch of research on teaching since 1989', *Educational Researcher*, 18, pp. 4–10.

Galston, W. (1991) *Liberal Purposes*, Cambridge, Cambridge University Press.

Galtung, J. (1967) *Theory and Methods of Social Research*, London, Allen and Unwin.

Gattone, C. (2006) *The Social Scientist as Public Intellectual*, Lanham, MD, Rowman and Littlefield.

Gaukroger, S. (2001) *Francis Bacon and the Transformation of Early-Modern Philosophy*, Cambridge, Cambridge University Press.

Gellner, E. (1968) *Words and Things*, Harmondsworth, Penguin.

Gibbons, M. (2000) 'Mode 2 society and the emergence of context-sensitive science', *Science and Public Policy*, 26, 5, pp. 159–63.

Gibbons, M., Limoges, C., Nowotny, H., Schwartzman, S., Scott, P. and Trow, M. (1994) *The New Production of Knowledge: The dynamics of science and research in contemporary societies*, London, Sage.

Gillam, R. (1977/8) 'Richard Hofstadter, C. Wright Mills and "the critical ideal"', *The American Scholar*, Winter, pp. 69–85.

Gillborn, D. (1996) *Racism and Antiracism in Real Schools*, Buckingham, Open University Press.

Gillies, D. (1993) *Philosophy of Science in the Twentieth Century*, Oxford, Blackwell.

Gitlin, A., Siegel, M. and Boru, K. (1989) 'The politics of method: from leftist ethnography to educative research', *International Journal of Qualitative Research in Education*, 2, 3, pp. 237–53.

Glaser, B. G. and Strauss, A. L. (1967) *The Discovery of Grounded Theory*, Chicago, Aldine.

Gonzalez, F. (1998) *Dialectic and Dialogue: Plato's practice of philosophical inquiry*, Evanston, IL, Northwestern University Press.

Goode, W. J. and Hatt, P. K. (1952) *Methods in Social Research*, New York, McGraw-Hill.

Goodson, I. (1999) 'The educational researcher as a public intellectual', *British Educational Research Journal*, 25, 3, pp. 277–97.

Gorz, A. (ed.) (1977) 'Sartre and Marx', in New Left Review *Western Marxism: A critical reader*, London, New Left Books.

Gottlieb, P. (2009) *The Virtue of Aristotle's Ethics*, Cambridge, Cambridge University Press.

Gouldner, A. (1965) *Enter Plato: Classical Greece and the Origins of Social Theory*, New York, Basic Books.

Gouldner, A. (1970) *The Coming Crisis of Western Sociology*, New York, Basic Books.

Gouldner, A. (1973) *For Sociology*, Harmondsworth, Penguin.

Gramsci, A. (1971) *Selections from the Prison Notebooks*, New York, International Publishers.

Gray, J. (1995) *Berlin*, London, Fontana.

Grice, P. (1975) 'Logic and conversation', in Cole, P. and Morgan, J. (eds) *Syntax and Semantics 3: Speech Acts*, New York, Academic Press.

Grice, P. (1989) *Studies in the Way of Words*, Cambridge, MA, Harvard University Press.

Griffiths, M. (1998) *Educational Research for Social Justice: Getting off the fence*, Buckingham, Open University Press.

Grondin, J. (2003) *Hans-Georg Gadamer: A biography*, New Haven, CT, Yale University Press. (First published in German in 1999.)

Gutmann, A. (1980) *Liberal Equality*, Cambridge, Cambridge University Press.

Gutmann, A. and Thompson, D. (1996) *Democracy and Disagreement*, Cambridge, MA, Harvard University Press.

Guttenplan, D. D. (2001) *The Holocaust on Trial*, New York, Norton.

Haack, S. (1984) 'Can James's theory of truth be made more satisfactory?', *Transactions of the Charles S. Peirce Society*, XX, 3, pp. 269–78.

Haack, S. A. (1997) '"The ethics of belief" reconsidered', in Hahn, L. E. (ed.) *The Philosophy of Roderick M. Chisholm*, Chicago, Open Court.

Haack, S. (1998) *Manifesto of a Passionate Moderate*, Chicago, University of Chicago Press.

Haack, S. (2009) *Evidence and Inquiry: Towards a reconstruction of epistemology*, Second edition, New York, Prometheus Press. (First edition published in 1993 by Blackwell.)

Habermas, J. (1968) *Knowledge and Interest*, English translation, Cambridge, Polity, 1987.

Habermas, J. (1975) *Legitimation Crisis*, Boston, MA, Beacon Press.

Habermas, J. (1985) *The Philosophical Discourse of Modernity*, English translation, Cambridge, Polity, 1987.

Habermas, J. (1989) *The Structural Transformation of the Public Sphere*, Cambridge, MA, MIT Press. (First published in German in 1962.)

Habermas, J. (2003) *Truth and Justification*, Cambridge, MA, MIT Press. (First published in German in 1998.)

Hague, D. (1991) *Beyond Universities: A new republic of the intellect*, Hobart Paper 115, London, Institute of Economic Affairs.

Halfpenny, P. (1982) *Positivism and Sociology*, London, Allen and Unwin.

Halfpenny, P. (1997) 'The relation between quantitative and qualitative social research', *Bulletin de Methodologie Sociologique*, 57, pp. 49–64.

Halsey, A. (2003) *Decline of Donnish Dominion*, Oxford, Oxford University Press.

Hamlyn, D. (1988) *A History of Western Philosophy*, London, Penguin.

Hammersley, M. (1984) 'The paradigmatic mentality: a diagnosis' in Barton, L. and Walker, S. (eds) *Social Crisis and Educational Research*, London, Croom Helm.

Hammersley, M. (1989) *The Dilemma of Qualitative Research: Herbert Blumer and the Chicago Tradition*, London, Routledge.

Hammersley, M. (1992a) *What's Wrong with Ethnography?*, London, Routledge.

Hammersley, M. (1992b) 'The paradigm wars: reports from the front', *British Journal of Sociology of Education*, 13, 1, pp. 131–43.

Hammersley, M. (1995) *The Politics of Social Research*, London, Sage.

Hammersley, M. (1997) 'Educational inequalities', in Block 5, Unit 1 (*EU208*) *Exploring Educational Issues*, Milton Keynes, The Open University.

Hammersley, M. (1998a) *Reading Ethnographic Research*, Second edition, London, Longman.

Hammersley, M. (1998b) 'Get real! A defence of realism', in Hodkinson, P. (ed.) *The Nature of Educational Research: Realism, relativism, or postmodernism*. Manchester, Crewe and Alsager Faculty, Manchester Metropolitan University. (Reprinted in Piper, H. and Stronach, I. (eds) (2004) *Educational Research: Difference and diversity*, Aldershot, Ashgate.)

Hammersley, M. (1998c) 'Telling tales about educational research: a response to John K. Smith', *Educational Researcher*, 27, 7, pp. 18–21.

Hammersley, M. (1999) 'Sociology, what's it for? A critique of the grand conception', *Sociological Research Online*, 4, 3. Available at www.socresonline.org.uk/4/3/hammersley.html (accessed 29.06.10).

Hammersley, M. (2000a) *Taking Sides in Social Research: Essays on bias and partisanship*, London, Routledge.

Hammersley, M. (2000b) 'Varieties of social research: a typology', *International Journal of Social Research Methodology*, 3, pp. 221–9. (Reprinted in Hammersley 2002a.)

Hammersley, M. (2000c) 'How not to engage in academic discussion: a commentary on Gillborn's 'Racism and Research', Unpublished paper.

Hammersley, M. (2002a) *Educational Social Research, Policymaking and Practice*, London, Paul Chapman.

Hammersley, M. (2002b) 'Induction: troublesome term, contested concept', Paper given at the Seminar on Induction: Fact or Fantasy?, Department of Education and Professional Studies, King's College, London, January.

Hammersley, M. (2003a) *Guide to Natural Histories of Research*. Available at www.tlrp.org/rcbn/capacity/Activities/Themes/Expertise/guide.pdf (accessed 4 February 2010).

Hammersley, M. (2003b) 'Can and should educational research be educative?', *Oxford Review of Education*, 29, 1, pp. 3–25.

Hammersley, M. (2004a) 'Action research: a contradiction in terms?', *Oxford Review of Education*, 30, 2, pp. 165–81.

Hammersley, M. (2004b) 'Teaching qualitative method: craft, profession, or bricolage?', in Seale, C. et al. (eds) *Qualitative Research Practice*, London, Sage.

Hammersley, M. (2004c) 'Reflexivity', in Lewis-Beck, M., Bryman, A. and Liao, T. F. (eds) *Encyclopedia of Social Science Research Methods*, Thousand Oaks, CA, Sage.

Hammersley, M. (2004d) 'Towards a usable past for qualitative research', *International Journal of Social Research Methodology*, 7, 1, pp. 19–27.

Hammersley, M. (2006a) 'Philosophy: who needs it? The case of social science research on education', *Journal of Philosophy of Education*, 40, 2, pp. 273–86.

Hammersley, M. (2006b) *Media Bias in Reporting Social Research? The case of reviewing ethnic inequalities in education*, London, Routledge.

Hammersley, M. (2008a) *Questioning Qualitative Inquiry*, London, Sage.

Hammersley, M. (2008b) 'Reflexivity for what? A response to Gewirtz and Cribb on the role of values in the sociology of education', *British Journal of Sociology of Education*, 29, 5, pp. 549–58.

Hammersley, M. (2009a) 'The sociology of the professions and the profession of sociology', Unpublished paper.

Hammersley, M. (2009b) 'Can social science tell us whether Britain is a meritocracy?', Paper presented at the Symposium on Methodological Issues in Research on Social Class, Education and Social Mobility, British Educational Research Association Annual Conference, Manchester, September.

Hammersley, M. (2010a) 'What's wrong with quantitative research?', Unpublished paper.

Hammersley, M. (2010b) 'On the concept of value-freedom or value-neutrality', Unpublished paper.

Hammersley, M. and Atkinson, P. (1983) *Ethnography: Principles in action*, London, Tavistock.

Hammersley, M. and Atkinson, P. (2007) *Ethnography: Principles in action*, Third edition, London, Routledge.

Hammersley, M. and Cooper, B. (2010) 'Analytic induction and qualitative comparative analysis', Unpublished paper.

Hammersley, M. and Gomm, R. (2000) 'Bias in social research', in Hammersley, M., *Taking Sides in Social Research: Essays on partisanship and bias*, London, Routledge. Ch. 6.

Harding, S. (1991) *Whose Science? Whose Knowledge? Thinking from women's lives*, Ithaca, NY, Cornell University Press.

Harding, S. (1992) 'After the neutrality ideal: science, politics, and "strong objectivity"', *Social Research*, 59, 3, pp. 568–87.

Harding, S. (1993) 'Rethinking standpoint epistemology: "What is strong objectivity?"', in Alcoff, L. and Potter, E. (eds) *Feminist Epistemologies*, New York, Routledge.

Harding, S. (1995) '"Strong objectivity": a response to the new objectivity question', *Synthese*, 104, pp. 331–49.

Harding, S. (ed.) (2004) *The Feminist Standpoint Theory Reader*, London, Routledge.

Harrington, A. (2001) *Hermeneutic Dialogue and Social Science: A Critique of Gadamer and Habermas*, London, Routledge.

Hartung, F. E. (1970) 'Problems of the sociology of knowledge', in Curtis, J. E. and Petras, J. W. (eds) *The Sociology of Knowledge: A reader*, London, Duckworth.

Haskell, T. (1998) 'Justifying the rights of academic freedom in the era of "power/knowledge"', in Menand, L. (ed.) *The Future of Academic Freedom*, Chicago, University of Chicago Press.

Hawkesworth, M. E. (1994) 'From objectivity to objectification: feminist objections', in Megill, A. (ed.) *Rethinking Objectivity*, Durham, NC, Duke University Press.

Hayman, R. (1986) *Writing Against: A biography of Sartre*, London, Weidenfeld & Nicolson.

Henry, F. and Saberwal, S. (eds) (1969) *Stress and Response in Fieldwork*, New York, Holt, Rinehart and Winston.

Hesse, M. (1972) 'In defence of objectivity', *Proceedings of the British Academy*, 4 October.

Hindess, B. (1987) *Freedom, Equality, and the Market*, London, Tavistock.

Hitchens, C. (2008) 'How to be a public intellectual: the world's fifth best public intellectual on the uses and abuses of the term', Prospect, 146, 24 May. Available at www.prospectmagazine.co.uk/2008/05/howtobeapublicintellectual/ (accessed 19 January 2010).

Hollands, R. and Stanley, L. (2009) 'Rethinking "current crisis" arguments: Gouldner and the legacy of critical sociology', *Sociological Research Online*, 14, 1. Available at www.socresonline.org.uk/14/1/1.html (accessed 6 February 2010).

Hollinger, D. A. (1983) 'In defence of democracy and Robert K. Merton's formulation of the scientific ethos', in Jones, R. A. and Kuklick, H. (eds) *Knowledge and Society: Studies in the Sociology of Culture Past and Present*, Volume 4, Greenwich, CT, JAI Press.

Hollinger, D. A. (1997) 'James, Clifford and the scientific conscience', in Putnam, R. A. (ed.) *The Cambridge Companion to William James*, Cambridge, Cambridge University Press.

Holmwood, J. (2007) 'Sociology as public discourse and professional practice: a critique of Michael Burawoy', *Sociological Theory*, 25, 1, pp. 46–66.

Holub, R. C. (1991) *Jürgen Habermas: Critic in the public sphere*, London, Routledge.

Horkheimer, M. (1972) 'Traditional and critical theory', in *Critical Theory: Selected essays*, New York, Seabury Press.

Horowitz, I. L. (1983) *C. Wright Mills: An American utopian*, New York, Free Press.

Horowitz, I. L. (1994) 'Critical responses to friendly critics', in Rist, R. (ed.) *The Democratic Imagination*, New Brunswick, NJ, Transaction Books.

Hoyningen-Huene, P. (1993) *Reconstructing Scientific Revolutions: Thomas S. Kuhn's philosophy of science*, Chicago, University of Chicago Press. (First published in German in 1989.)

Hughes, E. C. (1958) *Men and their Work*, Glencoe, IL, Free Press.

Hughes, E. C. (1960) 'Introduction', in B. H. Junker *Field Work: An introduction to the social sciences*, Chicago, University of Chicago Press.

Hughes, E. C. (1971) *The Sociological Eye*, Chicago, Aldine.

von Humboldt, W. (1792) *The Limits of State Action*, English translation, Cambridge, Cambridge University Press, 1969.

Hume, D. (1739) *A Treatise of Human Nature*, London, Penguin, 1969.

de Huszar, G. (ed.) (1960) *The Intellectuals: A controversial portrait*, Glencoe, IL, Free Press.

Hutchinson, P., Read, R. and Sharrock, W. (eds) (2008) *There is No Such Thing as a Social Science: In defence of Peter Winch*, Aldershot, Ashgate.

Ignatieff, M. (1997) 'The decline and fall of the public intellectual', *Queen's Quarterly*, 104, 3, pp. 395–403.

Jacoby, R. (1987) *The Last Intellectuals: American culture in the age of academe*, New York, Basic Books.

James, W. (1897) 'The will to believe', in *The Will to Believe and Other Essays in Popular Philosophy*, New York, Longmans, Green. (Republished in *Selected Writings*, London, Dent, 1995.)

Janesick, V. J. (1994) 'The dance of qualitative research: metaphor, methodolatry, and meaning', in Denzin, N. K. and Lincoln, Y. S. (eds) *Handbook of Qualitative Research*, Thousand Oaks, CA, Sage.

Jenkins, K. (ed.) (1997) *The Postmodern History Reader*, London, Routledge.

Jenkins, K. (2003) *Rethinking History*, Third edition, London, Routledge.

Jenkins, K. (2004) 'On history, historians and silence', *History Compass*, 2, pp. 1–4.

Jennings, J. (1997) 'Of treason, blindness and silence: dilemmas of the intellectual in modern France', in J. Jennings and A. Kemp-Welch (eds) *Intellectuals in Politics: From the Dreyfus Affair to Salman Rushdie*, London, Routledge.

Joffe, J. (2003) 'The decline of the public intellectual and the rise of the pundit', in Melzer, A., Weinberger, J. and Zinman, M. R. (eds) *The Public Intellectual*, Lanham, MD, Rowman and Littlefield.

Johnson, J. M. (1975) *Doing Field Research*, New York, Free Press.

Johnson, V. (1975) 'Violence in marriage', MA qualifying thesis, University of New South Wales.

Joll, J. (1961) *Three Intellectuals in Politics*, London, Weidenfeld & Nicolson.

Joll, J. (1977) *Gramsci*, London, Fontana.

Judt, T. (1986) *Marxism and the French Left*, Oxford, Oxford University Press.

Judt, T. (2003) 'The peripheral insider: Raymond Aron and the wages of reason', in Melzer, A., Weinberger, J. and Zinman, M. R. (eds) *The Public Intellectual*, Lanham, MD, Rowman and Littlefield.

Junker, B. H. (1960) *Field Work: An introduction to the social sciences*, Chicago, University of Chicago Press.

Kahn, C. (1996) *Plato and the Socratic Dialogue*, Cambridge, Cambridge University Press.

Kampe, N. (1987) 'Normalizing the Holocaust: the recent historians' debate in the Federal Republic of Germany', *Holocaust and Genocide Studies*, 2, 1, pp. 61–80.

Kaplan, A. (1964) *The Conduct of Inquiry: Methodology for behavioural science*, New York, Chandler.

Keat, R. and Urry, J. (1975) *Social Theory as Science*, London, Routledge & Kegan Paul.

Kedward, R. (1965) *The Dreyfus Affair*, London, Longman.

Kendall, W. (1960) 'The "Open Society" and its fallacies', *American Political Science Review*, 54, 4, pp. 972–9.

Kenny, A. (1983) *Thomas More*, Oxford, Oxford University Press.

Kent, R. (1981) *A History of British Empirical Sociology*, Aldershot, Gower.

Knight, M. (1950) 'Introduction', in Knight, M. (ed.) *William James*, Harmondsworth, Penguin.

Kober, M. (1996) 'Certainties of a world-picture: the epistemological investigations of *On Certainty*', in Sluga, H. and Stern, D. (eds) *The Cambridge Companion to Wittgenstein*, Cambridge, Cambridge University Press.

Korsgaard, C. (1996) *The Sources of Normativity*, Cambridge, Cambridge University Press.

Koyré, A. (1957) *From the Closed World to the Infinite Universe*, Baltimore, MD, Johns Hopkins University Press.

Kristeva, J. (1986) 'A new type of intellectual: the dissident', in Moi, T. (ed.) *The Kristeva Reader*, Oxford, Blackwell. (First published in French in 1977.)

Kuhn, T. S. (1970) *The Structure of Scientific Revolutions*, Chicago, University of Chicago Press.

Kuhn, T. S. (2000) *The Road from Structure*, Chicago, University of Chicago Press.

Kvanvig, J. L. (1992) *The Intellectual Virtues and the Life of the Mind: On the place of the virtues in epistemology*, Savage, MD, Rowman and Littlefield.

Lacey, H. (1999) *Is Science Value Free?*, New York, Routledge.

Landsberg, P.-L. (1937) 'Réflexions sur l'engagement personnel', *Esprit*, 62, November, pp. 179–97.

Lane, J. (2006) *Bourdieu's Politics*, London, Routledge.

Larmore, C. (1987) *Patterns of Moral Complexity*, Cambridge, Cambridge University Press.

Lather, P. (1996) 'Troubling clarity: the politics of accessible language', *Harvard Education Review*, 66, 3, pp. 525–54.

Latour, B. (1987) *Science in Action: How to follow scientists and engineers through society*, Milton Keynes, Open University Press.

Law, J. (ed.) (1986) *Power, Action and Belief: A new sociology of knowledge*, London, Routledge & Kegan Paul.

Law, J. (2004) *After Method: Mess in social science research*, London, Routledge.

Lecourt, D. (2001) *The Mediocracy: French philosophy since 1968*, London, Verso. (First published in French in 1999.)

Lenin, V. I. (1947) *What Is To Be Done?*, Moscow, Progress Publishers.

Levinas, E. (1989) 'As if consenting to horror', *Critical Inquiry*, 15, 2, pp. 485–8.

Lewis, C. I. (1955) *The Ground and Nature of the Right*, New York, Columbia University Press.

Lichtheim, G. (1971) *From Marx to Hegel and Other Essays*, London, Orbach and Chambers.

Lincoln, Y. S. and Guba, E. G. (1985) *Naturalistic Inquiry*, Beverly Hills, CA, Sage.

Lindbergh, A. M. (1940) *The Wave of the Future: A confession of faith*, New York, Harcourt, Brace and Company.

Lipstadt, D. E. (1993) *Denying the Holocaust: The growing assault on truth and memory*, New York, Free Press.

Lobkowicz, N. (1967) *Theory and Practice: History of a concept from Aristotle to Marx*, Notre Dame, IN, University of Notre Dame Press.

Locke, J. (1975) *An Essay Concerning Human Understanding*, ed. P. H. Nidditch, Oxford, Oxford University Press. (First published in its Fourth Edition in 1700.)

Lofland, J. (1971) *Analyzing Social Settings*, Belmont, CA, Wadsworth.

Losee, J. (1993) *A Historical Introduction to the Philosophy of Science*, Third edition, Oxford, Oxford University Press.

Lovejoy, A. (1917) 'On some conditions of progress in philosophical inquiry', *Philosophical Review*, 26, 2, pp. 131–8.

Lovejoy, A. (1937) 'Academic freedom', in Seligman, E. (ed.) *Encyclopedia of the Social Sciences*, New York, Macmillan.

Lukács, G. (1971) *History and Class Consciousness: Studies in Marxist dialectics*, Cambridge, MA, MIT Press.

Lukes, S. (1985) *Marxism and Morality*, Oxford, Oxford University Press.

Lynch, M. (2000) 'Against reflexivity as an academic virtue and source of privileged knowledge', *Theory, Culture and Society*, 17, 3, pp. 26–54.

Lyotard, J.-F. (1986) 'Discussions, or phrasing "after Auschwitz"', Working Paper No. 2, Milwaukee, WI, Center for Twentieth Century Studies, University of Wisconsin–Milwaukee.

Lyotard, J.-F. (1988) *The Differend: phrases in dispute*, Manchester, Manchester University Press.

Lyotard, J.-F. (1993) *Political Writings*, London, UCL Press.

MacLure, M. (2003) *Discourse in Educational and Social Research*, Buckingham, Open University Press.

Madigan, T. (2008) *T. K. Clifford and the Ethics of Belief*, Newcastle-upon-Tyne, Cambridge Scholars Press.

Maier, B. (1998) *The Unmasterable Past*, Cambridge, MA, Harvard University Press.

de Maistre, J. (1862) *Considérations sur la France*, Lyon, Pélagaud.

Malachowski, A. R. (1990) *Reading Rorty: Critical responses to philosophy and the mirror of nature (and beyond)*, Oxford, Blackwell.

Malinowski, B. (1967) *A Diary in the Strict Sense of the Term*, London, Routledge & Kegan Paul.

Mann, M. (1981) 'Socio-logic', *Sociology*, 15, 4, pp. 544–50.

Marcus, P. (1999) *Autonomy in Extreme Situations: Bruno Bettelheim, the Nazi concentration camps and the mass society*, Westport, CT, Praeger.

Marcuse, H. (1964) *One Dimensional Man: The ideology of industrial society*, London, Routledge & Kegan Paul.

Martin, B. (1981) *A Sociology of Contemporary Cultural Change*, Oxford, Blackwell.

Matza, D. (1969) *Becoming Deviant*, Chicago, Aldine.

Mauthner, M., Birch, M., Jessop, J. and Miller, T. (eds) (2002) *Ethics in Qualitative Research*, London, Sage.

Maxwell, J. (2004) *Qualitative Research Design*, Second edition, Thousand Oaks, CA, Sage.

May, T. (1994) *The Political Philosophy of Poststructuralist Anarchism*, University Park, PA, Pennsylvania State University Press.

McCarthy, P. (1985) 'Sartre, Nizan and the dilemmas of political commitment', *Yale French Studies*, 68, pp. 191–205.

McKinney, J. C. (1966) *Constructive Typology and Social Theory*, New York, Appleton-Century-Crofts.

McKinnon, C. (2006) *Toleration*, London, Routledge.

Melzer, A. (2003) 'What is an intellectual?', in Melzer, A., Weinberger, J. and Zinman, M. R. (eds) *The Public Intellectual*, Lanham, MD, Rowman and Littlefield.

Menand, L. (ed.) (1998) *The Future of Academic Freedom*, Chicago, University of Chicago Press.

Merton, R. K. (1973a) 'The normative structure of science', in Merton, R. K., *The Sociology of Science*, Chicago, University of Chicago Press.

Merton, R. K. (1973b) *The Sociology of Science: Theoretical and methodological investigations*, Chicago, University of Chicago Press.

Michael, J. (2000) *Anxious Intellects: Academic professionals, public intellectuals, and Enlightenment values*, Durham, NC, Duke University Press.

Michelfelder, D. and Palmer, R. E. (eds) (1989) *Dialogue and Deconstruction: The Gadamer–Derrida Encounter*, Albany, NY: State University of New York Press.

Mies, M. (1991) 'Women's research or feminist research? The debate surrounding feminist science and methodology', in Fonow, M. and Cook, J. (eds) *Beyond Methodology: Feminist scholarship as lived research*, Bloomington, IN, Indiana University Press.

Mill, J. S. (1859) *On Liberty*, Harmondsworth, Penguin, 1974.

Miller, D. W. (1994) *Critical Rationalism: A restatement and defence*, Chicago, Open Court.

Mills, C. W. (1959a) 'On intellectual craftsmanship', in Gross, L. (ed.) *Symposium on Sociological Theory*, Evanston, IL, Row, Peterson.

Mills, C. W. (1959b) *The Sociological Imagination*, New York, Oxford University Press.

Mills, C. W. (1963) *Power, Politics and People*, New York, Oxford University Press.

Montefiore, A. (1975) Part 1, in Montefiore, A. (ed.) *Neutrality and Impartiality: The university and political commitment*, Cambridge, Cambridge University Press.

Montmarquet, J. A. (1993) *Epistemic Virtue and Doxastic Responsibility*, Lanham, MD, Rowman and Littlefield.

More, T. (1969) *The Yale Edition of The Complete Works of St. Thomas More, Volume 5, Responsio ad Lutherum*, ed. J. Headley, New Haven, CT, Yale University Press.

Moyal-Sharrock, D. and Brenner, W. (eds) (2007) *Readings of Wittgenstein's On Certainty*, Basingstoke, Palgrave Macmillan.

Mulkay, M. (1980) 'Interpretation and the use of rules: the case of the norms of science', in Gieryn, T. F. (ed.) *Science and Social Structure: A festschrift for Robert K. Merton*, New York, Transactions of the New York Academy of Sciences, Series II, Volume 39, April 24.

Munslow, A. (1998) *Deconstructing History*, London, Routledge.

Munslow, A. and Rosenstone, R. (eds) (2004) *Experiments in Rethinking History*, New York, Routledge.

Myrdal, G. (1969) *Objectivity in Social Research*, New York, Pantheon.

Nagel, T. (1989) *The View from Nowhere*, Second edition, New York, Oxford University Press.

Newell, R. W. (1986) *Objectivity, Empiricism and Truth*, London, Routledge & Kegan Paul.

Nichols, R. (1978) *Treason, Tradition, and the Intellectual: Julien Benda and political discourse*, Lawrence, KS, The Regents Press of Kansas.

Nichols, R. L. (1965) 'The intellectual and modern politics: Julien Benda and the case of France', PhD dissertation, Princeton University.

Nielsen, F. (2004) 'The vacant "we": remarks on public sociology', *Social Forces*, 82, 4, pp. 1619–27.

Niess, R. (1956) *Julien Benda*, Ann Arbor, MI, University of Michigan Press.

Nisbet, R. A. (1963) 'Sociology as an art form', in Stein, M. and Vidich, A. (eds) *Sociology on Trial*, Englewood Cliffs, NJ, Prentice Hall.

Nisbet, R. A. (1971) *The Degradation of the Academic Dogma*, London, Heinemann.

Nizan, P. (1972) *Watchdogs: Philosophers and the established order*, New York, Monthly Review Press. (First published in French in 1932.)

Norris, N. (1995) 'Contracts, control and evaluation', *Journal of Education Policy*, 10, 3, pp. 271–85.

Novick, P. (1999) *The Holocaust in American Life*, Boston, MA, Houghton Mifflin.

Nowotny, H., Scott, P. and Gibbons, M. (2001) *Re-Thinking Science*, Cambridge, Polity.

Nowotny, H., Scott, P. and Gibbons, M. (2003) 'Introduction: "Mode2" revisited: the new production of knowledge', *Minerva*, 41, pp. 179–194.

Oakes, G. (1975) 'Introductory essay', in Weber, M., *Roscher and Knies: The logical problems of historical economics*, New York, Free Press.

Oakeshott, M. (1962) *Rationalism in Politics*, London, Methuen.

O'Leary, Z. (2009) *The Essential Guide to Doing Your Research Project*, Second edition, London, Sage.

O'Neill, J. (1972) 'On theory and criticism in Marx', in O'Neill, J., *Sociology as a Skin Trade*, London, Heinemann.

O'Rourke, K. (2001) *John Stuart Mill and Freedom of Expression*, London, Routledge.

Olson, G. and Worsham, L. (eds) (2004) *Postmodern Sophistry: Stanley Fish and the critical enterprise*, Albany, NY, State University of New York Press.

Palmer, R. E. (1969) *Hermeneutics*, Evanston, IL, Northwestern University Press.

Palmer, R. E. (2003) 'Gadamer's hermeneutical tolerance', Paper given at the 15th Conference of the InterAmerican Congress of Philosophy and 2nd Conference of the Iberian–American Congress of Philosophy, Pontifica Universidád Católica del Peru, Lima.

Passmore, J. (1961) *Philosophical Reasoning*, London, Duckworth.

Patai, D. (1994) 'When method becomes power', in Gitlin, A. (ed.) *Power and Method: Political activism in educational research*, New York, Routledge.

Pearson, G. (1975) *The Deviant Imagination: Psychiatry, social work, and social change*, London, Macmillan.

Peim, N. (2009) 'Thinking resources for educational research methods and methodology', *International Journal of Research and Method in Education*, 32, 3, pp. 235–48.

Pels, D. (2003) *Unhastening Science*, Liverpool, Liverpool University Press.

Pels, D. (2004) 'Strange standpoints, or how to define the situation for situated knowledge', in Harding, S. (ed.) *The Feminist Standpoint Theory Reader*, London, Routledge.

Phillips, D. L. (1973) *Abandoning Method: Sociological studies in methodology*, San Francisco, Jossey-Bass.

Phillips, E. and Pugh, D. (2005) *How to Get a PhD*, Fourth edition, Maidenhead, Open University Press.

Pincoffs, E. (ed.) (1975) *The Concept of Academic Freedom*, Austin, TX, University of Texas Press.

Poincaré, H. (1908) *Science and Method*, London, Nelson. (First published in French in 1908, English translation published in 1914.)

Polanyi, M. (1958) *Personal Knowledge*, Chicago, University of Chicago Press.

Polanyi, M. (1962) 'The republic of science: its political and economic theory', *Minerva*, 1, 1, pp. 54–73.

Pollit, C. (1990) *Managerialism and the Public Services*, Oxford, Blackwell.

Pomerantz, A. M. (1984) 'Agreeing and disagreeing with assessment: some features of preferred/dispreferred turn shapes', in Atkinson, J. M. and Heritage, J. (eds) *Structure of Social Action: Studies in Conversation Analysis*, Cambridge, Cambridge University Press.

Popper, K. R. (1945) *The Open Society and its Enemies, Volume 2, Hegel and Marx*, London, Routledge & Kegan Paul.

Popper, K. R. (1959) *The Logic of Scientific Discovery*, London, Hutchinson.

Popper, K. R. (1963) *Conjectures and Refutations: The growth of scientific knowledge*, London, Routledge & Kegan Paul.

Popper, K. R. (1966) *The Open Society and its Enemies*, Volumes 1 and 2, Fifth edition, London, Routledge & Kegan Paul.

Popper, K. R. (1987) 'On toleration and intellectual responsibility', in Mendus, S. and Edwards, D. (eds) *On Toleration*, Oxford, Oxford University Press.

Porpora, D. (2004) 'Objectivity and phallogocentrism', in Archer, M. S. and Outhwaite, W. (eds) *Defending Objectivity: Essays in honour of Andrew Collier*, London, Routledge.

Posner, R. (2003) *Public Intellectuals: A study in decline*, Cambridge, MA, Harvard University Press.

Power, M. (1997) *The Audit Society: Rituals of verification*, Oxford, Oxford University Press.

Price, H. H. (1969) *Belief*, London, Allen and Unwin.

Prokopczyk, C. (1980) *Truth and Reality in Marx and Hegel: A reassessment*, Amherst, MA, University of Massachusetts Press.

Quinton, A. (1980) *Francis Bacon*, Oxford, Oxford University Press.

Rabinow, P. (1977) *Reflections on Fieldwork in Morocco*, Berkeley, CA, University of California Press.

Radford, M. (2007) 'Prediction, control and the challenge to complexity', *Oxford Review of Education*. Available at http://dx.doi.org/10.1080/03054980701772636 (accessed 29.06.10).

Ragin, C. (2008) *Redesigning Social Inquiry: Fuzzy sets and beyond*, Chicago, University of Chicago Press.

Ratner, C. (2002) 'Subjectivity and objectivity in qualitative methodology', *Forum Qualitative Sozialforschung/Forum: Qualitative Social Research*, 3, 3. Available at www.qualitative-research.net/index.php/fqs/article/view/829/1801 (accessed 29.06.10).

Ravetz, J. R. (1971) *Scientific Knowledge and its Social Problems*, Oxford, Oxford University Press.

Rawls, J. (1971) *A Theory of Justice*, Cambridge, MA, Harvard University Press.

Readings, B. (1993) 'Foreword', in Lyotard, J.-F., *Political Writings*, Minneapolis, University of Minnesota Press.

Redfern, W. D. (1972) *Paul Nizan: Committed literature in a conspiratorial world*, Princeton, NJ, Princeton University Press.

Reed, J. S., Doss, G. E. and Hurlbert, J. S. (1987) 'Too good to be false: an essay in the folklore of social science', *Sociological Inquiry*, 57, 1, pp. 1–11.

Rescher, N. (1977) *Dialectics: A controversy-oriented approach to the theory of knowledge*, Albany, NY, State University of New York Press.

Rescher, N. (1978) *Peirce's Philosophy of Science: Critical studies in his theory of induction and scientific method*, South Bend, IN: University of Notre Dame Press.

Rescher, N. (1993) *Pluralism: Against the demand for consensus*, Oxford, Oxford University Press.

Rescher, N. (1997) *Objectivity: The obligations of impersonal reason*, Notre Dame, IN, University of Notre Dame Press.

Ringer, F. (1969) *The Decline of the German Mandarins*, Cambridge, MA, Harvard University Press.

Robbins, B. (1993) *Secular Vocations: Intellectuals, professionalism, culture*, London, Verso.

Robinson, R. (1953) *Plato's Earlier Dialectic*, Second edition, Oxford, Oxford University Press.

Robinson, R. (1954) *Definition*, Oxford, Oxford University Press.

Rogers, C. (1982) *A Social Psychology of Schooling: The expectancy process*, London, Routledge & Kegan Paul.

Root, M. (1993) *Philosophy of Social Science*, Oxford, Blackwell.

Rorty, R. (1982) *Consequences of Pragmatism*, Brighton, Harvester.

Rorty, R. (1991a) *Essays on Heidegger and Others*, Cambridge, Cambridge University Press.

Rorty, R. (1991b) 'Solidarity or objectivity?', in *Objectivity, Relativism and Truth*, Cambridge, Cambridge University Press.

Rose, G. (1996) *Mourning Becomes the Law*, Cambridge, Cambridge University Press.

Rosenbaum, A. (ed.) (1996) *Is the Holocaust Unique?*, Boulder, CO, Westview Press.

Rosenthal, R. (1966) *Experimenter Effects in Behavioral Research*, New York, Appleton-Century-Crofts.

Rosenthal, R. and Jacobson, L. (1968) *Pygmalion in the Classroom*, New York, Holt, Rinehart and Winston.

Rossi, P. (1996) 'Bacon's idea of science', in Peltonen, M. (ed.) *The Cambridge Companion to Bacon*, Cambridge, Cambridge University Press.

Rubinstein, W. (1981) 'Chomsky and the neo-Nazis', *Quadrant* (Australia), October, pp. 8–14. (A reply from Chomsky and a rejoinder by Rubinstein are published in the April 1982 issue of the same journal.)

Rule, J. B. (1997) *Theory and Progress in Social Science*, Cambridge, Cambridge University Press.

Rule, J. B. and Besen, Y. (2008) 'The once and future information society', *Theory and Society*, 37, 4, pp. 317–42.

Rüsen, J. (1997) 'The logic of historicization: metahistorical reflection on the debate between Friedländer and Broszat', *History and Memory*, 9, pp. 113–44.

Russell, C. (1993) *Academic Freedom*, London, Routledge.

Ryle, G. (1949) *The Concept of Mind*, London, Hutchinson.

Said, E. W. (1994) *Representations of the Intellectual*, The 1993 Reith Lectures, London, Random House.

Sargent, R.-M. (1996) 'Bacon as an advocate for cooperative scientific research', in Peltonen, M. (ed.) *The Cambridge Companion to Francis Bacon*, Cambridge, Cambridge University Press.

Sartre, J.-P. (1948a) *What is Literature?*. (English translation, London, Methuen, 1950.)

Sartre, J.-P. (1948b) *Existentialism and Humanism*, Methuen, London.

Sartre, J.-P. (1952) *The Communists and the Peace*. (English translation, New York, Braziller, 1968.)

Sartre, J.-P. (1972) 'A plea for intellectuals', English translation in Sartre, J.-P., *Between Existentialism and Marxism*, London, New Left Books, 1974.

Sartre, J.-P. (1974) 'Intellectuals and Revolution', *Ramparts*, IX, 6, pp. 52–5.

Schalk, D. (1979) *The Spectrum of Political Engagement*, Princeton, NJ, Princeton University Press.

Schatzman, L. and Strauss, A. L. (1973) *Field Research: Strategies for a natural sociology*, Englewood Cliffs, NJ, Prentice Hall.

Schutz, A. (1970) *Reflections on the Problem of Relevance*, New Haven, CT, Yale University Press.

Schwandt, T. A. and Halpern, E. S. (1988) *Linking Auditing and Metaevaluation: Enhancing quality in applied research*, Newbury Park, CA, Sage.

Schwartz, H. (2003) 'Data: who needs it? Describing normal environments – examples and methods', in Lynch, M. and Sharrock, W. W. (eds) *Harold Garfinkel*, Volume IV, London, Sage.

Seale, C. (1999) *The Quality of Qualitative Research*, London, Sage.

Sedgewick, P. and Tanesini, A. (1995) 'Lyotard and Kripke: essentialisms in dispute', *American Philosophical Quarterly*, 32, 3, pp. 271–8.

Seeskin, K. (1987) *Dialogue and Discovery: A study in Socratic method*, Albany, NY, State University of New York.

Sharrock, W. and Read, R. (2002) *Kuhn: Philosopher of scientific revolution*, Cambridge, Polity.

Shermer, M. and Grobman, A. (2002) *Denying History: Who says the Holocaust never happened and why do they say it?*, Berkeley, CA, University of California Press.

Shils, E. (1972) *The Intellectuals and the Powers*, Chicago, University of Chicago Press.

Shils. E. (1997) 'The Academic Ethic', in E. Shils, *The Calling of Education*, Chicago, University of Chicago Press.

Simon, R. L. (1994) *Neutrality and the Academic Ethic*, Lanham, MD, Rowman and Littlefield.

Skagestad, P. (1981) *The Road of Inquiry*, New York, Columbia University Press.

Smead, V. S. (1984) 'Self-fulfilling prophecies in the classroom: dead end or promising beginning?', *Alberta Journal of Educational Research*, XXX, 2, pp. 145–56.

Smith, J. K. (1989) *The Nature of Social and Educational Inquiry*, Norwood, NJ, Ablex.

Smith, J. K. (2004) 'Learning to live with relativism', in Piper, H. and Stronach, I. (eds) *Educational Research: Difference and diversity*, Aldershot, Ashgate.

Smith, J. K. and Deemer, D. K. (2000) 'The problem of criteria in the age of relativism', in N. K. Denzin and Y. S. Lincoln (eds) *Handbook of Qualitative Research*, Second edition, Thousand Oaks, CA, Sage.

Sohn-Rethel, A. (1978) *Intellectual and Manual Labour: A critique of epistemology*, London, Macmillan.

Sperber, D. and Wilson, D. (1986) *Relevance: Communication and cognition*, Oxford, Blackwell.

Stanley, L. and Wise, S. (1983) *Breaking Out: Feminist consciousness and feminist research*, London, Routledge & Kegan Paul.

Stanley, L. and Wise, S. (2002) *Breaking Out: Feminist consciousness and feminist research*, Second edition, London, Taylor & Francis.

Stehr, N. (1978) 'The ethos of science revisited: social and cognitive norms', in Gaston, J. (ed.) *Sociology of Science*, San Francisco, Jossey Bass.

Stehr, N. (1994) *Knowledge Societies*, London, Sage.

Sterba, R. (1982) *Reminiscences of a Viennese Psychoanalyst*, Detroit, IL, Wayne State University Press.

Stokes, D. (1997) *Pasteur's Quadrant: Basic science and technological innovation*, Washington, DC, Brookings Institution Press.

Stokes, D. E., 'Completing the Bush model: Pasteur's quadrant' Available at www.dcc. uchile.cl/~cgutierr/cursos/INV/Stokes.pdf (accessed 16 March 2009).

Strauss, L. (1953) *Natural Right and History*, Chicago, University of Chicago Press.

Sullivan, R. R. (1989) *Political Hermeneutics: The early thinking of Hans-Georg Gadamer*, Philadelphia, Pennsylvania University Press.

Summers, J. (ed.) (2008) *The Politics of Truth: Selected writings of C. Wright Mills*, Oxford, Oxford University Press.

Suppe, F. (ed.) (1974) *The Structure of Scientific Theories*, Chicago, University of Chicago Press.

Taylor, C. (1979) *Hegel and Modern Society*, Cambridge, Cambridge University Press.

Thompson, W. (2004) *Postmodernism and History*, Basingstoke, Palgrave Macmillan.

Todorov, T. (2001) 'The uses and abuses of memory', in Marchitello, H. (ed.) *What Happens to History: The renewal of ethics in contemporary thought*, New York, Routledge.

Travers, M. (2009) 'New methods, old problems: a sceptical view of innovation in qualitative research', *Qualitative Research*, 9, 2, pp. 161–79.

Tuchman, G. (2009) *Wannabe U: Inside the corporate university*, Chicago, University of Chicago Press.

Tudor, A. (1982) *Beyond Empiricism*, London, Routledge & Kegan Paul.

Turner, F. M. (1974) *Between Science and Religion: The reaction to scientific naturalism in later Victorian England*, New Haven, CT, Yale University Press.

Turner, S. P. (1990) 'Forms of patronage', in Cozzens, S. and Gieryn, T. (eds) *Theories of Science in Society*, Bloomington, IN, Indiana University Press.

Urbach, P. (1987) *Francis Bacon's Philosophy of Science: An account and a reappraisal*, LaSalle, IL, Open Court.

Vidal-Naquet, P. (1981) 'A paper Eichmann', *Democracy*, I, 2, pp. 70–95. (Originally published in French in *Esprit*, September 1980, pp. 8–56.)

Vidal-Naquet, P. (1992) *Assassins of Memory: Essays on the denial of the Holocaust*, New York, Columbia University Press. (First published in French in 1987.)

Vision, G. (1988) *Modern Anti-Realism and Manufactured Truth*, London, Routledge.

Von Wright, G. H. (1971) *Explanation and Understanding*, London, Routledge & Kegan Paul.

Wachterhauser, B. (2002) 'Getting it right: relativism, realism and truth', in Dostal, R. J. (ed.) *The Cambridge Companion to Gadamer*, Cambridge, Cambridge University Press.

Warburton, N. (2009) *Free Speech*, Oxford, Oxford University Press.

Wax, M. (1971) 'Tenting with Malinowski', *American Sociological Review*, 37, 1, pp. 1–13.

Weber, M. (1949) *The Methodology of the Social Sciences*, New York, Free Press.

Weber, M. (1974) *Max Weber on Universities: The power of the state and the dignity of the academic calling in Imperial Germany*, Chicago, University of Chicago Press.

Weber, M. (1975) *Roscher and Knies: The logical problems of historical economics*, New York, Free Press.

Weber, M. (1977) *Critique of Stammler*, New York, Free Press.

Webster, F. (1995) *Theories of the Information Society*, London, Routledge.

Weinberg, J. (1965) *Abstraction, Relation, and Induction*, Madison, WI, University of Wisconsin Press.

Weinstein, R. S. (2002) *Reaching Higher: The power of expectations in schooling*, Cambridge, MA, Harvard University Press.

Wernham, J. C. S. (1987) *James's Will-to-Believe Doctrine: A heretical view*, Kingston, McGill–Queen's University Press.

Wernick, A. (1984) 'Structuralism and the dislocation of the French rationalist project', in Fekete, J. (ed.) *The Structural Allegory: Reconstructive encounters with new French thought*, Manchester, Manchester University Press.

Westoby, A. (1987) 'Mental work, education and the division of labour', in Eyerman, R., Svensson, L. and Söderqvist, T. (eds) *Intellectuals, Universities and the State in Western Modern Societies*, Berkeley, CA, University of California Press.

White, H. (1966) 'The burden of history', *History and Theory*, 5, 2, pp, 111–34.

Whyte, W. F. (1955) *Streetcorner Society*, Second edition, Chicago, University of Chicago Press.

Whyte, W. F. (1993) *Streetcorner Society*, Fourth edition, Chicago, University of Chicago Press.

Wiesel, E. (1985) *Against Silence*, New York, Schocken Books.

Williams, B. (2002) *Truth and Truthfulness: An essay in genealogy*, Princeton, NJ, Princeton University Press.

Wirth, L. (1938) 'Urbanism as a way of life', *American Journal of Sociology*, 44, 1, pp. 1–24.

Wittgenstein, L. (1969) *On Certainty*, Oxford, Blackwell.

Woolgar, S. (1988) *Science: the very idea*, London, Routledge.

Woolgar, S. and Pawluch, D. (1985) 'Ontological gerrymandering: the anatomy of social problems explanations', *Social Problems*, 32, pp. 314–27.

Wyschogrod, E. (1998) *An Ethics of Remembering: History, Heterology and the Nameless Others*, Chicago, University of Chicago Press.

Zagorin, P. (2001) 'Francis Bacon's concept of objectivity and the idols of the mind', *British Journal of the History of Science*, 34, pp. 379–93.

Zagzebski, L. T. (1996) *Virtues of the Mind: An inquiry into the nature of virtue and the ethical foundations of knowledge*, Cambridge, Cambridge University Press.

Ziman, J. (1994) *Prometheus Bound: Science in a dynamic steady state*, Cambridge, Cambridge University Press.

Ziman, J. (2000) *Real Science: What it is and what it means*, Cambridge, Cambridge University Press.

Zola, E. (1996) *The Dreyfus Affair: J'Accuse and other writings*, New Haven, CT, Yale University Press.

NAME INDEX

Note: Page references followed by 'n' relate to footnotes

Adorno, T.W., 62
Althusser, L., 59–60, 69m
Ankersmit, F., 35
Anscombe, E., 90n
Arendt, Hannah, 139n
Aristotle, 36n, 75, 134–5, 135n, 138, 140n
Aron, Raymond, 59, 73
Aschheim, S., 175–6

Bacon, Francis, 18n, 91n, 138–40, 140n
Ball, S.J., 79
Bataille, G., 36n
Bauer, Y., 178
Bauman, Z., 52, 163n, 175
Beauvoir, Simone de, 54
Becker, H.S., 17, 69, 80n
Bell, C., 26n, 27–8, 37n
Benda, Julien, 47–57, 62–4, 76–7, 87
Bentham, Jeremy, 65
Bernstein, R., 91n
Bettelheim, B., 181–2
Blum, Léon, 52n
Bohannon, Laura, 25n
Bourdieu, Pierre, 59n
Bourg, J., 62n, 71
Bridges, D., 116n
Bridgman, P., 31, 92
Bruun, H.H., 8n
Bruyn, S., 22
Burawoy, M., 43n, 45, 74

Chamberlain, K., 31
Chomsky, Noam, 167–8
Clavel, Maurice, 62n
Clifford, W.K., 105, 110–14, 110n, 112n,
    116n, 118–19
Cobban, A., 53
Cohen, A., 176
Collier, A., 90n

Darwin, Charles, 123
Daston, L., 89–90
Dear, P., 90n
Deemer, D.K., 123
Deleuze, Gilles, 86n
Denzin, N.K., 6n, 29–30, 36
Descartes, René, 139n
Dewey, J., 135
Diner, D., 175
Douglas, H., 114n
Durkheim, E., 46–7

Eaglestone, R., 165–7, 166n, 173–4, 177
Eichmann, Adolf, 164
Elashoff, J.D., 107, 109
Emmet, Dorothy, 114
Enstein, Albert, 159
Evans, R.J., 166n
Eyerman, R., 45n

Farrell, F.B., 90n
Faurisson, Robert, 162n, 166–8
Feyerabend, P., 31
Finkelstein, N., 174
Fischer, M., 142
Fish, Stanley, 31, 65, 159, 160n, 165, 174n
Foster, P., 109
Foucault, Michel, 46, 60–1, 62n, 68–71, 86n
Freud, Sigmund, 17
Friedländer, S., 176, 179

Gadamer, Hans-Georg, 13–14, 124, 135,
    141, 143n
Gage, N., 107
Galison, P., 89–90
Glaser, B.G., 22
Goodman, Nelson, 165
Gouldner, A., 18, 44, 68, 73–4
Gramsci, Antonio, 43, 46n, 54n, 55, 77, 77n

Grice, Paul, 13, 150, 150n, 155–6, 155n
Grobman, A., 165n, 169, 171
Gutman, Israel, 174

Haack, S., 111–16, 112n, 114n, 119, 145
Habermas, Jürgen, 13, 82, 86, 141
Hague, Douglas, 3n
Halsey, A., 161n
Hamlyn, D., 138
Harding, S., 100–1
Haskell, T., 185–6
Hawkesworth, M.E., 94–5
Hegel, G. W. F., 76, 78, 98, 134–5, 135n
Heidegger, Martin, 135
Hesse, Mary, 19
Hitler, Adolf, 53
Holmwood, J., 74
Horowitz, I.L., 69, 69n
Hughes, E.C., 27, 161n
Hume, David, 133
Huxley, T.H., 110n

Irving, David, 162n, 164n

Jacobson, L., 106–9, 119
James, William, 105, 110–12, 110n, 111n,
    112n, 135
Janesick, V.J., 18
Jenkins, K., 177, 179
Joll, J. 52n

Kant, Immanuel, 13, 57, 76, 90, 129, 160n
Kaplan, A., 18
Keats, John, 149
Kendall, Willmoore, 144–5
Kierkegaard, Søren, 57
Kristeva, J., 61n
Kuhn, Thomas, 6, 23–4

Lacey, H., 14n
Latour, B., 106n, 107
Law, J., 30, 32, 40n
Leibniz, Gottfried, 139n
Lenin, V.I., 45, 69, 69n
Levinas, E., 162, 182
Lewis, C.I., 112, 114n
Lincoln, Y.S., 29–30, 36
Lindbergh, A.M., 43, 71n
Lipstadt, D.E., 164–7, 164n, 170–3
Locke, John, 110n
Lovejoy, A., 6n
Lukács, G., 55
Luther, Martin, 145
Lyotard, J.-F., 46, 61–2, 63n, 70–1, 86n, 166–7, 173

McCarthy, P., 56
Mach, Ernst, 128–9

de Maistre, J., 66
Malachowski, A.R., 139n
Malinowski, Bronislaw, 26n
Mann, M., 124n
Marcuse, H., 78
Marx, Karl, 76, 78, 98, 134–5, 135n
May, T., 61
Merton, R.K., 81–2, 114n
Mill, John Stuart, 58, 140n, 160n
Mills, C. Wright, 18, 30, 37, 39, 44, 68–9, 73–4
Mongin, Olivier, 62n
More, Thomas, 145
Mussolini, Benito, 53
Myrdal, G., 96

Newby, H., 26n, 27–8, 37n
Newman, John Henry, 110n
Nietzsche, Friedrich, 57, 60, 99, 135
Nisbet, R.A., 18
Nizan, Paul, 45, 53–7
Nora, Pierre, 62n
Nowotny, H., 4

Oppenheimer, Robert, 60

Palmer, R.E., 143n
Park, Robert, 124
Passmore, J., 22
Pawluch, D., 78, 146
Pearson, G., 9
Peim, N., 161
Peirce, Charles Sanders, 110n, 135, 179
Phillips, D.L., 32
Plato, 63n, 138, 140n
Poincaré, H., 17
Pomerantz, A.M., 149n
Popper, Karl, 1, 13, 75, 116n, 139–49, 140n, 157

Quinton, A., 140, 140n

Radford, M., 94
Ragin, C., 186n
Ratner, C., 91n
Rawls, John, 84n
Readings, B., 62
Redfern, W.D., 54
Reed, J.S., 105–6, 110
Renan, Ernest, 50
Rescher, N., 89, 138, 140, 140n
Ringer, F., 22n
Rogers, C., 107–9, 108n
Rorty, Richard, 6n, 111, 114n,
    139n, 141–2, 142n, 165
Rose, Gillian, 173, 176, 178–9
Rosenthal, R., 106–9, 119
Rüsen, J., 176–7
Russell, C., 3n, 160

NAME INDEX

Said, Edward, 44
Sartre, Jean-Paul, 45–6, 46n, 56–60,
    68–9, 135
Schalk, D., 55
Schwartz, Howard, 17n
Seale, Clive, 30
Sedgewick, P., 166n, 173
Shermer, M., 165n, 169, 171
Smead, V.S., 108n
Smith, J.K., 25, 123
Snow, R.E., 107, 109
Socrates, 62–3n
Solzhenitsyn, Aleksandr, 59
Sperber, D., 127
Strauss, A.L., 22, 177, 180
Sullivan, R.R, 141

Tanesini, A., 166n, 173
Taylor, C., 128
Thorndike, R.L., 107

Toqueville, Alexis de, 63
Tudor, A., 34
Turner, F.M., 110n

Vico, Giambattista, 134
Voltaire, 160, 168

Weber, Max, 8, 14n, 18, 59n, 79, 86n,
    95, 174n, 177, 180
Weinstein, R.S., 108n
Wernham, J.C.S., 111n
Whyte, William Foote, 25, 27–8
Wilkomirski, Binjamin, 174
Wilson, D., 127
Wittgenstein, L., 35, 81
Woolgar, S., 78, 146
Wyschogrod, E., 166

Ziman, J., 4
Zola, Emile, 47

SUBJECT INDEX

Note: Page references followed by 'n' relate to footnotes

abstract methodological work, 37, 40, 123–4
academic discussion, 10, 138–58
    constitutive principles of, 146–57
    distinctiveness from other discourses, 158
    goal of, 179–80
    Grice's maxims for, 150–7
    virtues and vices of, 143–6
academic ethos, 5–6, 183
academic freedom, 7–8, 13, 159–60
    and Holocaust denial, 168–83
    limitation of, 159–62, 185
    and production of knowledge, 161
academic work
    key features of, 103
    subordination of, 69–72
    virtues required for, 8–12
accountability in research, 4
action research, 5, 25
anti-realism, philosophical, 128–9
anti-Semitism, 162, 164
'audit trails' for research findings, 29
auditing of research, 96–7, 100
autobiography see methodology-as-autobiography
autonomy of intellectuals, 14n, 58, 77

bias in research, 70, 80n, 82–3, 95, 102n
    wilful, 103
    see also 'file drawer' bias; motivated bias

capacity-building for research, 17
Chicago School of sociology, 124
child abuse, 85
Christianity and the Christian Church, 52n, 99, 181
citation of research findings, 105–6
clarity of presentation in academic discourse, 150
collective nature of academic research, 10, 37,
    81, 115, 117, 138, 140, 158, 172, 185
commercialisation of research, 4
common ground between researchers, 88, 149
common interest in political issues, 84
communism and the Communist Party, 53–60, 66
consensus, academic, 154
consequentiality, 113

'construction' model of the research
    problems with, 130–1
    process, 13, 123–4, 127–31, 135–7
conversation, 150
correlational analysis, 41
craft tradition in research, 30–1, 36–7
'critical' social research, 5, 12, 74–81, 87–8
Critical Theory, 76, 87
criticism
    role in politics and practical affairs, 82–8
    role in research, 79–82
    tolerance of, 149
cultural competence, 152
'cultural lag' concept, 98

data collection and analysis, alternative
    strategies for, 33
dedication to research, 8–9, 12
deductive reasoning, 132–3
democracy, 49, 82
detachment on the part of researchers, 5, 25, 148
disciplinary power, theory of, 60–1
discourse analysis, 41
'discovery' model of research, 13, 123–37, 140n
    problems with, 126–7, 132–3
dissemination of research findings, 10–11, 40, 72
division of labour
    in research work, 39–40, 81, 140
    within universities, 44
Dreyfus Affair, 45–7, 51, 63–6

eliminative induction, 140
emotional dimension of research, 28
empiricism, 126–9
epistemic justification, 111–13,
    112n, 113n, 119, 130
epistemic privilege, 98–101
epistemic virtues, 92–3, 104
epistemological radicalism, 5–6
epistemological scepticism, 78–9, 81–2, 116, 131–2
ethics of belief, 113–19, 116n
ethnic minority pupils, 109
ethnomethodology, 23

existential truth, 173–4
experimental method, 18, 23, 140
expressivism, 128

fallibilism, 116, 143
false positives and false negatives,
    12–13, 113–15, 114n, 159
falsification of theories, 139–40
fascism, 53
feminism, 66, 68, 70, 77–8, 87, 94–5, 98
'file drawer' bias, 105n
First World War, 53
Franco-Prussian War, 53
Frankfurt School, 76
freedom of expression, 159–61, 167–70

generalisability of research findings, 41
genetic fallacy, 81
government involvement in social
    science research, 2–4
Groupe d'information sur les prisons, 61

hermeneutic model of the research
    process, 13, 123, 134–7
'hinge' assumptions of social
    enquiry, 35–6, 116, 186
Historians' Debate in Germany, 163
Holocaust, the, 19
    'normalisation' of, 163, 176, 178, 181–4
Holocaust denial, 13–14, 159, 162–85
    and academic freedom, 168–83
    responses to, 163–8
hypothesis-testing, 33, 140

'ideal speech situation', 141
intellectual occupations, 63–5, 64n, 72
intellectual property, 4
intellectual work
    purpose of, 47, 52
    value of, 54
intellectuals
    conceptions of, 11, 63, 72
    role of, 44–59, 62, 62n, 72
    see also organic intellectuals; public
        intellectuals; specific intellectuals
'investment' model of research, 3

justice, definition of, 65

knowledge claims
    assessment of, 12–13, 75, 78–82,
        85, 87, 96, 104, 113–19, 114n,
        146, 148, 185
    clarity of, 150, 154
    credibility of, 152
    fallibility of, 115–16, 132–3
knowledge
    definition of, 133
    as distinct from belief, 130, 133
    problem of, 66–9
    pursued for its own sake, 6–7, 186–7

legal process, 80
liberal political philosophy, 14, 159, 169n, 183–4

Maoism, 60
market forces, 3
Marxism, 4–5, 23, 55, 59, 61, 66, 68, 70, 76–7, 87, 98
maxim of manner for academic discussion, 156–7
maxim of quality for academic discussion, 153–5
maxim of quantity for academic
    discussion, 150–3, 156
maxim of relevance for academic discussion, 155–6
meaning, concept of, 134–7
media influence, 7
meta-statements in research reports, 153
methodological awareness, 9, 11, 185
methodological ideas, history of, 18–20
methodological literature, 38, 41–2
    scale of, 17–18
'methodologists', 17–18; see also
    specialisation in methodology
methodology
    argumemts against, 30–2, 41
    conclusion on need for, 42
    definitions of, 32, 38
    function of, 32–41
    limited and subordinate role for, 30–1
    normative nature of, 38–9
    writing about, 38
methodology-as-autobiography, 25–30, 36–42
    problems with, 38–9
methodology-as-philosophy, 22–5, 31, 34–6, 41
    problems with, 34–5
methodology-as-technique, 20–3, 28–34, 41
'Mode 1' and 'Mode 2' scientific enquiry, 3
motivated bias, 102, 102n

nationalism, 77
natural histories of research, 29
natural science, 1–2, 4, 6, 18–19, 23–4,
    29–31, 100, 110, 127, 181
    challenges to, 19
'natural' settings for research, 27
Nazi-Soviet pact (1939), 55
neo-liberalism, 73
neutrality in academic enquiry, 14
'new philosophers' in France, 66n
new public management, 3, 73, 86

objectivism, 91–5, 91n, 100–4
    alternatives to, 100
    problems with, 92–5
    rejection of, 104
objectivity in research, 6–9, 12, 24, 89–104, 144
    abandonment of the concept of, 104
    changing conceptions of, 89–90, 90n, 101–3
    meaning of term, 103–4
    reactions against, 94–101
    requirements for, 102–3
    strong and weak forms of (Harding), 100–1
    supposed impossibility or
        undesirability of, 95, 180

'ontological gerrymandering' (Woolgar and
    Pawluch), 78, 78n, 146
organic intellectuals, 46n, 52–6, 52n, 66–74, 77

paradigm wars, 6
paradigmatic assumptions, 23–4
patronage systems, 2–3, 3n
peer review, 146n
phenomenology, 129
'philosopher-king' role, 52
    Philosophes, 139n
philosophy of science, 22–3, 31, 140;
    see also methodology-as-philosophy
poiesis as distinct from *praxis*, 37n
policies and practices, public criticism of, 83–8
political aspects of research, 27, 79, 80m
political engagement, 52, 54, 56
political implications of research findings, 117–20
positivism, 21–3, 30, 35, 41, 91, 111, 124n, 128–9
positivist dispute in German sociology, 141
postmodernism, 6, 35, 63n, 66, 78–9, 82, 86–7,
    96, 100, 129, 164–6, 166n, 177–9, 184
postmodernity, 3–4
post-structuralism, 23, 60, 63n, 164
pragmatism, 23
praxis as distinct from *poiesis* and *theoria*, 37n, 49
preferences of researchers, error arising from, 101–4
procedural objectivity, 91–2, 96
proceduralism in research, 21, 33–4, 41, 92–4
professionalism, 11–12, 44, 74
prudence in political criticism, 86, 88
'pseudo-enquiry' (Haack), 145
public intellectuals, 12, 43–6, 52n, 56–60,
    63, 67–9, 72–4, 79, 86–7, 103
public sphere, 82, 86–8
publicity for research findings, 10–11

qualitative research, 6, 19–29, 21n, 32, 157, 186
quantitative research, 19–22, 21n, 186

realism, philosophical, 35, 39, 132, 135–6
realist objectivism, 92, 94
reflexivity, 11, 25–30, 36–41, 83, 96–7, 100, 153
    definitions of, 29n
relativism, 96–7, 131–2, 164, 165n
religious belief, 110–11, 110n
replication of research, 34, 97
research reports
    content of, 151
    length of, 152–3
rigour in research, 29
Russian Revolution, 53

scepticism
    and constructionism, 130
    as distinct from fallibilism, 116, 116n
    about fundamentals of truth and
        value, 36, 95–6, 151, 179
    about objectivity, 78
    'organised', 114n

scepticism *cont.*
    about the value of methodology, 41
    see also epistemological scepticism
Scholasticism, 139, 158
science
    academic and *post-academic*, 4
    current environment for research in, 4
    see also natural science
scientific method, 18–19, 21–2,
    25, 30–1, 136, 138–9
scientism, 68
social construction of knowledge, 5–6, 24
social critics, researchers as, 87–8
social research
    goal of, 24, 80
    nature of, 27–8
social science as an academic discipline, 1–11
    attitudes of researchers to, 4–7, 17–18
    challenges to, 1–2, 7, 74, 118, 196–7
    institutional environment of, 2–4
    necessary presuppositions of, 35–6
    skills needed for, 67–8
socialisation of researchers, 157
sociology of scientific knowledge, 129n
Soviet Union, 77
specialisation in methodology, 39–41
specific intellectuals, 60–2, 68–71, 74
'spin', 7
standpoint theory and standpoint
    epistemology, 70–1, 97–101
stepwise research design, 33
subjectivity, error deriving from, 91–3, 101–4
symbolic interactionism, 129

teacher-expectancy theory, 106–9, 108n, 117, 119
technological research, 7
'textbook' accounts of research, 26–8
theoria as distinct from *praxis*, 49
toleration, need for, 148–50
'too good to be false' findings
    from research, 12, 119–20
training of social researchers, 21
transactionalism, 135
transparency in the research process, 34, 38, 96–7, 153
truth, concept of, 116; *see also* existential truth

'understanding', use of term, 134–7
universities, changes in, 2, 44, 54, 160–1, 186–7
utilitarianism, 65

validity, concept of, 76
value-freedom, 14n, 95
value-neutrality, 14n, 174n, 180, 187
values championed by intellectuals,
    48–9, 51, 55, 63–6, 87
vocation, concept of, 160–1

'whistleblowing', 84

X-ray photographs, 152